HIRE ME, INC.

HIRE ME, INC.

Package Yourself to Get

Your Dream Job

ROY J. BLITZER

Ep
Entrepreneur
Press

Editorial director: Jere L. Calmes
Cover design: Beth Hansen-Winter
Composition and production: Eliot House Productions

This publication is designed to provide accurate and authoritative information in regard to the subject matter covered. It is sold with the understanding that the publisher is not engaged in rendering legal, accounting, or other professional services. If legal advice or other expert assistance is required, the services of a competent professional person should be sought.

Library of Congress Cataloging-in-Publication Data
  Blitzer, Roy J.
    Hire me, Inc.: package yourself to get your dream job/by Roy J. Blitzer.
      p.   cm.
    Includes bibliographical references.
    ISBN 1-59918-023-5 (alk. paper)
    1. Job hunting. I. Title.
  HF5382.7.B584 2006
  650.14—dc22   2006007971

Printed in Canada

11 10 09 08 07 06   10 9 8 7 6 5 4 3 2 1

CONTENTS

CHAPTER 6

CHANNELS OF MARKETING
The Distribution Mix _____ 141

CHAPTER 7

SUCCESSFUL SALES
The Pitch to Succeed _____ 157

ACKNOWLEDGMENTS
"It takes a village to...."

Writing this book cannot be compared to rearing a child, but the efforts of others made this text a reality.

First, I'd like to thank my colleagues in the career counseling profession, the friends and co-workers who worked side-by-side with me providing career counseling and outplacement services through the years—first at Syntex Corporation (now Roche Pharmaceuticals—F. Hoffman—LaRoche

Ltd.) then at de Recat/Interim/Spherion, and now at TMS (Torchiana, Mastrov and Sapiro). Special thanks to Al, Anna, Anne, Beth, Bert, Bill, Cheryl, Connie, Dave, Diane Enid, Eve, Gary, Gene, Helen, Holly, Jack, Jacquie, Janet, Kathy, Kristi, Laura, Lido, Linda, Margot, Marlys, Maryann, Mary, Maureen, Megan, Mike, Pat, Steve, Sue, Susan, and Susie. You have been unselfish in sharing your experiences, previously created notes, seminar exercises, written manuals/materials, and what-works tips of the trade. All have been lovingly massaged and painstakingly altered, and as a part of the content of this book, will now continue to help a whole new set of people. I am forever grateful and appreciative to you and your professionalism.

Special kudos to Matt Jones, whose skill at writing and editing substantially enhanced the material and whose firsthand knowledge of the search process was invaluable to the richness of the exercises, samples, and overall text.

All of the staff at Entrepreneur Media, my editor Karen Thomas in particular (and Karen Billipp in the background), deserve recognition for their patience and understanding, particularly of my limited—but constantly improving—word processing and computer skills.

And finally, thanks to my immediate family—my wife, Carol Blitzer, a seasoned journalist and the legitimate writer in our group, for her support and huge chunks of time in the final writing, proofing, and editing, and my daughters, Mara Blitzer and Hannah Blitzer, for the years of just listening and for starting their professional lives so successfully and admirably.

PREFACE

Welcome to *Hire Me, Inc.*, the complete resource to your ongoing career success. The information, advice, and exercises here (mostly in diagram-format throughout the text) serve as a guide to help clarify who you are (your unique skills), what you like to do (your interests), and what is important to you (your values). Understanding the best mix of these career keys can lead both to greater enjoyment in your work to become a better job candidate for your prospective employer.

This is just as much a "do" book as it is a "read" book. For you to get the most out of the text, you need to follow along, fill in the blanks, and focus your entergies. To help you along you'll also find some handy CEOs (Consultant Examples and Opinions) in each section of the book that provide either summaries or additional tips for your career enhancement. Here's an example:

CEO (Consultant Examples and Opinions)

Be sure to create:

- Strategy. It helps to have a plan or a picture of what you'd like to achieve in the long-term and what you see yourself enjoying at specific stages in your career. So make a flexible strategy—and follow it.

- Structure. It helps to set a routine. Set a specific amount of time each day for your job search (but make time for movies and popcorn, too). Organize how you will do what I recommend here.

- Support. It helps to test your assumptions and to talk about what you're feeling, thinking, and doing. Utilize your friends, family, and business colleagues as sounding boards, and listen to their advice when appropriate.

- Skills. It helps to freshen your job search skills if they're stale. Revisit your ideas on interviewing, building a resume, and presenting yourself. Push beyond your comfort level and experiment with new behaviors.

Finding work is hard work, yet the process can be exciting and exhilarating, filled with experiences that are ultimately valuable in a job. Building a rewarding career is not an easy chore, but if you maintain a sense of humor, you can lighten the load and see the fun, too.

Change of any kind is unsettling. If you have recently lost your job, there are lots of emotions that can surface, including everything from relief and disappointment to anger, embarrassment, hurt, and fear. Whether you are new to the workforce and looking for your first "real" job, are eager for a new work environment, want to continue what has been satisfying, are ready for a major shift in your established direction, or somewhere in between, similar emotions often apply. Your feelings are not easily adjusted and hardly predictable. You can wake up one day feeling terrific, and on another day feel angry or down in the dumps. Take account of how you're feeling, and learn more about what you want.

Being out of work is an especially good time to take stock of your career and to reflect on who you are and what you want to do for your future. To move more easily, and as painlessly as possible, through the job search process, think of yourself as a "product" ready to launch into the marketplace. (Hopefully, you're the new and improved model!) Now is your chance to renew, repackage, and revitalize yourself, and to showcase what you can do and how you can add value or become invaluable to an employer.

The aim of *Hire Me, Inc.* is to help you present yourself as a product, a unique item being launched into the work marketplace. As you begin your search, be mindful that there are a few basics to know before you start.

Looking for a job or new career is difficult work, a full-time job. There are lots of things to do when you're trying to find that ideal job or next work opportunity. Remember not to get too overwhelmed by the enormity of the project. It might be better to break things down into steps that are more easily manageable. Landing a position in today's job market is not a slam-dunk, make-one-phone-call, start-on-Monday proposition. It's tough out there because there's a lot of competition. Your search requires handling everything from a disciplined routine and follow-through plan to making solid decisions and choosing what is best for you and your situation.

Keep positive and upbeat. Try to roll with the punches, or at least learn how to duck. The process can be an emotional

---

VIP (Very Important Point)

You will soon see how to align your behaviors to the traditional Marketing Model.

- *Product.* Who are you, and what value do you bring to the organization?

- *Price.* How much are you worth, and what offer are you willing to accept?

- *Place.* Where are you willing to live; how much time are you willing to commute?

- *Promotion.* How are you going to present yourself and let people know you are available?

roller coaster ride, often jarring and bringing out both your best and worst. It impacts everything from how you cope with stress to maintaining your self-esteem: Can I deal with a tough interview? Am I really worth that salary?

It's also tough to think positively when you're feeling negative and recovering from rejection. Employers are looking for the best fit for their organizations. A lot of people can do the work, but not all of them can do it with an energetic, enthusiastic approach.

Distinguish yourself from others with a positive spin on what you say and do. Take a cue from some politicians here. Confidence is often the key to a job offer. So, let it shine for those considering you for a job.

Exuding confidence is a challenge at times when you just don't feel up to par. Remember that everyone who's hiring wants someone who's eager for the job, or at least appears to be. You'll need to smile like a beauty queen at times. So stay positive.

Asking for help is OK. People want you to succeed. But many job seekers are reluctant to call on friends and family for assistance. Excuses like "It's been too long since I've spoken to him," or "He's too busy to bother with me" are too often the out.

It's also a stretch for an introverted person to phone a contact. Remember that most people want to help you. It makes them feel good. They often are busy and pressed for time but also flattered that you've called them. Most will readily share their advice and suggestions. It's a win-win conversation. They feel good, and you get help. Accept input graciously, and try not to see it as an obligation. Remember to take the time to tell your contacts how they can help you most, whether by providing contacts or key information, identifying opportunities, or just listening to you.

Changing jobs or shifting careers is now an inevitable part of life. People with long careers at the same company, and often in the same position, may find this hard to believe and even tougher to accept. But most people do get bored or at least "routinized" in their work when they've been doing it seemingly forever—unless, perhaps, their high pay keeps them entertained. Typically, the itch for learning something new or taking on a challenging responsibility at work occurs about every two to three years. It's like products that are always enhanced and improved with the latest and greatest features and benefits. So change is both natural and inevitable, and you should be ready and open to adaptation in your work.

Some people just seem to flow with change better than others. Some love change and manage it wonderfully. Others have difficulty with any shift in routine or break in pattern. Knowing how you treat change and understanding that you're not alone may be the first step in managing the change you're facing.

There are lots of opportunities, and sometimes the presence of many choices makes it harder rather than easier. You are the only one who can take responsibly for your product and your positioning, despite the fact that very few people are born knowing what their careers will be and how they will plan for them.

Acknowledge your emotions—especially fear—and examine how you've dealt with changes in the past. Two books might help here. In *Feel the Fear and Do It Anyways*, Dr. Susan Jeffers suggests that fear is always part of growing, and the only way to eliminate fear of a task is to simply do it. She says pushing through the fear is easier than doing nothing and feeling helpless. William Bridges' *Transitions: Making Sense of Life's Changes* helps understand transitions. He describes transition as the unproductive time when you feel disconnected from people and things during a life passage. Bridges calls this circumstance the "neutral zone," a pause to overcome with fresh creativity and bold ideas for a new beginning.

Things happen for the best. It may be hard to accept this in the first few days after losing a job, but talk to someone who's been through the experience. She will acknowledge that the experience was good for her. Consider this: One door closing leads to another opening.

Trust the process, and trust yourself. When a job goes away, you have to redefine what you can control and what you can't. And you need to reconnect to your values and your personality. When you're not satisfied with what you're doing, a little voice inside tells you to look for more. Job loss often gives you the push for a change you were mulling over anyway but not quite ready to try.

> ## VIPP (Very Important Product Point)
>
> A job search is most similar to riding a roller coaster. There are ups and downs and lots of unpredictables. Try to see it as enormously fun and exhilarating rather than stomach-wrenching and frightening.

What you gain from the unemployment experience prepares you for the next important job in your life. And the next opportunity you win can be even better and more rewarding.

Consider your reaction to past changes. List five major changes you've experienced in your life so far. Then, answer the following questions for each change.

1. Was the change voluntary or involuntary? _____

_____

_____

2. What feelings surfaced when you confronted the experience? _____

_____

_____

3. What did you do to deal with the event? _____

_____

_____

4. How would you evaluate the impact the change made on your life? _____

_____

_____

5. What did you take away from the experience? _____

_____

_____

6. What would you do differently, if anything? _____

_____

_____

If your current thoughts are negative, try to change your perspective by creating the positive. Quite often creating the positive (or eliminating negative self talk) is an activity you can do periodically. Sometime, midway during your search, when you have been at it awhile and are feeling discouraged or disappointed at not getting the big one or losing a few close calls, try the technique again. Use it and work to look at the positives of what you've accomplished. Try to eliminate negativity that can bring you down or not present you as you want to be.

Replace these negative thoughts	with positive statements of a winner
"I'm never going to find what I want."	"I only need one job, and there is one out there for me that will match."
"I don't know anyone who can help me."	"Everyone has a network. Once I give some serious thought to my future, I'll be able to identify a lot of folks who can help me in this search."
"Competition is too tough for the job I want."	"I intend to be better prepared than my competition. I'll get the right job for me."
"My skills aren't very marketable."	I have been working successfully for years. I have education/training, experience, talent, and skills that make me valuable to any employer."
"No one is going to want me."	"I am a valuable individual who can make a contribution to any organization smart enough to get me."

List other concerns or negative feelings. Then, convert them into "winning" statements.

_____   _____

_____   _____

_____   _____

_____   _____

_____   _____

A final thought about control to ponder. You're in charge of this process, and you're the person ultimately responsible for its outcome. Certainly, you can use consultants to help you in all phases of this marketing project, but you make the ultimate decisions. A job loss may have been beyond your control. Put yourself back in the driver's seat. There is very little in life you have to do, really. Choice is what makes the search for a new position and/or career both colorful and commanding. Think of everything in your life and your work as a choice — activities you choose to do, not must do. It can be a liberating experience.

Now, list those chores or responsibilities that seem like musts or givens. In reality, they are choices, too. If you can see what you do and how your actions are always a choice, you will be in control of your campaign and in charge of the entire experience. Try switching the word "have" to "choose" for an entire week, and check to see what your reaction and responses are.

Have to	**Choose to**
Write three cover letters today	Write three cover letters today
Clean the backyard	Clean the backyard
Live in a 3,000-sq.-ft. home	Live in a 3,000-sq.-ft. home
_____	_____
_____	_____
_____	_____
_____	_____
_____	_____

Now that you've had a sample of what's to come, be prepared to master your job-hunting skills and to enjoy "the ride," as you package yourself to get that dream job.

Dedication

This book is dedicated to those people whom I may have helped in some way to discover their passion and to earn their livelihoods in jobs and careers they love. My hope is that they will bring inspiration to those still searching, and the future workplace will be filled with happy and productive individuals. The journey for job/career satisfaction is well worth the effort—your joy at doing what you're good at, what you love, and what's important to you can make an enormous long-term difference.

THE PRODUCT
Self Assessment/Product Analysis

People sell something all the time. In the world of work, it's often a product or a service. You interact within your own organization or in the marketplace, and the goal of the sale can be anything from realizing a profit, to adoption of a new plan, to a major shift in behavior. In the layman's world, you also "sell" to meet your objectives. You "sell" your friends and partners on the value of maintaining a lasting relationship; you "sell" your kids on the benefits of education and progress at school; and you "sell" your contractors on the value of cost-effective, reliable service for continued business.

Launching your search for a new job or career is no different than introducing a new product into the marketplace. It demands a sound marketing strategy and solid sales skills. Even if you're uneasy about selling yourself and have little or no marketing background, creating a realistic marketing plan and managing its step-by-step process can position your product—you—successfully in the marketplace. And you can make the sale.

ANALYZING YOURSELF

You need to begin by looking at the product and the marketplace objectively. That means taking a realistic view of your skills, growth areas, interests, pursuits, and values. In order to sell yourself, you must know your product's features and benefits and the buyer's needs and motivations. In other words, if your product is ice, you don't want to sell it to Eskimos. This rational and honest examination of your professional attributes, when linked with your job market research, will provide the true focus and the assurance to pursue legitimate career options. Figure 1.1 helps you discover which attributes are your strongest.

Note the skills, knowledge, and talents you've identified as a four (4) or a five (5), the higher scores. Understanding these as your better traits will come in handy in describing who you are, in distinguishing your product "qualities." Once you're comfortable and familiar with these unique strengths, you can emphasize them in many ways—as accomplishments, managing techniques, or strategic initiatives—to better promote yourself to interviewers looking to learn what you can do for their companies and why they should hire you.

It's also important to capture the attributes and traits that define your personality. Begin by checking 15 traits from the list in Figure 1.2. From that group, choose five and write them in the spaces that follow (see page 7).

VIPP (Very Important Product Point)

Self-assessment is only valuable if you are totally HONEST. Be sure you reply to all questions clearly and evaluate yourself as you really are vs. as you want to be. Remember, no one else is perfect either.

Figure 1.1: **Functional Skills Assessment and Inventory**

Rate the relative strength of each of your skills as:

(1) Weak   (2) Below average   (3) Average   (4) Above average   (5) Strong

Business Skills/Abilities	Score
Leadership (motivating, directing, delegating, hiring/firing)	
Communication (public speaking, selling ideas, negotiating)	
Planning (developing strategy, designing, improving)	
Organizing (seeing goals, scheduling, prioritizing)	
Organizational Skills/Abilities	**Score**
Administration (expediting, cataloging)	
Attention to detail	
Budgeting	
Buying/purchasing	
Calculating numbers	
Follow-through	
Memory	
Keeping good records	
Managing projects	
Precision	
Mechanical Skills/Abilities	**Score**
Assembling	
Assessing mechanics	
Building or crafting	
Constructing	

Figure 1.1: **Functional Skills Assessment and Inventory,** continued

Mechanical Skills/Abilities (continued)	Score
Installing	
Loading or shipping	
Repairing or maintaining	
Running or operating machines	
Working with hand tools	
Theory Skills/Abilities	**Score**
Designing systems	
Envisioning	
Estimating	
Evaluating or analyzing	
Formulating ideas	
Investigating	
Learning quickly	
Solving problems	
Artistic Skills/Abilities	**Score**
Aesthetic	
Artistic	
Compositional	
Entrepreneurial	
Idealistic	
Illustrative	
Imaginative	
Inventive	

Figure 1.1: **Functional Skills Assessment and Inventory,** continued

Social Skills/Abilities	Score
Advising	
Coaching	
Counseling	
Explaining concepts	
Facilitating	
Generating warmth	
Listening attentively	
Motivating	
Negotiating	
Sympathizing/Empathizing	
Teaching	

Figure 1.2: **Personal Traits Assessment and Inventory**

___ achiever	___ aware	___ conscientious
___ adaptable	___ calm	___ creative
___ adventurous	___ candid	___ curious
___ ambitious	___ cautious	___ decisive
___ analytical	___ cheerful	___ dependable
___ articulate	___ cheerleader	___ detail-oriented
___ assertive	___ civic-minded	___ diligent
___ astute	___ committed	___ diplomatic
___ authentic	___ confident	___ discerning

Figure 1.2: **Personal Traits Assessment and Inventory,** continued

___ dominant	___ level-headed	___ self-assured
___ dynamic	___ loyal	___ self-confident
___ easy-going	___ methodical	___ self-controlled
___ emotional	___ modest	___ sensible
___ empathetic	___ natural	___ sincere
___ energetic	___ open-minded	___ sociable
___ entertaining	___ optimistic	___ spontaneous
___ expressive	___ orderly	___ stable
___ firm	___ original	___ strong
___ flexible	___ outdoors person	___ tactful
___ focused	___ outspoken	___ talkative
___ formal	___ patient	___ task-oriented
___ friendly	___ persistent	___ tenacious
___ generous	___ physically strong	___ thorough
___ goal-directed	___ playful	___ tolerant
___ good with information	___ poised/confident	___ trustworthy
___ good with people	___ practical	___ versatile
___ hardworking	___ precise	___ well-organized
___ humble	___ predictable	___ willing to learn
___ humorous	___ productive	
___ imaginative	___ quick-learner	
___ impulsive	___ regular/rare traveler	
___ informal	___ reliable/dependable	
___ intelligent	___ resourceful	
___ leader	___ responsible	

1._____

2._____

3._____

4._____

5._____

Now take these five traits and apply them to Figure 1.3, which is the final step that helps you analyze your product and looks at the special skills and knowledge you have acquired in school or in previous positions. Read the examples below, and in the spaces provided, fill in your unique technical and knowledge skills from your previous work or life experiences.

Example 1. **Job Title/Activity: Life Guard**

Technical or Knowledge Skill 1: CPR certificate: EMT Training

Technical or Knowledge Skill 2: Red Cross Sr. Life Saving Certificate

Technical or Knowledge Skill 3: _____

Technical or Knowledge Skill 4: _____

Technical or Knowledge Skill 5: _____

Example 2. **Job Title/Activity: Administrative Assistant**

Technical or Knowledge Skill 1: Microsoft Word

Technical or Knowledge Skill 2: Excel

Technical or Knowledge Skill 3: _____

Technical or Knowledge Skill 4: _____

Technical or Knowledge Skill 5: _____

Example 3. **Job Title/Activity: Manufacturing Engineer**

Technical or Knowledge Skill 1: Proficient in ERP

Technical or Knowledge Skill 2: Trained in ISO 9000

Technical or Knowledge Skill 3: _____

Technical or Knowledge Skill 4: _____

Technical or Knowledge Skill 5: _____

Figure 1.3: **Technical/Knowledge Skills Inventory**

Your Technical or Knowledge Skill 1

Job Title/Activity: _____

Technical or Knowledge Skill 1: _____

Technical or Knowledge Skill 2: _____

Technical or Knowledge Skill 3: _____

Technical or Knowledge Skill 4: _____

Technical or Knowledge Skill 5: _____

Your Technical or Knowledge Skill 2

Job Title/Activity: _____

Technical or Knowledge Skill 1: _____

Technical or Knowledge Skill 2: _____

Technical or Knowledge Skill 3: _____

Technical or Knowledge Skill 4: _____

Technical or Knowledge Skill 5: _____

Take a moment to put these skills in perspective so you will be able to speak to them later on. The questions below will also help you.

Which of your technical skills are most marketable? _____

_____

Which technical knowledge skills must you build or strengthen to be more competitive? _____

_____

What must you do to obtain the technical skills knowledge cited above? _____

_____

STRENGTHS AND WEAKNESSES

Now that you've analyzed and assessed your personal traits, skills, special talents, and technical mastery, you can better summarize your overall strengths and gauge areas for improvement. Reflect on the skills that gained you frequent compliments, recall favorable performance evaluations (including the praises of your family and friends), and also note constructive critiques from your managers, clients, and peers. Remember, even the best products are often remarketed as "new and improved." (Just avoid throwing out your "brand" altogether as Coke did so disastrously by switching its popular flavor to Coke Classic). Use Figure 1.4 to help in this assessment.

The point is that it's OK to appreciate your talents, get feedback from trusted opinions, and continue to tinker—not tamper—with your recipe for success. The more you understand about yourself as a product, what you can and cannot do, and the fluctuating demands of the job marketplace, the better salesperson you'll be for your skills.

> ## VIPP (Very Important Product Point)
>
> People are all too often self-critical. For some people and in some cultures, looking to the positive is difficult. To help focus on your strengths, consider your past performance reviews: On what were you complimented? Where were you praised? Look for specifics and search out more than what your mom would say if asked about your positive qualities.

Figure 1.4: **Strengths and Areas to Improve**

Strengths (+)	Areas to Improve (△)

YOUR INTERESTS

Think about your job history and former work, and honestly assess those assignments and tasks that you especially mastered and enjoyed and that gave you genuine excitement and accomplishment. Now reflect on aspects of your work that you found boring, unpleasant, or pointless. When you compare these lists, you'll learn what interests you and what turns you off in a job, and you can then assess a potential position on this basis.

Liked Most	Recent Job	Liked Least
_____	_____	_____
_____	_____	_____
_____	_____	_____

Liked Most	Previous Job 1	Liked Least
_____	_____	_____
_____	_____	_____
_____	_____	_____

Liked Most	Previous Job 2	Liked Least
_____	_____	_____
_____	_____	_____
_____	_____	_____

Completing the exercise in Figure 1.5 will give you another way to look at types of work that bring you contentment or dissatisfaction. Figure 1.5 is similar to Figure 1.1, however, it approaches the interest from a different perspective, which can help you clarify your interests.

Figure 1.5: **Ranking Work Interests**

Rank each item in the list in a range from Like (4) to Dislike (1).

	Like			Dislike
Investigative Interests	4	3	2	1
To read and study				
To think through problems more than solve them				
To study math and science				
To investigate physical things				
To solve puzzles				
To tackle ambiguous challenges				
Total*				

Figure 1.5: **Ranking Work Interests,** continued

	Like			Dislike
Realistic Interests	4	3	2	1
To operate machinery				
To work outdoors				
To repair things				
To work with my hands				
To work with tools				
To do physical work				
Total*				
Artistic Interests	4	3	2	1
To avoid structure				
To work independently				
To search for creative solutions				
To express myself				
To discover unconventional answers				
To make aesthetic statements				
Total*				
Social Interests	4	3	2	1
To supervise people				
To care for others				
To work with people				
To help others				
To be part of a group				
To train others				
Total*				

Figure 1.5: **Ranking Work Interests,** continued

	Like			Dislike
Enterprising Interests	4	3	2	1
To manage projects				
To speak to groups				
To persuade others				
To accomplish tasks				
To sell things				
To be the leader				
Total*				
Conventional Interests	4	3	2	1
To have stability				
To be orderly				
To follow the chain of command				
To know what is next				
To have well-defined tasks				
To create systems and procedures				
Total*				

*To score your results, count each column's check marks and multiply that number by the point value of the column. Add the totals for each category together. Now fill in the scores for each below:

Investigative   _____

Realistic   _____

Artistic   _____

Social   _____

Enterprising   _____

Conventional   _____

List your top three work interests:

1._____

2._____

3._____

YOUR PERSONAL INTERESTS

A final way to look at your interests is to focus on what you like to do in your spare time. What are your hobbies? How do you relax? How do you entertain yourself? What brings you pleasure outside the job? They, too, are part of your product analysis, what makes you unique and special and, perhaps, how you position yourself in the job marketplace. List six or eight, or even more if you have wide-ranging interests.

Personal Interests

_____

_____

_____

_____

_____

_____

YOUR ACCOMPLISHMENTS

Look at your accomplishments as another way of assessing your product worth to a prospective buyer. A list of your key accomplishments can be compiled from experiences at school, work, or home and reflect your various satisfactions and fulfillments. (See more about this in Chapter 3 on how to build your resume.)

Think of your accomplishments as an OAR in the water, helping you row to your destination.

O *The opportunity.* What opportunity was there for you? What was the problem? What was the context or situation at hand?

A *The activity.* What action did you take? How did you solve the problem and address the situation? What specifically did you do, recommend, or initiate?

R *The result.* What did you achieve? What was the successful outcome? What is the metric that illustrates your accomplishment?

Complete the exercise below, considering the opportunity, activity, and result of each action noted. Choose four accomplishments that are important to you and make you proud; then explain them using the OAR format.

Sample Accomplishment Rating

Accomplishment: Increased the attendance at internal training programs.

O   As a corporate trainer, I was chartered with improving the participation of internally sponsored programs.

A   Generated a first-time online Needs Assessment document and a follow-up brochure of topics linked to corporate goals.

R   Attendance increased by 68 percent.

Accomplishment 1

O   _____

_____

A   _____

_____

R   _____

_____

Accomplishment 2

O   _____

_____

A   _____

_____

R _____

_____

Accomplishment 3

O _____

_____

A _____

_____

R _____

_____

Accomplishment 4

O _____

_____

A _____

_____

R _____

_____

YOUR LIFE AND CAREER VALUES

In large measure, who you are and what work you are best suited to do stems from your core values—those strongly held beliefs that are the foundation of your life and provide clarity to what you do and how you do it. Values may come from your parents and upbringing, religious beliefs, education, role models, and elsewhere. Many successful people attribute a rewarding personal life and apt career choices to an abiding appreciation of their core values.

Review each of the values in Figure 1.6, and check the column that best describes how consistently important each has been to you: Always, Often, Sometimes, or Rarely Valued. Limit yourself to the ten or fewer checks in the Always Valued column.

Figure 1.6: **Values**

	Valued			
	Always	**Often**	**Sometimes**	**Rarely**
1. Personal growth. Develop my potential and use my talents.				
2. Reward/achievement. Know accomplishments and mastery.				
3. Understanding/knowledge. Develop and use specific expertise and knowledge.				
4. Status. Hold a position of recognized importance in an organization.				
5. Competitiveness. Take part in activities in which people compete against each other.				
6. Variety and change. Do work with varied tasks and assignments.				
7. Making a difference to society. Give back and help contribute to a better society.				
8. Physical activity. Do tasks that require strength, agility, or physical stamina.				
9. Autonomy/independence. Control my own schedule/work.				
10. Leadership. Influence others to achieve their goals by helping direct and influence others.				
11. Creative expression. Express my creativity and imagination.				
12. Challenge. Find work that is mentally stimulating.				
13. Money. Reap substantial financial rewards.				

Figure 1.6: **Values,** continued

	Valued			
	Always	**Often**	**Sometimes**	**Rarely**
14. Security. Perform assignments without worry about loss of job.				
15. Management. Achieve work objectives as a result of other efforts.				
16. Collaboration. Work with others; belong to a collegial work team or group.				
17. Power. Manage work resources.				
18. Integrity. Work honestly and ethically.				
19. Balance. Establish an appropriate proportion of personal and professional activities/ responsibilities.				
20. Friendship. Develop personal/social relationships with colleagues at work.				
21. Career movement. Deserve promotion within the organization.				
22. Detail work. Work with assignments that meet and require specific and accurate attention to detail.				
23. Fast pace. Work under circumstances that are time pressured and demanding.				
24. Helping others. Involve myself in helping others and society.				
25. Location. Reside in a location that is convenient and in a suitable community.				
26. Recognition. Receive credit for work well done.				

Figure 1.6: **Values,** continued

	Valued			
	Always	**Often**	**Sometimes**	**Rarely**
27. Excitement. Experience novelty and innovation.				
28. Moral fulfillment. Contribute to moral needs.				
29. Aesthetics. Appreciate the beauty of ideas and things.				
30. Vigor/health. Maintain physical and mental fitness.				
31. Positive environment. Work in a supportive, pleasing, and harmonious setting.				
32. Efficient organization. Experience a time-efficient environment, with little bureaucracy.				
33. Family harmony. Maintain good balance between work and family life.				

VIPP (Very Important Product Point)

Remember that the assessment information you generate is to be seen as a guideline rather than a hard and fast set of rules. Interpreting deep meaning, analyzing or judging your data too harshly may not be productive. You need not narrow your search too early in the process. Sometimes your goals may appear to be in conflict—and yet you may find a way to match your values of making money and of saving the world.

Now, write your ten Always Valued criteria below, and then rank your top five.

My Priority Values	Rank
1. _____	_____
2. _____	_____
3. _____	_____
4. _____	_____
5. _____	_____
6. _____	_____
7. _____	_____
8. _____	_____
9. _____	_____
10. _____	_____

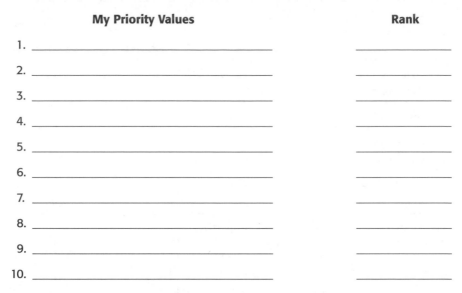

VIPP (Very Important Product Point)

Take a deeper look at what's important to you. Here are some questions that might help put things into place:

- What do you daydream about?

- What would you do if you couldn't fail and didn't have to be paid?

- Where do you get a sense of ultimate pleasure?

PUTTING IT TOGETHER TO PROMOTE A SOLID CAMPAIGN

Research validates that setting goals can be the key to getting the product to the right marketplace at the right time. Once more, consider yourself the product and try to answer the questions below.

What professional goals do you want to accomplish? Become a Director? Own your own business some day? Other? _____

_____

_____

What are your personal goals? Find a life partner? Gain more family time? Buy a new/bigger home? Other?   _____

_____

_____

What does your self-assessment indicate about your ideal job?   _____

_____

_____

What do you really want to do? Function? Industry? Tasks? Boss relationship? _____

_____

_____

Where do you want to do it? Location? Lifestyle non-negotiables—commute, etc.?

_____

_____

What are your minimum financial requirements?   _____

_____

_____

What is your time frame? How long should you be looking?* _____

_____

_____

*Outplacement data note that it can take up to one month per $10,000 income requirement, (e.g., you'll need to search five months for a $50,000 annual salary).

Think of your career search as a promotional event in which you present your unique combination of skills (personal traits and experience), interests (job motivators), and work/life values for an audience to appreciate and applaud (interview and hire). Everything you do, from creating your marketing tools (the resume, bio, cover letter, etc.), to designing your package (interview articulation and appearance), to closing the sale (negotiating the offer particulars) needs to emphasize and focus on your unique skills, interests, and values. Ideally, the mix of these components distinguishes you and provides your

> ## CEO (Consultant Examples and Opinions)
>
> 1. Look at the long-term value this product analysis or self-assessment process offers, minimizing any short-term effort in executing it:
>   - Your resume will be more organized and focused.
>   - You'll be better prepared to answer tough interview questions.
>   - Your assessment data may reflect patterns in your career history that will help your future decisions.
>   - You will most likely begin your campaign with more confidence and gain more poise later.
>   - You will have a fresh perspective on your strengths and accomplishments.
>   - Your process will most likely be more organized.
>
> 2. Be honest with your answers and evaluations. An objective and candid assessment is needed now, not a sugar-coated, what-I-want-to-be-when-I grow-up response.
>
> 3. Consider additional assessments (some with special career data that require a certified professional to interpret) that are available free on the internet and can illuminate some of the data generated here. Some useful assessments are the MBTI (Myers-Briggs Type Indicator), Strong Interest Inventory, Kiersey Temperament, The Birkman, and Lominger's Career Architect Skill Sort Cards. Here, too, be sure your answers are honest—try not to supply the "right" answer or what you think the instrument is measuring.

unique advantage in the job marketplace, connecting you with the needs of your key customer.

✳ *Summary* ✳

✳ Knowing who you are is the most important part of the marketing mix. You are in control. You are the one in charge.

✳ Matching your interests, skills, and values should bring ultimate career and job satisfaction.

✳ Setting a solid foundation of your accomplishments and successes early on will make moving forward and the rest of this process easier.

✳ Learning your professional "edge" and how to promote it will help distinguish you.

CHAPTER

RESEARCH AND DEVELOPMENT

Understanding the Market/Landscape

Marketing 101 tells you that successful organizations introduce a new product only after having first researched the needs and wants of the marketplace. Your product introduction is no exception. Until you know what the market needs and desires, you're not ready to fully promote your unique combination of skills (experience), interests, and values. You wouldn't enter a beauty contest without knowing if it included a swimsuit competition, right?

New positions are created through expansion, that is, economic growth and development, or turnover, that is replacing new people in existing jobs. Research is an important tool in discovering these opportunities. It will help identify everything from company names and locations to specific job openings, product information, industry growth and trends, sales forecasts, and officer, board member, and key employee names.

Perhaps the market has changed since you were last looking for work, or technological advances demand more cutting-edge skills than you have now. If you've been in the same job for 20 years or more, you may even want to check out the latest styles and buy a new suit or two. Thorough research will help gauge how the market relates to your strengths, areas of improvement, and experience. It will help you to better evaluate your career objectives and determine if the job fit is appropriate.

Understanding the job market will also save you valuable time because you'll be able to sell yourself to the right market segment. Your presentation will include market research and data asserting your value to the organization and will illustrate how your qualifications meet the specific organizational requirements.

It helps to be mentally and physically ready for your marketing campaign and, most importantly, to have a vision of how your success will appear—and I don't mean consulting your horoscope. Experience says that visualization is vital to success. Athletes are trained to visualize positive results of their play—to see the ball in the cup before making the putt or to see the ribbon breaking at the finish line before the starting gun is fired. If you're not inclined for sports, see the audience stand as you take your bows.

Imagine yourself finding significant information about a job you want. See yourself in the interview. Picture the positive presentation of your skills. Envision yourself making the closed-deal handshake. And then, see yourself walking proudly into the lobby for your first day of new work.

So it makes perfect sense to study industry trends and look clearly at possible impediments to your successful product rollout. Time spent here will never, ever be wasted.

VIPP (Very Important Product Point)

Job search statistics vary. How people get employment is not a cut-and-dried science, so it is not easy to measure. Most outplacement organizations conduct post "landing" surveys and interviews of candidate participants. The data here reflect that often unpublished information.

CEO (Consultant Examples and Opinions)

1. Carve a slice of time each day to conduct your research.

2. Be sure your activities:

   · Generate a list of target companies and names of key decision-makers.

   · Increase your knowledge about companies and industries that reinforce your career decision.

   · Prepare you for job interviews by knowing company market and product activities, and/or recent events in the news.

   · Uncover job openings.

3. Remember these facts:

   · Owning your own business is still the American dream—nearly 700,000 new businesses form each year, but 62 percent of them fail. Generating a detailed business plan helps ensure viability. (Remember one of your options in this search is working for yourself.)

   · Seventy percent of all jobs are filled internally—more than 50 percent of the people getting work do so in jobs that are never advertised or posted anywhere.

   · Through networking, 70 to 80 percent of jobs are acquired and filled externally: 10-15 percent via the internet; 5 percent from target mailings; 5 to 10 percent from executive searches; 5 percent from ads and job fairs.

   · More jobs are available in suburban locations than ever before—education levels and affordable housing, in addition to favorable tax inducements, have attracted employers out of major urban areas.

   · More than 95 percent of all organizations in America have fewer than 100 full-time employees.

   · There are increasing numbers of contract positions and interim assignments in accounting, engineering, and information technology—125,000 interim executives are at work on any given day. Many contracts lead to full-time positions.

RESEARCH METHODOLOGIES: SOURCES AND RESOURCES

The most efficient and effective way to conduct your market research phase is to role play as an investigative reporter or a private detective. (I told you this could be fun.) Say you've been assigned to cover the launch of a brand new job, but you're not sure when or where it will be released. So, you need to find the clues and facts that will lead you to its appearance. The more data you collect through the internet, libraries, telephone calls, periodicals, journals, newspapers, your somewhat suspicious cousin, or even what you pick up in a casual conversation, the easier it will be to narrow your target search. Then, you're sure to be on the scene when it's time to nab the job.

The research process involves sourcing the information, sorting and penetrating these sources for additional data to help you discover your value added, and focusing your market information and self-assessment data to identify targets that offer job possibilities. Look to companies themselves, individuals, various organizations, networking, libraries, and, obviously, the internet to gather help and information.

Parameters

Contact companies with the high probability of buying your product, that is, of hiring someone with your skills, experience, interests, and values. There are a variety of resources readily available to you, sources where you can get the information you need and uncover the hidden job market.

Individuals

There are a number of people who can provide you with relevant background and insight into industry trends, opportunities within specific organizations, and changes in functional fields. Other colleagues may become part of your network or research database. Remember those 70 to 80 percent of jobs gained through networking?

Other professionals, those outside your field, can also add an interesting perspective or pass on valuable career information. Talk with competitors, attorneys, venture capitalists, CPAs, consultants, professors, suppliers, vendors, stockbrokers, bankers, and recruiters.

Meetings and Networking

Look to people among your sports and hobby pastimes, community groups, college alumni, chambers of commerce, and professional associations for ideal information-gathering opportunities. Some churches, mosques, and synagogues, many civic groups such as Rotary, Odd Fellows, Elks, and fantasy football, and many schools have existing support groups as well. Check out the Forty Plus Group or the 5 o'Clock Club in your area.

Libraries

Local public, university, and business libraries offer internet access and have both hard copy and online documents of key research options and opportunities. Your business or reference librarian can point out these job-seeker resources, both online and via CD-ROM, and can also recommend internet use courses. Here's a break when you're out of work: some fee-based research databases on the internet may be available free at your local library.

THE WORLD WIDE WEB AND INTERNET

The internet, or the World Wide Web, is perhaps the world's largest library and offers a rapidly growing community of people to provide invaluable data as well. The breadth of information here is unsurpassed. The validity of information, however, is not always clear. Make sure to use reliable job hunting sites, not your cousin Mary's blog.

You can obtain reliable information through direct access to a company's web site, through search engines, company financial databases, and numerous employment opportunity sites. The internet is an especially helpful tool in gathering specific company information and industry trends, as well as the occasional e-trade you're banking on.

The internet is a positive supplement to a wide variety of strategies, but it should not replace meeting and connecting with people

> **VIPP** **(Very Important Product Point)**
>
> Beware of spending too much of your time on your computer. Valuable as it is, the internet is an activity you do alone (something introverts just love) and can suck up huge amounts of time, time you could be spending getting out there, meeting new people.

in person. It's always better to shake hands than to tap keys. Remember, only 10 to 15 percent of open jobs are landed via the internet. Try not to use the web as a too-comfortable substitute for quality face time with your contacts. If you find yourself always intoning, "I'm really spending a lot of time looking online," you've made your internet tool a crutch. Certainly, if you're more introverted and prefer spending time on the internet vs. sharing lunches or meetings for job contacts and referrals, then by all means use the approach that suits you best. In general, however, the internet is best for gathering job and career search counsel and advice, especially company and industrial stats and forecasts.

You can research career and occupational resources to confirm your objectives and find out the salary ranges and the educational/skill requirements for positions you're pursuing in the United States, Canada, and Europe. Through salary and relocation guides, you can also discover cost-of-living comparisons, compensation survey data, and other relevant career-related statistics and tips (e.g., negotiating strategies, interviewing recommendations, networking dos and don'ts, even sample cover and thank-you letters). You can stay up-to-date on recent trends and hot topics of interest in your field, such as the professional gossip of comings and goings in your competitor companies. You can use key internet resource lists to help you retrieve very specific information using keywords via search engines, find career information to clarify your goals, and gather additional information to build your resume.

1. Search engines
   - www.alltheweb.com
   - www.altavista.digital.com
   - www.excite.com
   - www.go.com
   - www.google.com
   - www.lycos.com
   - www.netcrawler.com
   - www.yahoo.com
   - www.vivisimo.com
2. Career information offers ways to gather additional career input:
   - www.jobhuntersbible.com
   - www.Quintcareers.com

- www.Rileyguide.com
- www.Plsinfo.com

3. Resume help
   - www.Damngood.com
   - www.Resumehelp.com
   - www.Resumeplace.com

Researching Company and Industry Information

You can research companies and industries via web sites prior to your job interview. You can also use databases to research products, services, financial information, news and press releases, and industry trends. You can generate a list of target companies using online databases and/or search and list web sites of companies that interest or intrigue you. Post your resume there as well if you can access their current opportunities job listings.

You can research a new city or town if you're considering a relocation for a job or job search. Find out everything from real estate values and school districts to newcomer sites and chamber of commerce listings. You can probably even learn about the best place for a good steak.

The following are some key internet resource lists that could help. Company financial and annual reports let you read about the company and can enhance your understanding of the organization.

1. Company financial reports
   - www.reportgallery.com
   - www.hoovers.com
   - www.yahoo.com/quotes
   - www/zpub.com/sf/arl/index.html

2. Salary and relocation guides
   - www.homefair.com
   - www.city.net
   - www.jobsmart.org/tools/salary/index.htm
   - www.rileyguide.com/salguides.html
   - www.salary.com
   - www.jobstar.org

- www.wageweb.com
- www.careerjournal.com
- www.salarysource.com
- www.salaryexpert.com

Job Leads

Networking online through web site discussion groups can help you exchange information and ideas with fellow professionals in your field. You can join online discussion or chat groups to exchange articles, information, ideas, valuable experiences, or humorous tidbits. But watch out, you never know for sure who you're corresponding with; it could be a peer or an unscrupulous recruiter. You can also use online groups as an additional source for job leads and as an exchange resource for names and networking leads.

To uncover job listings in your field, you can use government and commercial job sites, newspaper classifieds, recruiter sites, and professional associations and their electronic journals. You can look for sites that will e-mail job openings to you. A number of job listing sites do this free of charge, and it can be a real time saver once you have set it up.

Below are some key internet resource lists that could help with job leads:

1. Mailing lists/newsgroups. These provide easy-to-adapt electronic mailing lists and news feeds.
   - www.paml.net
   - www.groups.google.com
   - www.yahoo.com/economy/organizations/professional
2. Online classified services. Most newspaper listings can be accessed through the newspaper's home page.
   - www.craigslist.org
   - www.bostonglobe.com
   - www.sfgate.com
   - www.careerbuilder.com
   - career.wsj.com
3. Employment opportunity sites.
   - www.dice.com
   - www.monster.com

- www.search.com
- www.careerbuilder.com
- www.careers.wsj.com
- www.careermag.com
- www.careershop.com
- www.joboptions.com
- www.jobsonline.com
- www.myjobsearch.com
- www.directemployers.com
- www.jobstar.org
- www.grassisgreener.com
- www.jobfactory.com/index.htm
- www.simplyhired.com

4. Not-for-profit sites
   - www.idealist.com
   - www.nonprofitjobs.com
   - www.opportunityknocks.com
   - www.pnnonline.org (click on "career center")
   - www.uwccr.org
   - www.craigslist.org (click on "non-profit" under jobs)
   - www.philanthropy.com
   - www.nonprofitabout.com
   - www.volunteermatch.com

5. Specific fields
   - Biotech sites
     - www.biospace.com
     - www.bioview.com
     - www.medzilla.com
     - www.bio.com
   - Hi-tech sites
     - www.brassring.com
     - www.itcareers.com
     - www.techies.com
     - www.jobhub.com

- www.netview.com/svg/about
- Government sites
  - www.fedworld.gov
  - www.jobsfed.com
- Executive sites for C-level and Senior staff positions
  - www.futurestep.com
  - www.6figurejobs.com
  - www.execunet.com
  - www.chiefmonster.com
  - www.the-office.com/board/jobs.htm
- Contract or temporary work sites
  - www.nettemps.com
  - www.prosavy.com
  - www.msquared.com

Resumes

You can market your resume (the honest one, right?), and post it on one of the many commercial resume databases that are reviewed by both human resource departments and recruiters. You can also direct mail your paperwork to companies and recruiters and/or post it on their sites.

E-mail is the most common communication means for employers, recruiters, and discussion group exchanges. If you don't have a designated site already, you can easily create a free e-mail account, with dedicated folders to capture your custom-arranged blocks of mail, and use it just for your search activities.

Online resume banks let you post your resume (often at no charge) and secure your privacy, as well. Most sites require that you submit your resume in an ASCII/text only format. So open your resume in Word on

VIPP (Very Important Product Point)

Some sites will not activate your paperwork unless you include all the salary data requested, that is, a complete salary history. However, for a paper application, which is often asked for when you go for an interview or as a final HR requirement, there is no law that requires you to include that information. You can leave it blank, put N/A, or use the term "negotiable" for the current salary question. If the information is really required, you will be contacted to provide it. Your goal at this stage is to get the in-person interview; you can provide the salary data then.

your desktop, and save it as "text only." Then, you can either upload it onto a resume bank site or cut and paste the document into the site's appropriate field(s). Hint: Choose a site that allows you to revise and/or refresh your resume regularly. That way, recruiters who missed it earlier can see it again as a "new" posting every time you update it—about every two weeks. Some sites will also let you post several resumes targeted to various positions at once and will even record for you the number of times and dates recruiters view your resume.

1. Resume sites
   - www.careerbuilder.com
   - www.hotjobs.com
   - www.employmentguide.com
   - www.monster.com
   - www.joboptions.com
   - www.jobbankusa.com
   - www.monstertrak.com
2. E-mail sites with free e-mail accounts
   - www.yahoo.com
   - www.hotmail.com
   - www.excite.com

Other Information Sources

Other sources of information range from databases to your local newspaper. Be sure to check out trade shows and job fairs in your town as well as surrounding ones.

- *Electronic databases.* Business Dateline and InfoTrac databases are both available at most local libraries. They allow you access to full text articles from 800 business magazines and journals. If you're interested in learning the financials of publicly-traded companies, you can access the EDGAR database as well. CareerSearch and Career Advantage are other proprietary databases that allow you to identify companies by product, industry, and geography.
- *Chamber of commerce listings.* Your local chamber of commerce lists the locations of companies in your area.

- *Classified advertisements*. Recent newspaper and journal advertisements are often indicators of a company's fresh growth, especially if there are multiple ads for the same organization. Check out these sources to learn more about your target company's latest enterprises, even if the company's business doesn't intrinsically match your background.
- *Job fairs and hotlines*. Both these venues can provide information on a specific organization's hiring and open job categories. Job fairs, especially, can connect you with a company insider (no, not a CIA-like mole, but often an interested hiring manager). More important, a job fair can also be a fun way to meet others with similar goals and expand your job search network. (See Chapter 4 for more details.)
- *College career placement centers*. Many hiring organizations use local universities and colleges as sources for job talent and make their list of job openings available.

HELP IN PRINT

You can enhance your marketability by staying informed and in touch. In other words, put down the remote and pick up a book. Useful books, magazines, guides, and directories are readily available—sometimes they can be found in your own house.

Business sections of local and national newspapers are excellent sources of data on everything from new ventures (overall growth) and product launches to reorganizations and key promotions. Professional newsletters and college alumni publications share news of employee shifts, product inventions and enhancements, convention and meeting information, and even job opportunities.

Reading annual reports and the financial reports of publicly-held corporations can reveal valuable information on business philosophy, current priorities, long-term contracts, and business volume and growth. Professional and trade journals often identify major changes in company personnel and direction that can lead to possible job sources. Reading them regularly could help you reconnect with industry peers.

National magazines are a big source of data, too. They are especially good at highlighting trends and forecasts.

- Each spring, *Fortune* magazine publishes the *Fortune 500 Directory* of the largest industrial corporations and the top 1,000 firms.
- *Fast Company, Business Week, The Industry Standard, Business 2.0,* and *Forbes* run timely articles on the job market and employment trends.
- *The Wall Street Journal* and *Barron's Index* publish alphabetical lists of articles.
- *Predicasts* compiles and indexes company, product, and industry articles from more than 750 financial publications, business-oriented newspapers, trade magazines, and special reports.

Directories

The publications listed below are available in both book and online formats and can provide you with a variety of invaluable source data. Remember that the organizations listed here are typically medium- to large-sized organizations.

- *ABI/Inform*. A CD-ROM database that indexes and abstracts 800 worldwide management and business journals.
- *Business Periodicals on Disc.* The ABI/Inform database of article references and abstracts are combined with the ability to view or print the complete text from an extensive number of the periodicals.
- *Corporate 1,000 Yellow Book*. A directory of who runs the top 1,000 U.S. companies.
- *Corporate Technology Directory*. A list of high-tech companies with indexes that include product data, technology, and geography.
- *Directories in Print*. Offers a list of broad subject categories, with both subject and title/key word indexes.
- *Directory of American Firms in Foreign Countries*.
- *Directory of Corporate Affiliations*. Parent company and subsidiaries information.
- *Directory of Executive Recruiters*. A yearly updated list of more than 2,000 U.S. search firms. A Kennedy publication, it is sold in most bookstores and available in libraries as well.
- *Directory of Foreign Manufacturers in the U.S. (4th Edition)*. Offers a list of 6,000 foreign-owned manufacturers with U.S. operations, coded by state location, parent company location, and product.

- *Dun & Bradstreet.* Offers in three volumes an alphabetical list of companies, subsidiaries, and officers, with a brief description of size, products, and services. See also *Dun & Bradstreet Market Identifiers/Online Service, Dun & Bradstreet Financial Records/Online Service,* and *Dun's Consulting Directory.*

- *Encyclopedia of Associations.* A guide to more than 2,000 associations in nearly every field. Some provide separate classified sections and an extended calendar of convention dates.

- *Encyclopedia of Business Information Sources.* Vital source of information on such key topics as oil, real estate, and finance.

- *Encyclopedia of Careers.* Three volumes of basic information on thousands of professions, occupations, and positions.

- *Environmental Industries Marketplace.* Detailed data on organizations in the environmental industry.

- *European Consultants Directory.* Access to 5,000 European consultants and their specialties.

- *Gale Globalaccess Associates.* Offers information on not-for-profit membership organizations at the international and U.S. regional, state, and local levels.

- *Guide to American Directories.* Information on more than 5,000 directories and 200 topics.

- *Hoover's Business Resources.* Offers a database of more than 1,600 of the largest and most powerful public and private organizations in the United States and the world.

- *Laser Disclosure.* A full-text database of exact reproductions of original SEC filings for more than 6,000 organizations.

- *MacMillan Directory of Leading Private Companies.* Information on more than 12,000 companies and wholly owned subsidiaries with sales of $10,000,000 or more.

- *Marquis Who's Who.* Biographies, locations, and public mailing guides to more than 75,000 professionals in entertainment, arts, science, government, sports, and business.

- *Moody's Industrial Manual.* Information on history, lines of business, mergers and acquisitions, subsidiaries, and joint ventures on more than 3,000 manufacturing industries, public utilities, banks, financial institutions, international, OTC, and transportation industries.

- *National Directory of Addresses and Telephone Numbers.*
- *National Newspaper Index.* A detailed index and internet access of eight major newsources, including the *New York Times*, the *Christian Science Monitor*, and *The Wall Street Journal*; updated monthly, the materials include four years of coverage.
- *Occupational Outlook Handbook.* A detailed overview of 200-plus fields of work.
- *Over-the-Counter 1,000 Yellow Book.* The names of NASDAQ-listed growth companies, with their addresses and phone numbers, and the titles of more than 20,000 of their managing executives.
- *Polk's Bank Directory.* A comprehensive list of financial and banking organizations.
- *Pratt's Guide to Venture Capital Sources.* Information and insight on every-thing from how to raise venture capital funds to additional business development activities to going public.
- *Principal International Businesses.* Annual information on more than 55,000 leading companies in 140 countries (a Dun's Marketing Services publication).
- *Small Business Sourcebook.* Information provided by venture capital firms, trade show data, franchisers, government agencies, educational programs, consultants, and professional associations on more than 100 types of small businesses.
- *Standard and Poor's Register of Corporations.* Volume I is an alphabetical list of companies, employee numbers, products, offices, and SIC sales volumes; volume II includes bios of the senior staff and directors.
- *Standard Directory of Advertisers.* An alphabetical list of more than 16,500 organizations by classification, company

> **VIPP** (Very Important Place Point)
>
> Remember, there is often a time lag between when a position requisition has been approved and when the advertisement or announcement appears in a newspaper, journal, or monthly publication. Some companies post openings that have already been filled as a way to generate resumes for the future and to telegraph that business is solid. Try not to get discouraged if there is never a reply. AND, if you are among the lucky few who get a fast response, react quickly.

name, and brand name, with entries that also include important contact particulars and advertising specifics.

- *Thomas Register*. A 12-volume list of national company products and services.
- *Ward's Business Directory of Major U.S. Private Companies (Vol. 2)*. A ranking of companies with $500,000 to $11,000,000 sales volume, with addresses and CEO names.

IDENTIFY TARGET ORGANIZATIONS

Start with the broad industry, and narrow your scope to specific organizations. Be sure you examine trends in your current field of interest or industry that could impact your campaign and/or the sale of your product. Answering the questions below will help identify trends.

Is my current industry going to shrink or expand in the next five to ten years? Why?

_____

_____

_____

The greatest competitive threat to my industry is _____ because

_____

_____

My industry is booming in (location) _____ because

_____

_____

The markets served by my industry are shrinking/growing because _____

_____

_____

_____

The most exciting area for me in my field is _____

_____

_____

I/my product is well-suited to meet the expectations of changes in my industry because _____

_____

_____

Establish your geographic limitations or requirements, if any. Put the place part of your marketing mix in order. Many people are committed to current locations for a variety of personal reasons and preferences whereas others are open to relocate to a particular U.S. region or international site. Remember that the more you restrict your preferred job location, the fewer options you'll have among potential employers or buyers for your product. To access your geographic requirements, consider the following questions.

- Are you receptive to relocation for your next position? How important is place in your marketing mix?
- Do you have constraints on the geographic areas you are willing to consider? Northeast? San Francisco Bay Area? The Trump Tower?
- Do you have commuting restrictions if you stay where you are?
- Would you consider an airline commute or working somewhere during the week and returning home on weekends?
- At what point in your search might you reconsider these parameters?

Search target industries with your career potential in mind. It's often easiest to sell your product (or find a job) in your existing industry or field of interest. Many buyers (employers) prefer a product (or candidate) who has worked well or has extensive coverage in a given area. If you're new to the workforce or eager for a career change, it's more important than ever to stay current on your industry's growth. Some specialties such as administrative services, human resources, finance and accounting, and even information technology, however, are not always industry specific.

If research reveals your industry's future is limited, or if your skills, interests, and values no longer suit your industry's direction, you may consider moving or selling your product to a new or related industry that offers more promise and is a better career fit. For example, health care workers have many complementary subindustries they can migrate to for a change: pharmaceuticals, biotech, medical devices, retirement homes, management consulting, and government or professional services. And teachers may turn to corporate training, social work, employee relations, or employee assistance programs.

It is important too, to talk to other people and think about tangential industries you could explore. Answer the questions below for some guidance.

What is the industry's expected growth? _____

_____

_____

How can I utilize my skills and knowledge most effectively in these industries/functions? _____

_____

_____

_____

How can I prioritize my personal interests and preferences (geography, environment)?

_____

_____

_____

At this point, a review of your desires and requirements will also help your decision-making.

You Desire	You Require
Flexible schedule	Discipline
Independence	Counsel from colleagues
Quality of life	Balance of activities
Unlimited income	Good bank account/comfortable sleep
Professional freedom	Variety of experiences and skills

Perhaps your research so far shows employment options besides a traditional full-time position, options such as self-employment. (I mean purpose-driven entrepreneurship not a navel-gazing indulgence). Starting your own business, buying or purchasing an existing business or franchise, or working on a contract or temporary assignment are often viable options, too. Remember, assessing your need for security, taking risks, flexibility, and hard work is as important as considering the financials.

If you are thinking now of starting your own business, some additional resources to consult are:

- *Working Solo* by Terri Lonier (Wiley, 1998).
- Paul and Sarah Edwards, "Making It on Your Own" online newsletter and Torcher, on CompuServe.
- National Association for the Self Employed, Hurst, Texas.
- *Buying Your Own Small Business* by Brian R. Smith and Thomas L. West (Stephen Greene Press, 1985).
- *The Complete Guide to Buying a Business* by Richard Snowden (Amacom, 1993).
- *Start Your Own Business, Third Edition* by Rieva Lesonsky (Entrepreneur Press, 2004).

Now you should be ready to select organizations within your industry and geographic parameters, companies with a high probability of hiring someone with your skills, experience, interests, and values. List several companies that you have targeted through your research, published openings, and talking to your friends and contacts. Be expansive and resourceful by including organizations of value for their products, research, market, or community-focused goals.

_____

_____

_____

_____

_____

_____

_____

_____

You can also target your companies by industry.

Sample: **Target Companies by Industry**

Healthcare	**Nonprofit**	**Professional Services**
_____	_____	_____
_____	_____	_____
_____	_____	_____

Your Target Companies by Industry

_____

_____

_____

Now it's time to dig for inside information on these target organizations. Revisit your research and list the vital information on each of your targets. Include the key data for your top ten: everything from the company's purpose to bios of the senior officers you might recognize or contacts you may know. Be sure your data includes:

VIPP (Very Important Place Point)

The best way to get the real skinny about a company that interests you is to ask. Seek out someone who works at the organization or who interacts a lot with people there. The ideal would be someone with a style most similar to yours. Company reputations and culture analyses are perceptions, so calibrate the data as best you can. A competitive and aggressive environment for one can represent a jungle or shark-infested waters to another.

Name	Number of employees
Address	Product or service
Phone number	Key contact*
Web e-mail	Key contact's assistant
Sales volume	Comments
Organizational changes	New product developments
Major personnel changes	Trade show/convention plans
New facilities/location shifts	Call back time
Date of connection	

*If you know someone in the company, consider information you have in common as a topic to introduce yourself (your product) or arrange a meeting. If you need to meet someone there, ask yourself how you will initiate a first meeting. Use this mutual information connection to show how your product (you) can solve a problem, fill a skill gap, or demonstrate a special understanding for the company.

SWOT ANALYSIS

A SWOT Analysis covers Strengths, Weaknesses, Opportunities, and Threats, hence its name. It is a standard technique in corporate strategic planning and new product launches. You have already summarized your strengths and weaknesses (areas for improvement). To complete your research phase, it helps to acknowledge your product opportunities and threats. Complete an analysis for each threat that you see.

Sample: **Overcoming Threats, Maximizing Opportunities**

Overcoming Threats

Example: Educate future buyers (employers) about credentials required and experience needed.

My field is flooded with job seekers who call themselves coaches.

Maximizing Opportunities

Example: Strengthen value of experience and successful interventions to date.

Organizations see the value of executive development.

Threats: How will you overcome these?

_____

_____

_____

Opportunities: How will you strengthen these?

_____

_____

_____

✳ *Summary* ✳

✳ Methodically doing your research upfront helps you focus on what's important.

✳ Identifying target organizations can bring clarity to your planning and a method to your activities.

✳ Analyzing the present and future market is the key to a solid decision later on.

✳ Knowing the strengths, weaknesses, opportunities and threats helps you create marketing tools that solve problems and provide you with potential answers to tough questions and situations that could come up.

PACKAGING

Creating Tools of the Trade

Our society puts lots of emphasis on appearance—just check out the primping that goes on in many of today's popular reality TV shows. Your look during the career search process, however, should be much more than a superficial impression; it states your personal image. You want to be sure that your brand image—and the packaging to sell yourself—has a purpose and shares your primary message with your buyer. It is a significant part of the mix.

VISUAL APPEARANCE

Today, consumers evaluate many aspects of the total product offering, and packaging is a key part of any assessment. Companies now use packaging to change and improve their product offerings: a squeezable ketchup bottle that sits upside down on its cap for easy pouring, a salt container that ensures a uniform flow in all weather conditions, a square paint can with screw tops and built-in handles, and a toothpaste tube that pumps. In each of these examples, the product package told the consumer the product was new and improved, and this opened up larger market segments for the items. You need to consider what you can do to generate this kind of improved packaging and function in your product (without, of course, your being able to "leap tall buildings in a single bound").

Packaging can also make the offering more attractive to retailers. The Universal Product Codes and accompanying bar codes, for instance, provide valuable information on price, color, size, and sales volume. With the new RFD chip, products can now be tracked at all times and provide even more key data on visibility, attractiveness, and usefulness.

Items that were once sold by a sales force are now available online or at self-serve outlets, so packaging has an even more compelling role. New laws make content and safety issues more important, too, and you now get more information than ever before. Today, a product package must:

- Attract positive attention.
- Describe the contents and present information.
- Explain the benefits.
- Provide warranty and guarantee data.
- Give some price, use, and value facts.
- Protect the contents from damage and theft.

Some companies even package their services. Consider the Enterprise car pick-up, Virgin Airlines' door-to-door limousine option, and the financial institution that includes counsel on insurance or mutual fund purchases. But you should make sure the additional service doesn't inflate the price. In your job offer "service package," don't hide your real salary requirements from a prospective employer.

Your job in this process, no matter your desired field or position, is to broadcast an image of confidence and competence — in both your personal look and your sales materials (resume, bio, brochure, business cards). You want everyone you encounter to see that you can perform the work required and that you are the person you appear to be, both on paper and in person. If you don't believe this, just think of poor Mr. Brown, who misrepresented himself and accepted the position as head of FEMA only to be disgraced before the entire nation during the Katrina disaster.

As a consumer, you yourself buy products that look attractive, such as a sleek sports car or a high-tech digital watch. You also purchase products that look like they can do the job: Think of the heavy-duty vacuum cleaner or the easy-grip knife. Now put yourself in the position of your future employer, who on hiring you wants to show off the shiny new product to the staff and hopes it will work well right away.

Your marketability always depends on good grooming and demeanor. As stand-up comedians say, know your audience. If you've ever told an off-color joke to the wrong crowd, you know what that means! So if doing your job well involves wearing loud, baggy clothes, body piercing, tattoos, and eccentric hair, make sure the job you just took is as a roadie for a rock group, not as an assistant for an investment firm.

Attracting Positive Attention

Choose clothes that make you feel good—and are both clean and well-tailored for your body type. Much has been offered in the media about determining the right color and style that looks good on each person. Perhaps the most important tip is simply to choose a wardrobe that makes you feel comfortable and good about yourself. Remember, good grooming is more than what to wear at an interview (see Chapter 7 for interviewing). You can meet a future contact at a number of places—on the soccer field, at a dinner party, or at a business seminar.

Your goal is to look your best at all times. Mom set you on the right track years ago. Wear lipstick for a trip to the supermarket, clean underwear for the car accident that puts you in the hospital, and shined shoes when you rake the leaves. No matter what your size, all of your clothes should be stain- and wrinkle-free and fit appropriately. Avoid making any unintentional statement that flashes wild colors or exaggerated style—unless that look is your business. Stay well groomed, and accessorize without drawing undo attention.

VIPP (Very Important Product Point)

Any week could be your lucky week. Be prepared: your shoes shined, your hair cut, your interview outfit clean, pressed, and ready to roll. Have your day care lined up and your transportation secured, as well. You need to be available.

Be sure to take good care of yourself by maintaining your personal hygiene: Shower and shave regularly, trim and clean your nails, and pick a hairstyle that flatters you and presents the image you want. Ponytails and scraggly beards for men or long, unshaped hair for women may not work. Neither would four-inch nails manicured with happy-face images or rhinestones. Some over 50 also wonder about the "to color or not to color" question. Age discrimination can be very subtle and is often more in behaviors than in looks. Once again, choose what makes you feel comfortable and be sure to ask an honest and trusted friend to critique any major personal makeover you wish to try.

Make sure your eyeglasses fit your face properly and suit your image. The Elton John jeweled look or the huge, lens-take-over-the-face style might not work. Jewelry can also mislead your customer. Huge hoop earrings, four studs in one ear, dangling gold chains, and that four-carat diamond ring could give others the wrong impression (especially if you're a social worker visiting less-privileged clients).

Behave graciously at all times; show your positive self. Remember that loud commotion you caused at the supermarket checkout counter or the screaming dressing down of your son's soccer referee? Such outbursts can come back to bite you. You never know who is listening or observing you, so stay calm, be positive, lower your voice, and keep your temper in check. For example, one senior executive candidate lost a job opportunity when his Monday interviewer turned out to be the referee he had yelled at during Saturday's soccer playoffs. Another marketing manager was rejected for a position when the HR screener behind her in line witnessed her berate the teenager bagging groceries. Life, during this search phase, has been compared to a performance appraisal at work—everything you do may be under scrutiny.

How to Explain the Benefits of What's Inside

Prepare a 30- to 60-second infomercial. Some call this an "elevator speech" because it's a presentation you can give in the time it takes to get to your floor on an elevator. Others call it "a reason for availability." This descriptor is your sound bite, a short delivery telling what you have done successfully to date and what you plan for the future. If your pitch runs much more than a minute, though, and your subject wanders, you risk boring the person you're talking to. The point is that when asked, "How are you doing?" you have an invitation to make your job needs clear to someone who may be able to help you (see more details below and in Chapter 4).

> **VIPP** (Very Important Promotion Point)
>
> Practice your material. Gather some friends together to test how it sounds. You need to be prepared but not canned, articulate but not stiff. It's best to weave in data that will interest your listener and encourage a dialogue or discussion that could lead to something.

BUILDING YOUR RESUME

Perhaps your most valuable marketing tool/aid is your resume. Although your resume is often the first opportunity hiring managers have to judge you, it alone does not get you the job. The main goal of a powerful resume is to get you an interview. The resume provides the summary you need to sell yourself and to highlight your background and accomplishments to the hiring team. It also serves as a road map the interviewer can use to craft questions that test your skills, knowledge, and value-fit for the job.

Your resume needs to generate a compelling marketing message at a glance on just a page or two (the average time for a resume review is merely 25 seconds). In our fast-paced, information-overload times when everyone is accustomed to getting just the gist, the high-speed download, or the instant highlight, a hiring manager won't read your resume unless intrigued by a catchy presentation. It should play up your strengths and present results and accomplishments that address the needs of the marketplace. The buyer (or hiring organization) is looking for an ideal candidate fit, and your resume needs to maximize your marketability for both his present and future needs. It is the literature, ad, or commercial that drives one to check out the product firsthand, in person.

Your references read your resume as a refresher statement, a way for them to recall your unique accomplishments or to see where you have succeeded since you last worked together. Your network partners read your resume to help

VIPP (Very Important Promotion Point)

A two-page resume is just fine nowadays, especially for someone who has been in the workforce for many years. Be sure your second page has your name on it (Blitzer, page 2) and a paperclip is usually the best way to keep the pages together because the next step may be a scanner and the operator needs to separate them quickly.

you validate your job goals and real successes. Employment agency staff and recruiters scan your resume to standardize their candidate presentations; and in general, it is the best way to screen applicants not meeting their qualifications. Remember, although many who read your resume may draw individual conclusions about your career, your resume needs to reflect the criteria that you believe make your work special and valuable to many employers.

Overall Appearance

Your resume's appearance (design and verbal organization) is almost as important as its content. Your package must be distinctive but not outlandish, inclusive but not confessional. (Save confessions for your partner or the clergy.) Unless you're in the creative fields or are a huge risk taker, avoid shocking pink paper, pictures, and fanciful punctuation. None of these tricks enhance your message, and they could easily backfire for a more serious hiring manager. There are, of course, always exceptions like the sports reporter who sent his resume to the newspaper editor inked on a basketball. OK, it was clever, marginally appropriate to the role, and he got the job, but you should generally reserve your distinctive resume presentation to perhaps placing the resume in an extra-large envelope that stands out.

To attract positive attention, keep the following four points in mind:

1. Select a high-end, standard 8½ x 11-inch paper stock (rag content bond). White is often the best and most sensible; soft grey, cream/off-white, and light blue also work well.
2. Print your copies on a letter-quality (laser) printer or professional photocopy machine—in black type only.
3. Select an easy-to-read type face (Helvetica or Times Roman) and point size (12 point is preferred).
4. Provide adequate white space and generous margins, and use bullet points and indentations to add emphasis or to highlight accomplishments.

All CAPS BOLD can be used for headings and highlighting company names nicely. Using a lot of italics or underlines can be too busy.

Structure and Style

Before you begin building the contents of your resume, you need to decide which type and format is best for you. With the increasing use of technology, you need to be mindful of how your resume is really used. Human resource professionals and hiring managers still read and screen paperwork manually, but most organizations capture the contents of your resume electronically, using computer keyword-searching techniques. You need a resume, then, that is both attractive and sales-focused. It also should be in hard copy/presentation format, easy to scan, and computer-friendly. Also remember, if you are over 50, there is no need to put your year of graduation on any of your degrees.

There are two basic hard copy formats: chronological and functional. The chronological presents your experience and accomplishments from your most recent position to your first. This is the most common and acceptable format because it is a direct and straightforward picture of your work history and accomplishments. This resume style is most suitable for a search in your existing field. See Figure 3.1 for an example of a chronological resume. The Appendix also has other, more involved examples of chronological resumes.

The functional or skills format (Figure 3.2) leads with emphasis on your successful experiences and skills, with a summary of your job history and positions listed at the end. This resume style can be an especially powerful tool when changing fields or switching industries. It can also be seen as a way to hide a checkered career or hard-to-transfer skills. Remember to check the Appendix for more detailed examples of functional resumes.

If your previous job experience meshes well with your current career objective, consider creating a resume that combines the two formats to showcase all relevant achievements that support your new objective, and make sure to bold and bullet point the transferable functional skills and expertise.

Should you be considering posting a resume online, there are two computer-compatible (soft copy) formats to try:

1. *ASCII.* This is an unformatted version, without underlines, bolds, bullet points, etc., and is understood by any computer regardless of the software

Figure 3.1: **Sample Chronological Resume**

FLORENCE NIGHTINGALE
57 Health Lane
Longlife, Louisiana 30303
(564) 333-3367 (564) 333-3368 (Mobile)
fn@wecare.net

SUMMARY PROFILE

ADMINISTRATIVE/CLINICAL NURSE with more than 10 years' experience in ambulatory care services and skilled nursing facilities. Background in clinical care, triage, patient education. Proven ability to work effectively under pressure. Bilingual—English and Russian.

EXPERIENCE

University Health Care, Baton Rouge, Louisiana   1991–2005
Administrative Nurse/Supervisor—Otolaryngology/Head and Neck Surgery
  • Developed and maintained a high standard of ambulatory nursing care, sustained a safe physical environment for patients and staff

Operational Management
  • Redesigned patient charts to tab system that increased efficiency by 10 percent
  • Oriented new residents and staff to the practice
  • Purchased, tracked, and maintained medical and surgical supplies adhering to capital budget

Clinical Care

Coordination

Mt. Scopus Medical Center, Baton Rouge, Louisiana   1990–1991
Staff RN—Outpatient Ambulatory Care Department
  • Provided a high standard of comprehensive nursing care for …

Figure 3.1: **Sample Chronological Resume,** continued

Get Well Convalescent Hospital, Baton Rouge, LA   **1987–1989**

  Nursing Supervisor—100-Bed Skilled Nursing Facility
   • Directed activities of licensed and unlicensed personnel …

Saint Valentine Memorial Hospital, Longlife, Louisiana   **1981–1987**
  Primary Care Nurse—300-Bed Acute Care Hospital

EDUCATION

PROFESSIONAL ASSOCIATIONS

LICENSURE AND CERTIFICATIONS

SKILLS

Particulars in each category to follow

Figure 3.2: **Sample Functional or Skills Resume**

STAR PERFORMANCE, CHA, CFE

549 Spotlight Avenue

Oscar, California 94510

email: winner@hotstuff.com

Home (707) 555-3546

Office (925) 555-4428

SUMMARY OF EXPERIENCE

International and domestic bank management experience including Auditing, Private Banking, Retail/Consumer Operations and Wholesale Compliance. Has demonstrated skills in strategic planning, foreign and domestic acquisitions, corporate restructuring, process flow improvements, premises optimization, and organizational effectiveness. Proven leadership in building teams and personnel management. Trilingual—English, Spanish, and Portuguese.

HIGHLIGHTS OF ACCOMPLISHMENTS

STRATEGIC PLANNING

- Planned and established strategic administrative and support offices in: Panama, Colombia, Argentina, and Brazil.
- Downsized and restructured operations in Argentina, Brazil, and Mexico. Strategically organized compliance and operational support service units for the Global Private Bank, Latin America, Europe, and Asia.

MANAGEMENT

- Implemented efficiency improvements through training and guiding subordinate staff to attain high quality levels of performance. Ensured team player concepts were learned and practiced by peer and subordinate management.
- Instilled client service quality standards to ensure independent and impromptu satisfaction surveys were always of the highest standards.
- Units reviewed for fiscal and operational purposes were always rated superior or outstanding under the corporation's performance rating criteria.
- Managed with compliance control emphasis without sacrificing the premium service standards demanded by sophisticated clientele.

AUDIT/FRAUD

- Led and participated in 5 acquisition due diligence reviews in the U.S. and abroad. Acquisition activities involved foreign and domestic financial entities that were subsequently purchased or removed from the bidding process based on recommendations made to senior management.
- Directed, participated in, and completed more than 300 fraud-related investigations. Administered audit services provided to 236 retail/consumer branches and to more than 30 overseas banking units.

Figure 3.2: **Sample Functional or Skills Resume,** continued

---

EMPLOYEE RELATIONS
- Attracted and retained key staff through training, mentoring, guidance, and promoting ongoing career development.
- Planned/organized quarterly, semi-annual recognition events for staff. Retained associate satisfaction while achieving profit objectives.
- Reduced staff in Latin American location from 180 to 3. Managed the process to ensure successful transition of employees.

CAREER PROGRESSION

MEGABUCKS BANK, 1964–1999
Held multiple, progressively responsible positions in U.S., Mexico, Central/South America, and the Far East.

Vice President & Group Manager Administration
- Provided support as interim Implementation Manager of the Lockbox efforts for clients and operations in Dallas, Arizona, Nevada, Chicago, and Atlanta.

Vice President & Country Operations Manager for Megabucks Bank—Mexico, S.A.
- Managed staff of 150. Operationally responsible for country's loan, deposit, and treasury banking functions. Combined unit client portfolios were up to $2 billion with earnings growth from $45 to $58 million.

Vice President & Manager, Megabucks Bank Private Bank Wholesale Operations Worldwide
- Provided Administration/Operations/Compliance and Client Support. Developed operations and international compliance procedures and provided quality control evaluations.

Vice President & Manager, Megabucks Bank World Banking Corp. (held several auditing positions)
- Involved in all aspects of corporate audit activities including trust audits, employee fraud investigations and training, country and regional audit manager assignments.
- Foreign assignments included Panama, Central America / Caribbean, and Comptroller in Colombia, Regional Manager in Brazil.
- Managed audits of 236 retail units in Southern California and the Special Fraud Investigations desk. Audited Assets from $2–2.5 billion.

Operations Officer/Assistant Operations
- Ten Retail/Consumer branches with staff of up to 97. Assets $2.5 to 25 million.

EDUCATION
BS, Science and Literature, Humanities Courses, National University of Costa Rica

PROFESSIONAL MEMBERSHIP
National Association of Certified Fraud Examiners

---

or platform used to generate it. It is much easier to use as an attachment or copied into the body of an e-mail. Instructions for converting your resume to ASCII are:

– Open resume in MS Word.

– Change margins to reflect one inch (from top, bottom, and sides). In Page Set Up, delete headers and footers. Then "Select" the entire document, left justify, unbold any words and select Courier 12 point for the font.

– Choose FILE and SAVE AS (in the SAVE AS TYPE—choose "text only with line breaks"). Disregard warning that some formatting may be lost. Exit Word.

– Open your resume in Notepad™ (a software program usually bundled with Windows) by going to Desktop, "click" START, PROGRAMS, ACCESSORIES, NOTEPAD.

– In Notepad, select FILE and OPEN (your document will have a ".txt" extension).

– ASCII documents should not contain "characters" (i.e., %, &, bullet points). Use space between paragraphs and sections of text for emphasis.

2. *HTML or Web.* This is a formatted version that permits hard copy options (bullet points, bolds, etc.) and is becoming an increasingly popular way to demonstrate and showcase your accomplishments and achievements by linking your resume with various web sites. It is a way to market yourself online. This version can, however, be time-consuming to generate and may include everything from just a web page equivalent of your word-processed document (with some links, too) to several pages with an index and links to different resume sections. Consult with a web designer about how to set one up or check out various sites that not only offer you templates and techniques to generate your piece (great for the noncomputer savvy techno nerd) but also an opportunity to host free of charge.

When writing any resume, describe the contents and explain the benefits by:

• Using strong verbs—"implemented," "generated," "created," etc.

• Using technical terms only if they enhance the description of your work. Avoid jargon—assume the reader does not know it.

• Using abbreviations cautiously and carefully.

- Using the third person voice—avoid "I."
- Avoiding any personal information about your race, martial status, religious, or political affiliations, etc.
- Avoiding the inclusion of your references. There is no need for "References Available Upon Request" either.
- Avoiding your salary expectations and history.
- Avoiding exclamation marks (unless you are in the entertainment world).
- Presenting only the truth. Be honest about everything or be prepared for an immediate termination if falsehood is discovered.
- Sticking to two pages and using a third only if you have an extensive publication list.

The Template or Components

You should use the template presented in the following pages and in your resume, whether following a chronological or skills/functional format. Make sure you include all the components.

Contact Particulars. Identify yourself at the top:

First Name, Middle Initial, Last Name

Street Address

City, State, Zip Code

Mobile Phone: Home Phone: E–Mail Address:

If you're uneasy about including too much personal information—tempting identity theft—present only your e-mail address and a mobile phone number. If you're really worried, use a special e-mail address set up specifically for your job search.

Objective or Background Summary. For an objective statement, use the data generated from your assessment research, combined with your market analysis and employment options, to create a definitive statement or summary profile for the position you want. Craft an answer to the question, "What is my employment goal?" Provide a clear presentation of the level and function you hope to perform. The well-written objective tells your potential buyer that you're looking for an exclusive position, and you are crystal clear about how your credentials and skills match the requisition title and requirements.

The disadvantage of using an objective is that it can restrict you to one particular opening and take you out of the running for other functions and opportunities in an organization where you could be successful. Also, many objective statements sound like canned textbook descriptors or pie-in-the sky expectations and thus can annoy the reader. They can be hard to write, too. Nowadays, a large majority of job seekers, especially those with a variety of skills and more life experiences, eliminate them completely. They use the background qualifications summary instead and work the objective into a cover letter (see more details below). Another disadvantage of the objective format is that you need to have numerous versions of your resume to serve the various positions you seek.

If you choose to include a career objective, remember not to make it too vague, too broad, or too restrictive.

Too vague. Looking for a challenging senior management position in a growth-oriented organization.

Too broad. An opportunity that offers growth and supervisory potential in customer service, marketing, or sales.

Too restrictive. Accounts payable lead for a key division of a multinational consumer product manufacturer.

You can write an effective objective.

First, review your plan and look at your assessment data for that ideal situation (title or function you are seeking). _____

_____

Second, condense and combine what you want and where you want it. (Be sure to include the skill and experience you bring, too.) _____

_____

Third, write the objective again, and repeat it aloud to hear how it sounds. _____

_____

Some examples of effective objectives are:

Entry level Human Resources position in a manufacturing environment.

A Quality Assurance Engineer position in the diagnostics and medical instrumentation industry.

Sales Manager in the telecommunications arena.

Customer Service Representative in the biotech industry.

Now, practice writing an objective.

_____

_____

_____

There are lots of positive reasons to do a background qualifications summary or a summary profile of your skills besides your extensive life experiences and multiple skill sets. Creating the content of this summary helps you prepare for a future interview, often stimulates interest and helps people remember you, provides an overview that positions your product match, and includes key words that identify you early on to the screener. A well-written summary sets the tone of your resume and does a good job of preparing the reader for what is coming next: it capsules who you are and what you have accomplished.

Some sample summary statements that work are:

SOFTWARE CONFIGURATION MANAGEMENT PROFESSIONAL with more than 20 years' experience in all phases of development. Technical skills include source code control with ClearCase, PVCs; scripting with DOS Batch, Linux Bourne, and C Shell, and software environments for build—Windows, Linux, UniWare, SCO, Mac/OS.

SALES AND MANAGEMENT PROFESSIONAL with 10 years' experience in all aspects of sales and sales management. Energetic, results-driven leader capable of consistently meeting and exceeding sales and departmental targets and directives. Grew people and territories with a solid combination of interpersonal sophistication and tenacious follow-through.

EH&S MANAGER with an extensive operational, technical, and materials background. Strong leadership, project management, problem-solving, analysis, and people skills— seen as a perceptive, hands-on manager who gets things done, thinks independently, and likes challenges.

HUMAN RESOURCES PROFESSIONAL with extensive experience in generalist functions and specialization in Human Resources Information Systems. Areas of expertise include strategic planning, leadership, re-engineering, change management, and team development. A results-oriented team player with strong management and problem-solving skills.

Persuasive and polished MARKETING PROFESSIONAL with excellent presentation skills. Innovatively developed and marketed products, people, and services for three *Fortune* 100 Companies. A natural team-builder with a high energy level and tenacity for detail. Especially skilled in:
- Market Segmentation
- Special Events Promotions
- Supervisory Training
- New Product and Package Introductions

In order to write a summary statement that works, open with your professional moniker, such as production manager, sales engineer, or corporate trainer. Select your marketable skills from your previous assessments that link to the professional identity—"with five years' experience in high-tech manufacturing" (for the production manager), or "ten years of stand-up supervisory training delivery" (for the corporate trainer). You can sell yourself here even more with another descriptor sentence that includes your marketable personal strengths: "Clever problem-solver with two successful ISO certifications," or "Exceptional writing skills with a strong background in program design and evaluation." Now, you try:

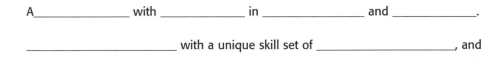

The following phrases might also help in writing your summary:

Broad range of experience in . . .

Worked effectively in . . .

A proven performer in . . .

Extensive expertise in . . .

Innovative

Creative

Committed

Tenacious

Additional training in . . .

Attended

Drove

Grew

Achieved

Demonstrated

Launched

Captured

Now, you prepare your background summary or profile.

_____

_____

_____

Professional Experience, Experience/Accomplishments, or Experience. This component is the heart of your resume, the opportunity you have to tell your buyer not only what you were responsible for, but also what you were able to accomplish. This is your chance to distinguish yourself and to tell your story by responsibilities and describing results.

You started this process in Chapter 1 when you created your accomplishment and achievement statements. Now, it's time to take these OARs (Opportunity/Problem, Activity, and Result) and begin to row. Polish them for use in this experience component of your resume.

First, consider each previous employment—what were your activities on a daily, weekly, monthly, and periodic basis? Second, gauge the value you brought to your department and your organization. Third, focus on how you contributed to any significant changes. Finally, note how you resolved these challenges. Where were you most successful?

Refer to your old job descriptions and performance reviews to refresh your memory on the role you played and the impact you made. See this as a Responsible/Results Were exercise. For the discriminating buyer, it's the results you achieved—the measurable accomplishments—that make the difference. It is also an ideal opportunity to include as many key words as you can to trigger scanning- and user-recognition. Check current employment ads for the latest terminology or words to include. There is no need to repeat terms.

To transform your accomplishment statements to your resume results:

- Keep it short and sweet.
- Begin with verbs (e.g., managed, created, controlled, directed, etc.) and remember to check with synonym dictionaries in order to vary job descriptors (e.g., authorized, sanctioned, justified, warranted, allowed).
- Include the activity and the benefits of your efforts.
- Whenever possible, use quantifiable metrics and key words in each statement.

For example, say:

Created an inventory control and recording system that improved department productivity by 24 percent.

Attained a $62,000 monthly gross margin in first year.

Drove company to increase its corporate product PR initiatives, increasing published PR by 60 percent within a year.

Built a strong working relationship with marketing to allow aggressive pursuit of configuration information ahead of project milestones. This increased manufacturing visibility, reduced engineering and materials issues, and consistently increased on-time delivery to near 100 percent.

Some verbs create attention:

Reduced turnover	Improved reliability
Expanded customer base	Designed new technique
Reduced cycle time	Increased productivity
Revamped . . .	Streamlined . . .
Turned around . . .	

Some metrics generate discussion:

Increased sales by 20 percent.

Reduced response time by 50 percent.

Prevented $2-million customer from defecting.

Reduced underutilization by 45 percent.

Read the examples below, and then practice writing your own using the sample presentation in Figure 3.3.

Action Taken	Result
Crafted all form letters	Handled more than 40 percent of customer correspondence and negated need for additional staff.
Conducted shipper audit	Corrected 135 original invoices and regained $65,000 in billing mistakes.
_____	_____
_____	_____
_____	_____
_____	_____

Remember, your resume is NOT a complete biography of your life. As a sales tool, it needs to reflect the background and experience you bring to your current career objective. If it looks like this component might make your resume three pages, limit your achievements to the past 10 to 12 years' experience and include only the most noteworthy or relevant achievements. Edit scrupulously, and if you want to include all of your previous jobs and there is space, consider creating a list as below:

Other Related Experience:

    Flight attendant, US Airways

    Desk Clerk, Trump Tower

    Customer Service Manager, InfoWorld Inc.

Figure 3.3: **Sample Format**

Company: _____ Location: _____

Position title: _____ Dates: _____

(Years only preferred)

Responsible for: _____

_____

Results (or accomplishments): _____

_____

Position title: _____ Dates: _____

Responsible for: _____

_____

Results (or accomplishments): _____

_____

If all of your experience is with one company, be sure to highlight the periodic changes you managed in the interview and emphasize your varied expertise for any reviewer who may question your work range.

If there are significant gaps in your job history (like that year you spent helping a charity or globetrotting for adventure), be prepared to answer interviewer questions with a positive spin on your engagements (perhaps emphasizing volunteer work that tapped new skills or travel that increased your understanding of diversity). If you were in drug rehab, incarcerated, or returned home to manage the household, skip any details and simply explain it as a maturing experience.

Sometimes your job title isn't an accurate reflection of what you really did. In this case, emphasize your responsibilities or focus on the function.

Responsibilities. Senior Secretary: Coordinated the company's activities in five trade shows—designed and set up booths, created demonstrations, and scheduling.

Function. Trade Show Coordination: Coordinated the company's activities in five trade shows—designed and set up booths, created demonstrations, and scheduling.

A note on the job title: Senior Secretary. DO NOT CHANGE YOUR JOB TITLE. Your company often provides this information to anyone who calls, and falsification can be grounds for termination or a fast rejection.

Education, Training, and Professional Development. It's important to consider how much education and continuous learning is valued in your field of interest or industry. Telling your buyer that you have not only studied formally but also continued to take classes is an advantage. Be sure to begin with your highest degree and include your major, name of college or university, and its location.

Sample:

MBA, University of California, Berkeley, Berkeley, CA

B.A., English Literature, University of Massachusetts at Amherst, Amherst, MA

Master Trainer, Zenger-Miller, San Jose, CA

Negotiation Skill, Karass Seminars, Los Angeles, CA

Now, you do the same, using the same format: degree first, certifications second, and continuing education third.

_____

_____

_____

_____

Your education and professional development data can trigger future interview questions, so you need to prepare answers. If you did not go to college, present more professional development activities that point to your eagerness to learn and to master skills that ensured your accomplishments. There is no need to apologize for not continuing a formal degree. If you went to college and did not graduate, present the degree you were studying for but DO NOT LIE about receiving it. Lying is another cause for termination or a fast rejection, and there's no need for a defensive reaction. Stress your experience and talents and steer the conversation toward your accomplishments and special talents. On the resume, just put:

Engineering Curriculum, University of the Pacific, Stockton, CA

VIPP (Very Important Promotion Point)

Pedigree and educational credentials can be important (in some environments more than others), but lifelong learning and a willingness to study new things can distinguish you. Take the seminar, read the book, complete the tutorial, and visually feature the most relevant ones (the most applicable) proudly and prominently with your formal degree(s).

Some people are concerned that their major does not relate to their current occupation or the job in consideration. If this mismatch comes up in an interview, just mention that your career plans have shifted since your formal education, and that what you learned as a student has helped you in your career so far and goes well beyond your major field.

Additional Information. Provide data here such as your technical or computer skills, licenses and certifications, military service, professional associations, and publications. For example:

Proficient in Microsoft™ Word, Excel, and Access

Organization Development Network, Regional Vice President

U.S. Army Reserve, Lt. Colonel

Now you.

_____

_____

There is no need to include any personal information (marital status, age, parking tickets, softball league batting average) or unique interests and clever hobbies. Some resume experts recommend you include these as a way to connect and perhaps network with your buyer's personal interests—say, as fellow adventure traveler and Cordon Bleu master chef—but there is too great a risk your favorites don't mesh. If you are that gourmet cook who loves to travel and are interviewing with a hiring manager whose spouse ran way with the Italian cooking school teacher, you'll have to ad lib from there.

Using Figures 3.1 and 3.2 as examples, put it all together in Figure 3.4.

> **VIPP** (Very Important Promotion Point)
>
> Never, never, never change or alter the facts for your resume. Honesty is not only the best policy, it is the ONLY policy. Rejection and termination are the consequences. It isn't worth it.

BUSINESS CARDS

Remember that your resume is just one of the marketing tools you have at your disposal. A business card can make a statement that starts a buzz. If you're no longer working (and are without a company business card), it's important to create one. Generate a card that reflects who you are or who you want to be. Keep this new card handy at all times, and use it often. Hand it out at networking events; include it with correspondence. If you meet someone at a formal networking event, at a dinner party, or on a weekend holiday, make it a point to hand her this new business card. Deliver a card that states your marketing message clearly and declares your specialty. Often, this card is best as your first contact follow-up. Your resume, too, follows.

If possible, design the card in keeping with the brand identity of your other marketing materials so you present an organized, cohesive, sure image. If you prefer an off-white or cream paper for your resume and stationery and a block typeface, use a coordinating color and type for your business card.

Local and national copy centers and large office supply chains offer business cards at reasonable prices (200 one-sided pieces for about $15). There are

Figure 3.4: **Sample Resume**

Identity: Name _____

Address _____

City, state, zip _____

Home phone _____

E-mail _____ Mobile phone _____

OBJECTIVE (optional)

_____

_____

QUALIFICATIONS SUMMARY

_____

_____

EXPERIENCE/PROFESSIONAL DEVELOPMENT

Organization, Location   **Years**

Job Title

- Description: _____

  _____

- Achievements: _____

  _____

Organization, Location   **Years**

Job Title

- Description: _____

  _____

- Achievements: _____

  _____

Figure 3.4: **Sample Resume,** continued

EDUCATION/PROFESSIONAL DEVELOPMENT

_____

_____

_____

_____

ADDITIONAL INFORMATION

_____

_____

_____

_____

also web sites that will print your cards for free, with colorful designs and a variety of options—but they also include their company info on the card's reverse side, advertising their benefits as well as yours. Some may see your card, then, as a frugal venture (maybe those hiring a budding accountant) and others as a cheap shortcut (perhaps those hiring a creative graphic artist).

It's fun to create your own card, but it can be challenging, too. Like your elevator pitch (discussed later in this chapter), you want to put your career story in sharp focus, in this case using about 12 to 15 words emblazoned on a small card. (If you have two to three legitimate skill sets to share, you can put a bulleted list of them on the back of the card, too.)

The artwork says much about you as well. Block type says orderly; elegant type says creative; crayon type says, well, let's not go there. Any additional color background, texture, and/or pictures all convey your message. But don't overdo the artwork (you'll appear indulgent) or try too hard to make it capture the whole you (it's a blurb not a birth certificate). If you're looking for work as a

VIPP (Very Important Product Point)

Treat yourself to a distinctive calling card holder: real leather or a clasped, brushed metal piece. Go the extra mile to ensure that your card is clean, not dog-eared. Even in presenting it, you could create a classy impression. Accessories might make a difference.

charter boat captain, it's OK to use a picture of a fishing boat. If you work in computer programming, the mouse photo on your card is fine. The business card is for gaining business, not telling the world about your favorite hobby. There are cases where a clever card can win you attention and lasting recognition as many boring cards get tossed and forgotten: A professional woodworker at a building products trade show, for example, offered business cards made from a thin slip of real wood—now that's class!

Consider the business card samples in Figure 3.5.

Figure 3.5: **Sample Business Cards**

PENNY CILLAN

Immunologist

303 Helpful Avenue
Biotech, CA 94104   (650) 424-4000

BLANCHE DUBOIS

MANAGEMENT ENGINEERING
For Improved Productivity, Quality, and Safety

3661 Williams Way   Days 607-239-6023
New Orleans, LA 56709   Eves 512-689-5600
Bdubois@gentlemancaller.com

Figure 3.5: **Sample Business Cards,** continued

IGOR VRONSKY, PH.D.

Strategic Alliance • Technical Marketing
Business Development • Technology Consulting

E-mail: ivronsky@tolstoy.com
14278 Novel Lane • King of Prussia, PA 60689

MICHAEL JORDAN

210 Basketball Lane   Tel: 312-888-8900
Bulls, Illinois 30303   Fax: 312-888-8901
                               mjordan@bulls.com

HAROLD ("HOP") A. CASSIDY
Engineering & Project Management

725 Cowboy Way   HACassidy@whitehorse.com
Hollywood, Florida 914007   Phone: (213) 654-5407
                               Fax: (213) 654-5408

Experience with development and manufacture of
- Specialty Chemicals & Materials
- Drug Substances & Pharmaceutical Dosage Forms
- Disposable & Consumable Devices/Supplies
- Electronics Components

Figure 3.5: **Sample Business Cards,** continued

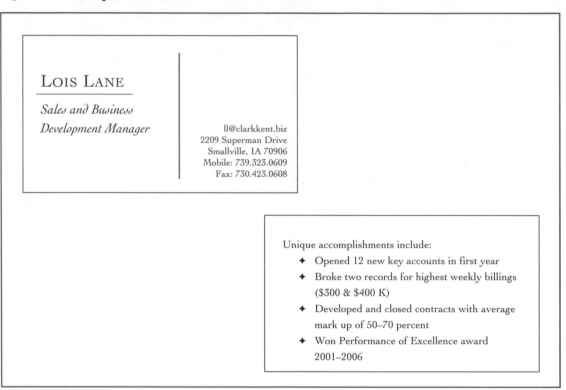

BROCHURES NO ONE IGNORES

In many ways, your resume is your key brochure, but you can certainly create other tools that serve the same purpose. Try sharing a one-page biography that summarizes your skills and accomplishments in a more conversational, less formal way than a resume. This format is similar to the copy you might use to introduce yourself at a speaking engagement or include in a letter requesting a meeting with a key leader in your field. Figures 3.6 and 3.7 give you examples. A sample format is:

- Personal Descriptor (a little bit about you and what you have done).
- Accomplishments (a list from your achievement statements).
- Your education (special credentials and key work assignments).
- Contact information (mention that a detailed resume is available).

Figure 3.6: **Standard Short Biography**

Roy J. Blitzer, an Executive Coach and Management Consultant, has more than 30 years' experience as a human resource and business management professional. He has held numerous positions, such as Manager of Training and Corporate Communications, Vice President, and Executive Consultant.

Roy's accomplishments include:

- Coordination and delivery of worldwide training services, from career management seminars for individual contributors and skill building sessions for managers to strategy and team development activities for senior staff.

- Creation of a corporate-wide climate survey that included all levels of feedback collection, dissemination, and action planning.

- Serving as Vice President and Executive Consultant for Zenger Miller, a training, education, and consulting company (now Achieve Global International), contributing to annual growth from 50–100 percent per year. As chair and creator of the Instructor Certification process and Customer Service Operations, he also established the Human Resource system for a 300-person staff.

- Consulting organizations implementing organization change with service quality, self-managing teams, and other high-employee interventions.

- Counseling senior industry leaders in executive development and career management activities that resulted in meeting personal improvement goals.

Roy works with numerous assessment tools (MBTI, Strong, Birkman, FIRO-B, 360 Feedback, etc.) and has a BA from the University of Massachusetts at Amherst, and an MBA from the University of California at Berkeley. He is an adjunct faculty member at the University of San Francisco, San Jose State University, and Menlo College; he sits on the Board of Directors for the Institute of Social Responsibility and the Institute for Effective School Leadership; and he is former chair of the Palo Alto, CA, Human Relations Commission. The author of two books, *Office Smarts: 252 Tips for Success in the Workplace* and *Find the Bathrooms First*, Roy has been published in numerous journals and magazines. He produces and hosts his own television show, *Ask "Dr." Business*, is a regular guest on NBC Channel 11's *Bay Area Saturday*, and is a frequent speaker at national professional conferences.

Figure 3.7: **More Creative Short Resume or Biography**

CHRISTOPHER COLUMBUS

Who is this guy?

Chris recently served as Vice President of Corporate Marketing for Quiles Corporation.

Prior to that, he …

What more has he done?

Prior to his sales work, Chris ran a $290 billion division of Spanish maritime organization …

Where's he from?

Chris, who speaks fluent Spanish and French, grew up in Barcelona, Spain, but has also lived in Belgium and Holland. He graduated from …

What's his work history?

2005–2001: Vice President of Corporate Marketing, Quiles Corporation

1993–2001: Vice President of Sales …

Contact information   Detailed resume available
3 Spanish Armada Circle
Typo, Florida 30922
Mobile: (631) 676-0900
CC@isabella.com

A marketing professional took this concept, included a photo and generated more clever headings, to create greater interest and illustrate creativity in his craft. See Figure 3.7.

Another brochure option includes creating a CD ROM. Circulating a custom-made CD, which includes your career info/marketing pitch as text, images, and even video of your elevator pitch (more on this below), puts you on the leading edge of info materials and adds an extra dash of excitement for those reviewing your e-brochure. A CD is also a better presentation tool for a busy hiring team who can see your materials together at one time but from different locations—and if you're really impressive (lucky?), your reviewer may copy your CD material and e-mail it to others who have similar interest in you. Be careful, however, not to play with this fun toy by doing some activity such as singing your resume in the CD video, unless you are trying out for the *American Idol* TV show talent judges. If you don't know how to burn a CD (it's just as easy as copying a file), have a tech-savvy friend create one for you (see Chapter 5 for more details).

PROPOSALS AND PITCHES

In addition to a well-crafted resume and business cards that generate a buzz, there are other verbal marketing tools you need to help you move forward. The first is your Reason for Job Availability. This is your formal, for-the-public "job exit" statement. It helps to tie your dismissal to that of others in your group, if that was the case. It's a courteous but concise reply to folks' wondering, "What's going on?" It's short on details and focuses on the future. Some examples are:

> CSI merged with CCL & A, and my position was impacted. I chose to leave the organization rather than move to Manhattan as required.

> My position was eliminated when the product assigned to me was discontinued and removed from the 2006–2007 offerings.

> Our division was closed by Corporate, and my entire group was eliminated. I'm now looking elsewhere.

> After 15 years in finance, I'm taking advantage of the new restructuring at the bank and leaving to pursue new interests.

Now, you practice.

_____

_____

_____

_____

_____

The second verbal tool is your 60-second elevator speech, sound bite, or infomercial. This is great for networking. Many formal networking organizations limit members to 60-second presentations. It also works in social situations when you're asked the usual icebreakers, such as "What do you do?" or "What job are you looking for?"

The elevator pitch suggests your career history, current job situation, and future options. It can position you in the job market and encourage the listener to open a door or two and provide other assistance. It can also serve — if expanded to emphasize your resume — as part of a response to the typical interviewer's core question: "Tell me about yourself" (see Chapter 7). The goal of this presentation or pitch is to persuade others that you have valuable skills and significant work experiences and that you are clear about your next steps and career direction. It can help with cover letters and recruiters, too, and is often the means for positive attention in your telemarketing efforts and phone calls.

There are three basic parts to the piece:

1. *Career history*. That is, a brief overview of your professional work life, with emphasis on your most recent experience, key skills, and strengths.
2. *Current status*. Where you are in your search process or what transpired.
3. *Future goals*. Where you want to be next; focus here and springboard from a possible negative comment to a positive outlook on your future employment and how others can help you reach your goals.

The elevator pitch should include:

- Your name
- What you've been doing
- What you're looking for
- What kind of support, information or help you'd like

The following are two examples.

I'm Florence Nightingale, a Senior Health Care Leader with more than 20 years' experience in ambulatory care services and skilled nursing. I recently left University Health

Care after 10 years as Head Nursing Supervisor, where I reported to the Department Chair and managed all aspects of clinical care, triage, and patient education. Under my leadership, our group of 13 received the highest overall satisfaction and effectiveness rating for patients and staff. Now that University has merged with College Community, I'm looking to apply my skills to another medium-sized hospital or health care facility. Please let me know whom you suggest I talk to as I'm looking for three new contacts.

Hi, I'm Pat Tent. I'm looking for a Senior Level Sales position in telecommunications. I just completed a 12-year "career" at UCALL, where for the past three years, I ran the Northeastern region as Senior Sales Director and drove revenues up 30 percent to $6 million annually. The organization both downsized and reorganized, and my position, along with many others, was eliminated. I'm eager to take my years of sales experience, plus exposure to marketing and human resources, and apply them to a start-up or second-stage telecommunications company. I'd appreciate your introducing me to some VC contacts to begin my search for new work in business development.

Now, you practice.

_____

_____

_____

_____

_____

_____

_____

_____

_____

_____

For busier occasions, you might only have time for a simple personal slogan:

I help make hospitals better for patients and patients better for hospitals.

I manage sales professionals by collaboration and manage to meet profit goals by task and customer focus.

Again, practice one that fits your circumstances.

_____

_____

_____

_____

Practicing your 60-second statement aloud is vital. Include your friends and family as aides (OK, guinea pigs). It's important for the minipresentation to flow naturally, and for you to sound confident and comfortable in your delivery, not pat or staged (leave that slick delivery to the huckster who sold you the used-car lemon). Write it out and read it aloud several times for practice, memorizing it as you would a short speech. Then tape record your delivery, listen to it several times, and rehearse, rehearse, rehearse.

Another tool that might be useful is a special cover letter response for a specific ad or internet posting. If you are responding to a particular position and are well suited, try the T-letter response or echo letter. Because you use the ad posting's exact wording—the computer will pick this up—and make the match easy to see, your response rate should increase greatly. For example:

I am interested in applying for your position of _____.

A partial list of how your requirements match my qualifications appears below:

Your Requirements	My Qualifications
* _____	* _____
* _____	* _____
* _____	* _____

I look forward to meeting with you and detailing the information above and the accomplishments in my attached resume.

Feel free to contact me at_____. May I call you on _____ to arrange a meeting time?

Thank you for your consideration.

A personal fax form designed to highlight your strengths and/or experience might also be helpful as an innovative way to present yourself. For an example, see Figure 3.8

Figure 3.8: **Personal Fax Form**

FAX
Cover Sheet

PROVEN BUSINESS LEADER

Igor Vronsky, Ph.D.
14278 Novel Lane
King of Prussia, PA 60689
Phone: (650) 356-0695
Fax: (650) 356-0694
E-mail: ivronsky@tolstoy.com

To: _____

Company: _____

Date: _____

From: ___Igor Vronsky, Ph.D._____

Number of pages (including cover sheet): _____

Subject

_____

_____

_____

_____

_____

_____

(left margin, vertical) TECHNOLOGY CONSULTING

(right margin, vertical) BUSINESS DEVELOPMENT

STRATEGIC ALLIANCE • TECHNICAL MARKETING

CEO (Consultant Examples and Opinions)

- You must be prepared to back up everything in your resume with authentic examples and data.

- Proofread your paperwork obsessively—no typos, no misspellings whatsoever (think of Mrs. Crabapple in fifth grade for your discipline).

- Remember that some screeners see the functional resume as a way to hide something.

- Some key words are especially attention-grabbing, i.e., marshaled, championed, demonstrated, spearheaded—and when you post online, key words only appear once, so there is no need to repeat them.

- Respond openly and honestly—and with confidence—to queries about your work status, especially if there are implications that you are no longer working because of poor performance or interpersonal conflict.

- Practice your 60-second infomercial in front of a mirror. It's an ideal way to see how you really look and sound when delivering it.

✳ *Summary* ✳

✳ Staying well groomed, in good shape, and prepared for any kind of encounter eliminates possible disasters.

✳ Practicing what you will say for various kinds of situations can only help the real encounters be more powerful and successful.

✳ Keeping your resume, cover letter, business cards, and any other for-the-public materials consistent in style and in look can help distinguish you and can create a brand, or image, that people remember.

MARKETING

Product Roll Out

Before you begin the process of selling and marketing yourself, it helps to understand traditional means that have proven successful. Perhaps the most valuable are reach, message, and frequency. Your reach connects with as many buyers or those who influence buyers as you can, through as many avenues as possible. Message helps create and communicate a consistent theme that will not only trigger a positive recall from your customer but also lead to a purchase of the product. Frequency repeats your message regularly so your buyer remembers it. Successful sales professionals report that they typically connect with a customer up to six times before the sale is closed. Persistence pays off: People may only remember your message if told multiple times.

Your goal, then, is to connect with as many people as you can, as often as you can, with a message that is consistent and clear about your career objective. Promoting your name, expertise, and targeted industry is a must, for example: Ivan Help, Product Manager, Medical Instrumentation. Your objective is to have your contacts remember you now and in the future—you want referrals for opportunities during this present search process as well as years from now when you might be ready for another move.

You need to develop a strategy that will maximize your energy and bring you the best results. Searching for a job in today's market is especially competitive, and if you know what you need to do and plan your approach appropriately, you can win a good job. Remember the following steps in your job search:

1. Networking
2. Responding to published openings on the internet or in a classified advertisement
3. Attending job fairs and seminars
4. Collaborating with recruiters
5. Doing targeted mailings
6. Making cold calls or contacting organizations directly

NETWORKING

Primary research gathered by the 1980s publication *Parting Company* (though now rather dated), recent exit data from outplacement agencies, and existing market conditions suggest that 70 to 80 percent of job seekers obtain new employment through networking, 5 to 15 percent through responding to published ads, 10 to 20 percent via collaborating with recruiters, and 5 to 15 percent from mailings, cold calling, and job fairs.

Using this data, you may want to chart your strategy for your week giving approximately the same amount of time to each general category. See Figure 4.1 for an example.

Figure 4.1: **Scheduling**

Technique	Percent of Time	Hours per Week	Day(s)
Networking	70–80%	28–32	6–7
Responding to published ads	5–15%	2½–7½	30–90 min.
Collaborating with recruiters	10–20%	5–10	1–2
Mailings, cold calling, fairs	5–15%	2½–7½	30–90 min.

By balancing your time and energy to suit the most effective methods, you will be able to commit each day and all your resources to generating productive leads and contacts.

Networking Rules

Lose the schmoozing and develop a dialogue. Critical hiring decisions are generally made by a committee. Key managers meet to decide on the person they want for their group, and someone often responds readily when the question pops up, "Who do we know that could fill this role?" (And, no, it's not always the boss's nephew or niece who is mentioned.) Hiring managers are human, so like most of us they naturally turn to friends or acquaintances they can trust, those who may enhance their reputations as judges of reliable talent. This means that your next position will most likely come from someone you know or who knows someone you know, not from a recruiter, through the internet, or via an advertisement.

Your "friends" are your strongest marketing allies; they are your sales force and need to be involved in your campaign as much as possible. Most people looking for a job just call peers and say, "I've been let go—let me know if you hear of anything" or "I'm now committed to becoming a party planner, do you want to help?" The friendly reply is typically, "Sure, I'll keep you in mind." "I'll let you know if I hear of anything." But that's often the end of it. Friends want to help, but many don't know the kind of help you need. Tell them: Call, post an e-mail, or send a letter. Eventually, you will want to meet as many people as you can in person, at his/her place of business, at a café for a cup of coffee, or at a restaurant for dinner or an after-work drink.

In your job search, a friend is almost everyone you know—not just your nearest and dearest pals, but everyone who knows your name. If you've seen *Cheers* reruns about the place where "everybody knows your name," that's the camaraderie you're looking for with those in your personal and professional sphere who have shared your activities, from coaching soccer to launching special work projects.

Check out these statistics on those who find work via networking:

- 48 percent of those under 40
- 66 percent of those over 50
- 70 percent of those earning more than $100,000
- 51 percent of those earning less than $100,000

And take note also that 80 percent of all jobs are not advertised but obtained in the hidden job market through networking.

Despite these compelling numbers, many are still reluctant to network. Some see it as a bother or an imposition, using people, or taking advantage of others. There are definitely lots of stories about people who pushed too hard or offended someone along the way, like that office guy who badgered people for days to get tickets to the big concert. Try to see networking as simply talking to others and gathering information. If you think about it, most people enjoy helping each other, giving advice, and passing on their special tips.

Certainly, the process can be a stretch for the more introverted personality or for those who find cold calling stressful or making new contacts a chore. Yet, if you see the experience as a way for you to add value, pass on information, volunteer services, or

VIPP (Very Important Promotion Point)

In real estate, the mantra is location, location, location. In the job search, it's networking, networking, networking. Remember, this is not a singular event. Networking is a process that is ongoing and neverending.

For an introvert, who might get his energy from within, networking is a constant push to leave his comfort zone. For an extrovert, who might get his energy from the external or others, this process can be fun. Either way, try to stretch yourself and make it happen.

provide key market and competitive data, it might be easier to implement or tolerate. Skipping this tactic is clearly not an option.

Contacts

The first step in organizing your networking strategy is building your list of contacts. Consider and capture as many names as you can, without bias, so you won't prematurely rule out anyone who may be helpful. Begin by creating a list. Strive for a list of 75 individuals. The following list of titles and groups may help you recall names that can go on your list.

- Administrative assistants
- Attorney
- Aunts
- Banker
- Builders
- Chamber of commerce staff
- Church groups
- Classmates
- Close personal friends
- Club officers
- Consultants retained
- Cousins
- CPA
- Current and former employers
- Customers, clients
- Dentist
- Distant relatives

- Doctor
- Dry cleaner*
- Editors, staff, and reporters of your local newspaper
- Electricians
- Ex in-laws
- Favorite waiters/bartenders
- Fellow jurors
- Fellow vacationers/travelers
- Financial planner
- Former buyers and suppliers
- Fraternity sisters/brothers
- Friends of your parents
- Hairdresser
- High school buddies
- Hobby groups
- Insurance agent

---

* A Silicon Valley CEO between jobs brought laundry to his favorite dry cleaning store near home at 2:00 in the afternoon. The owner was surprised to see him at mid-day and she asked what was going on. He explained his situation. She told him that her brother in-law, a Taiwanese entrepreneur, was coming to the states to look for new ideas and talent for some of his investors. She asked for his resume and offered to make an introduction. The entrepreneur and the CEO met and they found a great match; the CEO has now been working for him for 2½ years.

- Job headhunters
- Librarians
- Neighbors
- Organizations
- Parents
- Parents of your children's friends
- Peer employees
- Plumbers
- Professional societies
- Professors
- Psychologist
- PTA members
- Realtor
- Religious leaders (rabbi, pastor, priest)
- Security guards
- Shoe repair person
- Sports team participants (soccer, tennis, etc.)
- Sports team parents
- Store owners
- Students
- Uncles
- Veterinarian

Maintaining successful career partner relationships should include gathering information and ideas; soliciting advice, feedback, and recommendations; and collecting names and leads to contact. When you ask for help, focus on these means of support, not a specific job. Most people are more receptive and better able to answer these requests than to reply to petitions for a job interview.

Some things to do to make your networking efficient:

- Rate individuals by their capacity to help. Note those on your list as an A-, B-, or C-level helpers and decide how you will contact them. Put on your teacher's thinking cap when handing out the "grades." For example, A people might get a phone call and a check-in status report from you on how you're doing; B people might get an e-mail contact with your resume attached; C people might receive a letter and your resume in the mail. Work with your personal contacts first.
- Prepare your story or script and tap your infomercial or elevator speech material (see Chapter 3) to focus on your career goals and targets. Remember, your goal at this point is just to get job search information, not a job.

- Establish an easy rapport. For example, you might say, "Professor Duckert wanted us to meet. She was confident you'd be able to help me connect with some key people in our field."

- Find ways to repay the favor for their information, such as giving them some tips in their fields (share a book or an article clipping), and extend your offer to include special help or a favor in the future as well.

- Keep your commitments and promises. Pass on the resume you offered and always thank the person with a cordial follow-up (within 24 hours) that's most suitable for them. E-mail is not the only or always the preferred means.

- Take advantage of social events and public gatherings to make contacts. The July 4th barbecue picnic or your daughter's Brownie family meeting might include some valuable networking. The point is: BE PREPARED AT ANY TIME, ANY PLACE.

- Stay in touch with your network members on a regular basis. Reconnect every month or so. Going three or more months without any contact is too long—unless, perhaps, you still owe an individual some poker game money.

Scheduling Appointments

The second step is to schedule an appointment for your networking meeting. If possible, it's best to do so after you have a referral name from someone. Check your target company lists to see if you recognize an executive on the executive team, a hiring manager, or an HR professional. Next, check your new list of names and see if someone on it might be connected to a key person at the organization. You might also get good results by contacting your network of names periodically with a question like, "Do you know anyone at DEX Inc., Fall Corp., or Simple Ltd.?" You can even try networking online through a job search site's chat room.

If you begin your request with a letter, use the model in Figure 4.2 to seek a referral. To contact a recent acquaintance or renew a lapsed one, use the letter in Figure 4.3.

Figure 4.2: **Referral Request Letter**

Date

John Dorn
Vice President, Manufacturing
June Computers
3500 Brian Way
San Antonio, TX 78230

Dear Mr. Dorn:

Mike Rose of Idex Industries suggested we meet. I am exploring new professional opportunities, and he thought you would be able to provide helpful information.

I have 12 years' experience in financial management with two major manufacturing organizations in Toronto. Most recently, as a Senior Financial Analyst, I supplied comparative data from operating performance to forecasts and budgets to the VP of Finance.

I am eager to discuss the computer industry and its growth in the San Antonio area.

I would greatly appreciate any advice you can share, and I'll contact you next week to arrange a time to meet. I have attached my resume for your convenience.

Regards,

Charles Hacker

Charles "Woody" Hacker
14829 Pine Rose Circle
Toronto, Ontario, Canada V3AL6
woodyhac@sbcglobal.net.cn
(504) 375-8617 (cell)

Figure 4.3: **Acquaintance Referral Request Letter**

Date

Karen Foreperson
90 Happy Way
Shawnee, OK 33456
kfc@yahoo.com
(315) 555-3654 (home)

Mr. James Simone-Smith
Account Executive
Brookfield Automation
5000 Gamble Road
Mayeux, LA 66214

Dear Jim:

I've been remiss in not staying in touch. Forgive me, please, but so much has happened since we last spoke. My entire department at Crabapple Inc., including my position, was eliminated a few weeks ago, and I wanted your advice and insight into my search for new job opportunities.

I'm eager to find a financial analyst position in high-tech manufacturing, and your extensive experience and knowledge in the field could really make a difference in my hire.

I've attached my resume to help refresh your memory on my experience and accomplishments. I'll call next week to arrange a time for us to get together.

Best wishes, Jim, and thanks in advance,

Karen

Enclosure

After taking a look at the two examples, try writing your own sample letter.

_____

_____

_____

_____

_____

_____

_____

_____

_____

_____

_____

If you telephone your contact, prepare a script with message points, following the model below. Remember to be brief, direct, and positive. Show your contact specifically how she can truly help. Use Figure 4.4 to help you track your calls.

You: John? This is Woody Hacker. Mike Rose, our mutual friend, wants us to meet. You guys are connected through the Crestview Country Club, I believe.

John: Yes, and we also worked together ages ago at Hydro Electric.

You: After seven years in manufacturing organizations, I'm exploring the computer industry, also as a Senior Financial Analyst. Mike thought you could offer me some advice and information about industry growth and work in San Antonio. I have no expectations about a job at June Computers, nor does Mike. But I'm gathering information now and wanted about 15 to 20 minutes of your time to talk in person.

John: I'm not sure how I can help, really.

You: Mike said if there was one person I needed to meet in San Antonio it was you, John, probably because of your knowledge of the field and your many years in Texas.

John: Well, I have been around. Tell me about your background.

You: I've got an MBA from Wharton and 12 years' financial management experience, most recently as a Senior Financial Analyst for Hopkins. My comparative report to the VP Finance was a significant part of the company's successful outsourcing move. Some computer experience would broaden my career, and I hear San Antonio is now the best place to be for tech jobs. Can we meet some time next week—maybe Tuesday morning? I'm positive your perspective and counsel would be invaluable.

John: Sure, then, come to my office at 11:00.

You: Thanks so much, John. I look forward to meeting you, and I'll let Mike know about our meeting as well.

If you plan to make contact with some of your people by telephone, you should try to write a brief script now. Remember, it is flexible and can be rewritten if it doesn't work for you the first time.

_____

_____

_____

_____

_____

_____

_____

Figure 4.4: **Sample Call Tracking Sheet**

Date of call: _____ Time: _____ Message left: _____

Follow-up messages/calls: _____

Returned call (Y/N): _____ Date: _____

Contact name: _____ Returned call (Y/N): _____

Title: _____ E-mail: _____

Firm: _____

Address: _____

Referral source: _____

Objective: _____

Networking meeting date: _____

Possible questions to ask: _____

_____

_____

Comments: _____

_____

_____

_____

Referrals to: _____

Follow-up action: _____ Thank-you sent (date): _____

Your responses on the phone can make the difference in getting an appointment. Here are a few tips that telemarketing researchers say can help give you positive responses:

- *Stand up when talking on the phone*. This posture can open your diaphragm and produce a clear, well-projected voice.
- *Smile*. You'll feel more relaxed and your listener will hear that confident tone in your voice.
- *Move about if you are able and have a portable phone*. This activity can generate and increase your positive energy level.
- *Keep a copy of your resume handy and near your phone* (along with the coffee, of course) for easy reference. Make sure your accomplishments are highlighted so you have quick facts at your fingertips.
- *Reserve a quiet time and place*, if possible, for your networking conversation, especially if you initiate the call, to maintain a professional perspective. In other words, turn down the game on your desk radio and close your door if your kids or pets are shuffling through the house.

Below are some ways to handle objections to your networking overtures. Remember no one is successful on every call, so don't take rejection too personally. Our work world today makes many demands on us, leaving most with too much to do and too little time to do it. Even well-intentioned people may be overwhelmed and not as helpful as you would like. Check out the conversation scenarios below (some pointers are even good to use with your spouse!) and try rehearsing them to find out how you can customize them:

Comment	Counter
I'm swamped now. Bad time to talk.	When's a better time to call back? I'd enjoy meeting you in person. Can we schedule a time? Maybe a phone appointment would work?
We don't have any openings.	Thanks, I realize that. Right now I'm just looking for information, and I've learned you're a key person in the industry who's in the know.

Comment	Counter
I don't give information interviews.	I understand your time is limited. Do you have a couple of phone minutes now for a question or two?
I really can't help you.	I heard you were THE expert in _____. I would really value your insight.
Call Cecile, she can help you.	I appreciate that referral,____ May I use your name?
I'm tied up for the next two weeks on projects.	Could you check the week of ___ then? Can we schedule something now or would calling back be better?
My workdays are packed.	May I treat you to a coffee break for15 minutes one early morning?
E-mail me your resume.	Thanks. That's great, and. I'll do that. When it's convenient, I'd like to talk to you about it as well. Any time next week we could meet for a few moments?
We don't hire people with your skills.	That's fine. I understand. But I'm not necessarily asking about your firm. My goal is to get referrals from people who may have some specific information about hiring trends in the industry.
Get your resume to HR.	No problem. Is there a specific opening you have in mind? Who is the hiring manager, and may I use your name when we connect?
I'll call you back.	Better yet, if you name a specific time, I can call you back. It would be my pleasure.

The Meeting

The third step is conducting the meeting. Make sure you are prepared and are comfortable with what you will ask and how you will ask it. Begin by reassuring your contact that you are not hitting on him or her for a job but you are eager to learn about what he or she does, the industry/trends, and how your skills and talents fit into the current marketplace. Your goal is to build an ongoing career partner relationship rather than focusing only on your immediate need for a job.

Arrive on time and relaxed, comfortable with your objectives and accomplishments to date. Try to match your communication style with your contact's. See if you can pick up her language usage. For example, for those who talk in terms of images, offer "picture this" scenarios to help them visualize your talents in action, or for those who listen sharply, share quotes from references that let them hear the differences between you and your competition. Be gracious about your contact's needs but stay focused on your objectives. Take care to use the allotted time wisely. Leave both your business card and a copy of your resume. Follow up with a thank you and deliver on anything you promised to do. Perform professionally in the information interview process as if it were already your first day on a new job—without asking for the paycheck, of course.

Figure 4.5 contains sample questions to ask your contact to assure your networking success. Choose those that fit you best, but make sure you accept the input you get from your networking contact graciously. As an example of this, read the following story before examining the sample questions.

One Silicon Valley HR professional came to solicit advice and then proceeded to discount each recommendation given: "I can't do that because" "I already tried that and . . ." "I don't like that method." She closed the meeting by asking for feedback on our time together. I took the risk—checking that she did indeed want some straight talk—and informed her she would have come off better by accepting the input less judgmentally, even if she might choose not to use it later on: "I didn't consider that approach. Thanks." "I'll look into that. Glad you mentioned it." Feedback is like a gift at holiday time. You thank the person when you get it and only return it after you acknowledge and appreciate the gesture. She took everything in and thanked me for my honesty.

Figure 4.5: **Sample Questions for an Information Interview**

1. **Information/Data**
   - What are the possibilities for jobs in this industry?
   - What are the best career development opportunities in this industry?
   - What would it take to be hired by this company?
   - What are the major industry trends?
   - What are the best jobs?

2. **Ideas**
   - What key information should I know about this field?
   - What background do you usually require?
   - What do you find most rewarding about your job?
   - What do you find least rewarding?
   - What reference material would be pertinent for me to read about this industry?
   - What professional organizations recruit members in this industry?
   - What are the possibilities for doing volunteer work?
   - Since nothing is perfect, what are the problems in your group?

3. **Advice**
   - What strikes you most about my resume?
   - How can I spend my job-hunting time most effectively?
   - (To someone who knows you well enough) Given my experience, what is a key tip you have for me?
   - Given this interview, would your company hire me if there were an opening?
   - What would you do if you were in my position?
   - What did you do to gain your present role?
   - If you were in my position, which competitor would you interview with?

4. **Feedback/Recommendations**
   - How does someone with my experience enter this industry?
   - Reading my resume, how do you think I'd fit into your company or industry?
   - What suggestions do you have for me to enhance my chances (e.g., training, networking, promoting, etc.)?
   - What other questions might I ask to gain even more specific information about this industry's jobs?

Figure 4.5: **Sample Questions for an Information Interview,** continued

---

- What value did you get from our time together?
- May I contact you in the future?
- What is the key item you'd change on my resume?

5. Names to Contact

- Can you recommend others in your organization I may meet? (It's important to get additional new contact names as part of your current information interview.)
- Who can I talk to for a broader perspective on the company?

No one else had clued her in, and she realized that her approach might have alienated some of her network contacts. Three weeks later a huge plant arrangement arrived with another thank you and the news that she got a job from a lead she met right after our meeting.

Thank-you letters show good manners. They reflect on your upbringing and knowledge of what's the right thing to do. Think of your most proper relative (maybe Mom?) and know that etiquette is not old fashioned. Some families, like mine, insist that you cannot wear, deposit, spend, or "play with" presents unless your note is in the mail. The same holds true for business. A thank-you note reinforces any positive impression you may have made. See Figure 4.6 for a sample thank-you letter (or e-mail) for your information interview.

VIPP (Very Important Promotion Point)

Your information interview should include a mix of open-ended questions (what, where, why, when, and how), moderate-focus questions (explain, elaborate, tell me about), and closed questions (can you, will you, is it, i.e., those that only elicit a yes/no answer) and must gather data, ideas, advice, feedback/recommendations, and three names to contact to be successful.

Figure 4.6: **Sample Thank-You Letter**

Date

Mr. Billy Bob Wharton
Director, Okawalla Beverages
3 Indian Lane
Half Moon Bay, CA 54578

Dear Mr. Wharton:

Yesterday morning's meeting was an especially productive one. Thank you. I appreciate your finding time in your busy schedule to talk to me. I will gladly follow your suggestions to contact more trade officials and call Henry Wackler and Doris Weeks at Pepsi.

I have a meeting with Doris next week and already have calls into the DNA.

Again thanks for all your help. I'll keep you posted on my progress.

Regards,

J.D. Drink

P.S. My Mom sends her special best.

Next, try writing your own letter.

_____

_____

_____

_____

_____

_____

_____

_____

_____

_____

The following are some additional pointers that might help you make a favorable presentation.

- Test your firm handshake with several people.
- Note the career and personal interests of managers in your organization and/or profession.
- Find common interests with those you hope to include in your network.
- Learn who makes the decisions. It's not always the person with the lofty title, so be comfortable with those who may help, regardless of rank.
- Return all calls promptly.
- Take good care of your referral source. (Think of this relationship as if he is a celebrity and you are a doting personal assistant.) A formal thank you is a must. Small, thoughtful acknowledgments are even better. Consider giving your contact a box of candy, small bouquet, or a gift card for his favorite coffee shop.

- Save your major requests for the big needs. Don't overdraw your account by constantly asking for ever more favors. Your tracking sheet will help you keep a running balance of the requests.

COLLABORATING WITH RECRUITERS AND EMPLOYMENT AGENCIES

Between 10 to 20 percent of job seekers find a position via a recruiter or employment agency. These figures can fluctuate widely, depending on the economy. During the tech-industry boom years from 1998 to 2000, the job search firm business grew more than 20 percent per year. When the economy fell with the burst of the internet industry bubble, and investors finally felt all the hot air escaping from the bogus business plan balloon, more than 65 percent of recruiting agencies, mostly smaller, one- to four-person shops, closed their doors. But today the large national organizations are still in business, and many of the smaller shops are building back up with the improved economic outlook.

How much do recruiters help with job searches? Results are mixed. Job candidates often report that some recruiters don't acknowledge receiving their resumes or return phone calls. Other recruiters are seen as responsive and eager to build a relationship with the job seeker. Think of them as Hollywood talent scouts always angling to find a new star to sell to a studio—you've got one good shot to impress before they move on to other candidates. The bottom line is that RECRUITERS DON'T WORK FOR YOU. They are paid by client companies to locate and screen candidates for positions. Most do a fine job, but so do many bounty hunters!

Basically, there are three types of recruiters you may encounter: contingency, retained, and contract. Each has a particular function and style. It will help you to know with whom you are dealing.

Contingency Recruiter

Contingency recruiters earn their fees only after a client company hires a candidate they've referred. They usually handle a broader base of candidates for mid- to lower-level positions. Some more discriminating recruiters will, however, place executives and senior staff. The salary levels they fill are mostly up to $75,000 per year, and they often fill multiple vacancies with similar talent and work for more than one organization at once to "find the right hire/fit." Companies use contingency recruiters when they want to stay more involved in the screening, interviewing, and negotiating processes. Because their fees (ranging from 30 to 35 percent of the job winner's first-year compensation) are paid only when the candidate is placed, many contin-

> **VIPP** (Very Important Promotion Point)
>
> Check out your recruiter, your career counselor, and your seminar leader before entering a relationship. Remember, it is your right to ask questions, as many questions as you want, to ensure a comfort level of trust and professionalism. There is no need to succumb to pressure of any kind.

gency recruiters are highly sales-focused. They can push hard to get your interest and have an aggressive work style. Some of the less scrupulous recruiters tarnish the role's reputation for others.

Retained Recruiter

Retained recruiters (or search firms) are paid in advance by the organization to conduct a search. They also collect a fee from 30 to 35 percent of first-year compensation but often receive their pay up front or as a monthly retainer, even if the search doesn't produce a successful hire. Their market is the upper-middle to senior- level professional with a salary greater than $75,000. A great source listing these recruiters is the *Directory of Executive Recruiters* (see Chapter 2).

To fulfill your marketing strategy, it can help to mail your paperwork to as many retained search firms as possible, especially to those that specialize in your field. You may get a better response if you consult someone in your network who has had success with a particular recruiting organization or if you are familiar with the firm because in a former role you had a substantial budget and retained them to find top talent for your company.

Contract or Temporary Recruiter

Contract or temporary recruiters work for a corporation on a part-time, contract, or temp-to-permanent basis. In an effort to contain costs, many organizations use these professionals to augment their workforces and manage the peaks in their hiring requirements. Because major job hiring can ebb and flow with broad economic situations, these handy, low-commitment, on-demand recruiters are a growing segment of the personnel placement industry.

Remember, state employment agencies and college placement centers also provide free job listings, career development counseling, and company data.

There are a number of points to keep in mind when working with recruiters.

- You will interest a recruiter only if you meet the exact requirements of the position to be filled. Recruiters provide a service to client companies; contingency or retained, they are chartered to find the individual who best fits the often narrowly defined skill set.

- You must carefully select the firms you work with—reputable directories and your network can help—and there is no ideal number to have working for you. The quality of the relationship can help guide you in determining the number.

- You never need to give a contingency recruiter the "right" to work for you, but you do need to present yourself honestly (many people inflate their career qualifications and credentials) and treat the first meeting like a sales pitch, where you call attention to your special skills, talents, and accomplishments and provide a reason for him to represent you. Pay attention to how you are treated. Find out about the client base and how long the company has been in business, plus what special qualifications it has.

- For an initial contact, you may do best using a contact name for your introduction rather than relying on a less personal e-mail or letter overture. Always include a resume if your first approach is through a letter. See Figure 4.7 for a model letter to a recruiter.

- Be careful when distributing your reference list to recruiters. It is best to make your names available only after the recruiter indicates you are a very strong candidate. These colleagues are important to your long-term success, and you should not call on them prematurely or too often. They are the job application ace up your sleeve, and the more frequently you use them, the less enthusiastic they might be to endorse you. Explain to the recruiter that you reserve your list of contacts for only the best job opportunities, just as the recruiter saves her candidates for the ideal openings.

- You can certainly ask for a job description before your interview and request that the recruiter secure annual reports, marketing brochures, or any other data that might help you.

Figure 4.7: **Sample Letter to a Recruiter**

Christine Keller
2902 Calle Glorietta • Tucson, AZ 85716
Christinek@profumo.net • (502) 346-7689

Ms. Robin Hood
Harper and Watson
688 Highland Circle
Tucson, AZ 85710

Dear Ms. Hood:

Option #1: John Monroe of Classical Health Group suggested I contact you. I am a senior operations/financial professional interested in an executive officer position.

or

Option #2: If you are searching for a senior operations/financial executive, I would be interested meeting with you to explore how my skills and abilities may match your client's needs.

My expertise and skills include:
- Business Process Improvements
- Systems Integration
- Initial Public Offerings
- Mergers/Acquisitions/Divestitures
- Strategic Planning

I am committed to staying in the Tucson area, and my total compensation requirement is in the $180,000 to $225,000 range.

Attached is my resume for your review. I'll call this week to see if we can meet and discuss the details of my professional experience.

I'm eager to be considered for relevant assignments and trust you will not share my paperwork until we have spoken.

Regards,

Christine Keller

Enclosure

- You should make an effort to keep the recruiter informed of your progress and call to summarize and critique your performance after each interview. There's no need to be hesitant in pressing for specific feedback, too, whether the assessment is praise or correction. And you should use these times of analysis to identify for your recruiter how he or she is progressing in assisting you.

- Once you have a job offer in hand, you should negotiate directly with the hiring manager. Some companies want your recruiter involved at this point, and some recruiters insist on participation because he often sets the hiring goals for you. It's always your option to take charge and deal one-on-one with the hiring manager, not the intermediary agent, if you are not satisfied with the direction of the job negotiation (see Chapter 8).

- You need to keep accurate records of the recruiters you meet or contact and full notes on your shared conduct of the job search. Include the information in your contact tracking sheet (Figure 4.4) and remember to save copies of all your written correspondence with them.

Take the time now, to compose your own letter to recruiters.

_____

_____

_____

_____

_____

_____

_____

_____

_____

_____

RESPONDING TO ADS

Only 5 to 15 percent of job seekers find a position by replying to listings that appear as a classified advertisement—either on the web or via various publications or media.

Ads, as social commentators frequently note, are all around you, even ads for jobs. Just look at:

- billboards, TV, radio, movie media;
- college alumni and sorority/fraternity publications or university bulletins;
- industry and trade journals;
- local newspapers;
- magazines;
- professional journals; and
- special interest newsletters.

Ads are often displayed "blind," lacking a company identification. They often have just a P.O. box number for replies. Others are "open," with the company, and often the hiring manager, named. Your reply method and the amount of time you devote to it depend on the ad.

Expect little return on your effort if you reply to a blind ad. Job application follow-up, including offering samples of your work, references, or additional credentials, is always a key part of earning an interview, but an ad without a contact is just a case of the blind leading the blind.

To be sure, answering an open ad does not assure you'll get an immediate interview, but the clear opportunity for follow-up contacts keeps the two-way communication going. Review your research market data to refresh what you know already about the organization. Do you know anyone who works at the company that's advertising the opening? Do you know their key customer or a supplier/vendor? Do you know who might know someone there? Engage in your best networking to get an introduction to the hiring manager or a key decision-maker.

As I said above, replying to advertised positions is a low-yield effort—mainly because so many who lack a job search plan are competing for the same jobs. A typical job advertisement in a local newspaper can draw anywhere from 200 to 800 responses. Some internet postings bring as many as 2,000 replies. Your task, then, is to maximize the chances of your paperwork reaching the desk of a decision-maker or hiring manager. Keep in mind that an effective personnel staffer selects only about 25 to 35 resumes from the pile of submissions for management review. These are further narrowed to 10 to 12 resumes for the hiring manager to read, and then she selects the final few 3 to 5 candidates to be called in to interview. The hiring odds favor those who use innovative self-marketing to bypass the masses of resume mailers and get on the short list of a company's preferred candidates.

Some tips that will help your letter survive the culling process and reach the hiring manager's short list:

- Use your collected data and research on the organization to link your qualifications and skills to the organization's existing strategies and issues.

- Position yourself as one who solves problems and meets key goals.

- Look for as many creative ways as possible to encourage someone in your network to introduce you to the hiring manager or an employee at the organization. (You might reward—not bribe—them with a thoughtful treat: Get them passes to a big ballgame, help them make a small home repair, etc.)

- To schedule an interview, first call the hiring manager directly. Follow up with a letter that references this phone call (attach your resume) if you need to try again. As a final attempt, send your pitch/cover letter and resume to entice a meeting.

- Send a second letter if you later have another key name or have already responded to someone in the HR department. Timing is important—just mention that your paperwork might already be in the system. Every attempt requires a follow-up phone call.

- Personalize your follow-up phone calls as much as possible. Be upbeat and cordial and try to connect positively. Make a good name for yourself with all contacts in the job search process. Employers tend to favor people they come to know . . . and like.

- Pass on positions lacking an obvious fit with your skills and experience. But go all out (notice I didn't say go for broke) for the job description with at least three to four matches with your skills/experience and the company's requirements.

- Create pitches/cover letters that answer a company's key needs in the posting. Customize your qualifications with the listed requirements.

The Cover Letter

Your cover, or pitch, letter will have the most impact if it repeats the key phrases that appear in the job posting. Whether it is a blind or an open ad, you should use the echo technique or T letter. Here you match requirements to qualifications and background and make it easy for the reader to see your able fit. See Figures 4.8 and 4.9.

There's no need, of course, to include your salary requirements or salary history in your initial correspondence. Focus on the key phrases that will catch attention and generate a call to interview. Money talk is best left to later in the process. If pressed to quote a salary request—and to avoid the screener regarding you as reticent or expensive—briefly note your recent salary range, for example,"Most recently, my base pay was in the mid $60s."

There are some additional points that can help you write an effective letter. First, highlight or underline the requirements stated in the posting. Then, list them so you can easily see the matches. (Do this before you create the list to ensure including everything important.) Limit yourself to five to six paragraphs and no more than one page. (You have about ten seconds to grab your reader's attention—that's about the same instant it takes to buy a lottery ticket!)

Show your best ad jingle writer's creativity and grab the screener's interest with enticing points, such as: "I've developed some systems—that I will share exclusively with you—that have produced a 12 percent gain in market capture and helped Dorky and Torky produce $3 million in revenue over the last nine months."

End on a positive note, citing as many meeting arrangements as you can, such as: "I look forward to speaking to you about the results you can expect from me. I will call your office on Tuesday at 10:00 A.M. to answer any questions and learn when I can get on your calendar."

> **VIPP** (Very Important Promotion Point)
>
> Proofread every piece of correspondence that has your name on it. Remember that spell check is not foolproof and sometimes that perfect piece requires a break in time from when you create it to when you read it over and send it. Even the most minor error in grammar, spelling, or typography can do huge amounts of damage.

Figure 4.8: **Sample Job Posting and Reply Letter I**

Job Posting

HUMAN RESOURCE PERSONNEL OFFICER

We are a large real estate brokerage looking for a Human Resource Personnel Officer with seven-plus years' experience in recruiting and hiring industry professionals. Must be familiar with the business, have administrative experience, and the ability to work collaboratively under pressure. BA/BS required. Reference #23465.

Response

I am responding to your April 2006, posting #23465 for a Human Resource Personnel Officer and am eager to talk to you about the partial list below and how your requirements match my qualifications:

Your Requirements	My Qualifications
Recruiting and Hiring	Attracted and retained key talent with a turnover rate 50% below industry average.
Direct administrative activities	Assisted manager in planning and executing all company HR programs
Real estate industry knowledge	CA real estate agent license
Seven years' experience	8 years at G & G—3 years as an agent
BA/BS required	BS Business Management

This looks like an exciting opportunity, and I hope to meet with you to discuss the additional accomplishments in my attached resume (i.e., the design and implementation of a company-wide training program that helped increase individual productivity), and how I can contribute to your success as well.

Regards,

Brenda Starr

Figure 4.9: **Sample Job Posting and Reply Letter II**

Job Posting

WAREHOUSE SUPERVISOR

Customized food distribution corporation looking for a full-time Warehouse Supervisor. Excellent salary and benefits package provided. Applicant must be a self-starter, leader, willing to work night shift, and have three years' relevant experience. Degree preferred but not required. #505056

Response

Morgan Freedman
34 Shawshank Way • Milpitas, CA 94567
E-mail: mgf@hollywood.net • (408) 567-7893

Ms. T. Hanks
HIJ Distribution
7 Rebellion Place
San Jose, CA 95114

Dear Ms. Hanks:

Daniel Bower of Gilroy Fans suggested I apply for your Warehouse Supervisor position, as advertised on Monster.com, March 28, 2006, posting #505056.

I have more than four years' experience in the consumable products industry and want to meet with you to talk about the match below:

Your Requirements	My Qualifications
Self-starter	Designed and implemented two warehouse programs.
Leadership ability	Managed crew of 4 with 0% turnover.
Willing to work nightshift	Led nightshift staff 4 years (prefer those hours)

Figure 4.9: **Sample Job Posting and Reply Letter II**

Your Requirements	My Qualifications
3 years relevant experience	4 years in industry
Degree preferred but not required	BS Operations Management

I will call you next Thursday after lunch (1:30 P.M., PST) to schedule time to talk, not only about what looks like an ideal job fit here, but also the additional accomplishments noted on my attached resume, plus the stacking and retrieval system I devised that reduced download speed 30 percent.

Feel free to call me at (408) 567-7893 if you have any questions. Thanks for your consideration.

Sincerely,

Morgan Freedman

OTHER STRATEGIES FOR FINDING A JOB

Targeted mailings, cold calling, job fairs, and occasionally other strategies work for some job seekers. Yet, only 5 to 15 percent of job seekers find positions using these strategies, so be mindful of how much time and energy you put into each. Any direct mail marketing campaign, for example, is considered successful if it generates from a 1 to 3 percent response (each batch of 100 letters yielding 1 to 3 replies). To get significant results from this strategy, you need to limit your expectations; even if you mail to hundreds of organizations, your response rate may be even lower than the industry average. Your goal is to meet someone who will talk to you when there is no open position.

Targeted Mailings

To be effective in a targeted mailing, choose the person you hope to report to or think is the key decision maker. If you correspond with someone much above or below the job level you seek, your letter could be forwarded directly to human resources for filing in the future reference drawer—and never be read. (Job seekers have a special term for this place: the black hole, where all errant resume mailings go to oblivion. One industrious job applicant I know engaged in the great folly of addressing 700 resumes "To Whom It May Concern." How many people do you think ever read his resume? Oh well, at least he made the Post Office happy; many of his envelopes were sent via Next Day Air delivery.)

Compose a cover or marketing letter that will distinguish you and showcase your best abilities to contribute. Make your comments interesting, relevant, and creative, for example, "Resumes can't talk, but I can. I'm eager to speak to you about . . ." Then, follow up each targeted mailing with a phone call. Wait about two to three days after your mailing to call to be sure the letter has arrived; it is embarrassing to call too early and appear to be a pest, or too late and learn the letter got passed on to the black hole. Also practice some of the techniques presented here.

Mail your letters in batches of no more than 20 letters at a time. Remember your goal is an in-person interview, and there is no need to mail more inquiries than you can effectively track for timely follow up.

Cold Calling

Most of your job search communication will be by phone. Here's where you get to be a phone fan like your teenager. Your goal is a face-to-face meeting or interview, and applying the phone strategy well will increase your number of interviews. Remember, you are competing for your contact's attention with many others who are selling—real estate agents, stockbrokers, bankers, and other job seekers. Of course, telemarketing has a poor reputation, conjuring up images of frenzied callers interrupting dinners and barking about overzealous bargains. Nevertheless, in the pursuit of new work, effective telemarketing is a critical part of your marketing campaign.

To be effective, plan what you want to say, as you would any important telephone conversation.

- Develop a script and rehearse it, in front of a mirror, if possible.
- Craft a sequential list of meaningful questions, beginning with the most important. Ask questions that can actually be answered; people won't respond well to long, imposing, or confusing questions.

- Verify your research so you are knowledgeable and informed. Also, do your homework on the background of the person you're going to talk with, noting any special accomplishments to bring up, if that is appropriate, in the conversation.
- Relax and take some deep breaths. Even Olympic weight lifters do this before making a move!
- Mention your contact's name with your greeting.
- Check if it's a good time for the other to talk.
- Prepare answers for objections.
- Stay cheerful and focused on your objective.
- Take notes and listen carefully (confirm some facts if necessary).
- Ask specifically for what you want.
- Write down your follow-up steps—and follow up on them.
- Meet your commitments, that is, don't assent to something you can't provide.
- Compose and send your thank-you note on the same day.

With cold calling, you do not always know the name of the right person to contact. You need to do your research and bypass the voice mail system by learning the names and numbers of assistants who can refer your call directly to a preferred contact. To find the correct name, try the company's main number first, and ask the operator for the name of the vice president of human resources or the manager of customer service. If the above information is unavailable, and sometimes it truly is, ask to be transferred directly to the specific department and learn the name of the department head. Verify the correct name spelling and address. If you're unsure about the gender of a name—like Carol, perhaps—or only have the first initial, make sure you learn the person's gender, too.

If you are working through a company phone directory, experiment using a catch phrase, such as, "I have some correspondence with Brent Nichols—is he still your manager of customer service?" Try to get the name of your target's support person and use it if you can, too. Be clear and distinct when you give your name and number and alert her that you will be calling back. Your tone should be patient, courteous, and upbeat.

Finally, to increase your chances of talking to your target when you telephone, call during business off-hours: early in the morning, right before lunch, or late in the day. Your target is most likely to be at his desk then, not away at a meeting.

Practice your voice mail reply so that it is both brief and inclusive. Provide a time when you'll be available for a return call and leave your message citing your number slowly and distinctly. You've encountered fast talkers, not all of them selling used cars or leading an auction, so you can imagine how annoyed your contact will be if you leave a hasty voice mail that has to be played twice to hear the message correctly.

> ### VIPP (Very Important Promotion Point)
>
> Try not to lose the opportunity to talk with the recruiter or hiring manager who has contacted you. Sometimes it can be tough, especially with a cell phone and the tendency to take a call almost anywhere. Keep her on the phone rather than trying to call back. Put the person on a short hold if you are in a noisy spot or need a second or two to gather your composure and your thoughts.

For incoming calls, be sure you have a quiet room set aside to talk, including a desk or table for your contact records, calendar, and resume (or accomplishment sheet), with paper and pencil handy. Alert family members who answer the phone to be prepared to note accurate information, and sound as polite as possible. Your four-year old is charming for family and friends, but might not be the best choice as an administrator to answer your phone call from a job recruiter, unless you're a day care leader. Make sure your voice mail recording is rational, too, and not overly cute or off the wall. (Let the kids' cell phones have the answering modes with rapper-recorded messages.) The following story is an illustration of this type of situation.

A freelance single mother of a ten-year-old girl asked me for advice on expanding her business. I returned her phone call one morning, only to hear the daughter's recorded voice singing a "hello" message before asking for return call information. I met with the freelancer to tell her that this was neither professional nor a business-friendly message and she should consider a separate phone line or a revised recording. She told me she was reluctant to do this, fearing she would damage her daughter's self-esteem if the message were changed, nor did she want to pay the extra cost for another line. One month after reluctantly changing her voice message, her business began growing again.

VIPP (Very Important Product Point)

Job fairs require stamina, patience, and a good sense of humor. Wear your most comfortable shoes and your high-spirited smile. Measure your expectations, treat your time as an adventure, and try to think of the interesting people you will meet.

Job Fairs and Open Houses

Job fairs and open houses attract potential employees and help organizations fill a large number of open requisitions. Fairs are popular during periods of dynamic growth and even in downtimes draw those with can-do skills. Some job seekers see these as "cattle drives" to round up desperate people who will work cheaply, but others with a positive attitude like job fairs because the gatherings allow them to shop the companies they like.

Before the fair, you should practice your "reason for availability" or your 60-second infomercial/elevator speech, stay confident and positive, shake hands convincingly, and smile. Also, keep the following tips in mind.

- Research the companies attending—and also consider organizations not previously on your radar list.
- Dress professionally (tie and jacket for men; skirt/dress slacks and blouse for women). Save the Speedos and sweats for at-home networking. And always wear comfortable shoes.
- While at the fair, ask good questions of the recruiters and show enthusiastic interest in the organization. Take company literature available for future study/research.
- Write down the name of the person you meet and jot down the context of your conversation on the back of his business card. You may find, however, that some companies hire recruiters just for the day and instruct them to withhold any personal identification.
- Bring an ample supply of resumes (25 to 30 copies). Some astute product marketers fold their resumes in thirds to have them stand out in a file; others enclose them in plastic sheaths to distinguish them.
- Distribute your business card (see Chapter 3 on tools for specifics).
- After the meeting, follow up with the recruiter or hiring manager by telephone. Wait three to five days for smaller events, five to ten days for events with more than 100 attendees.
- If the lines are long and the waits are tedious, introduce yourself to others in line and start one or two new relationships. People looking for

work could have friends and contacts at companies that interest you, and you can often learn from them about the company's culture, salary range, and hiring needs.

Other Sources

There are numerous sources to help you find a job. Below are just a few for you to consider.

Job Hot Lines. Some large organizations, universities (and colleges), and government agencies have 24-hour job hot lines. They have recorded messages with current openings that include brief job descriptions, a few key requirements, salary ranges, and dates for submitting applications. Treat your responses as you would a published listing.

Computer Networks. Some institutions use a national computer network for their job listings and accept resumes online. Be sure to follow all of the directions to log on and to access the system exactly. There is always the danger that your paperwork will be cut off at the end of a couple of minutes or after 200 some odd words. Make sure your resume has key words that are used in the job description.

Interactive Voice Mail. Some firms are experimenting with a new interactive voice mail software. Here you are asked to submit your qualifications by touching your telephone keys (push 1 if you have an MBA, push 2 if you have a Ph.D.). It is used mostly as an elimination tool, so, again, follow directions precisely to avoid a mistake that could take you out of the running. Also, supplementing this with a follow-up mail response or direct phone contact with the hiring manager is a very good idea.

Faxing Your Resume. Never hesitate to fax your resume when asked or to use the medium to further distinguish yourself. One marketing executive created her own fax form, with her unique experience and skill set noted in the borders. Remember back to Chapter 3 and Figure 3.8. She also took a risk when she faxed her resume and marketing cover letter to a key number of important directors of marketing. Some offices do not welcome unsolicited fax communication, even from a candidate where creativity is expected.

ORGANIZATION AND FOLLOW-UP

You are probably ready to fire away and begin your marketing. Before you do, make sure you are organized and can keep track of your activities and responses to them. Create a daily and weekly work schedule and activity worksheets that reinforce how you are spending your time. See Figure 4.10 for an example. Keep track of what you do and those who support your efforts. Also schedule some personal escape and down time. A day or two break—not that world cruise you always wanted to take—here and there refreshes your thinking.

Order personal business stationery for cover letters and thank-you notes. Some shops will create a letterhead that can be used for your resume as well. Match these to your brand by using the same color, typeface, and graphic design on your business cards.

Set up a record-keeping system that is easy to organize, label, and adapt. For example, using a system of color-coded folders works for hard ·copy records. Software spreadsheets help arrange and transfer information. You definitely need to set up a tracking system to monitor your progress. Link it to your weekly goals and overall marketing plan. See Figure 4.11.

CEO (Consultant Examples and Opinions)

- Be prepared at all times. Every setting is a potential networking opportunity. Have your business cards with you at all times and be generous in distributing them. They are much easier to hand out and can be stapled to a 3-by-5 card or put into a PDA case. Your resume could be distributed, too, so have a supply in your car, as well.

- Keep a thorough list or spreadsheet table of everyone you contacted, what you sent, what took place, and the follow-up action. Thank anyone who gives you a name.

- Be honest about your referral source. Never claim to be a close buddy of a friend of a friend you just met. Be prepared to answer a question like, "How well do you know Greta?"

Figure 4.10: **Marketing Plan**

Marketing Plan for the Week of _____

Published Listings _____

_____

Time I will spend _____

Sources

Goals _____   1. _____

           _____   2. _____

           _____   3. _____

Networking Contacts _____

_____

Time I will spend _____

Recruiters _____

_____

Time I will spend _____

Target Organizations _____

_____

Time I will spend _____

Organizations Researched_____

_____

Time I will spend _____

Figure 4.11: **Tracking System**

Week in Review for the Week of_____

Key goals accomplished _____

_____

_____

_____

Hours spent on search_____

Results _____

_____Interviews

_____Job leads

_____Marketing letters sent

_____Networking contacts

_____Published listings replied

_____Recruiters contacted

_____Referrals received

_____Target organizations contacted

_____Target organizations studied

Other _____

_____

_____

_____

Issues and concerns—Possible solutions _____

_____

_____

_____

CEO (Consultant Examples and Opinions)

- Use the holiday time (Thanksgiving to Christmas) to distinguish yourself and take advantage of the warm spirit. The idea that no hirings happen between Thanksgiving and New Years is partly a job search myth. This could be the best time to meet and connect with key people. Not everyone is traveling. Managers often use the time to catch up on paperwork. Some companies want to recruit and hire people before the end of the year to maintain their department's head count budget.

- Join a networking group that matches your lifestyle interests as well as your job search so those who share your hobbies may also become friends eager to help in your job search. Remember not to fake it. Join a church group only if you like going to church.

- Remember the janitor's cousin could be as helpful as the CIO's neighbor. Tips on jobs can come at any time from anyone at any level.

- Always ask the recruiter how he is compensated. Conduct your own interview. Learn how he or she operates and never be bashful about asking for client references (and number of positions filled with the average company), verifying technical qualifications, and matching the firm's mission statement with your own goals and objectives.

- Make a salesperson your friend and pick up some of their special sales techniques to apply to your marketing job search.

❋ *Summary* ❋

❋ Mastering a knockout 60-second infomercial or elevator pitch can make a big difference. Practicing is worth the effort.

❋ Networking, networking, networking is *the* mantra. You can never do too much of it.

❋ Choosing who will represent you and deciding discriminatingly can put you in front of the right people.

* Creating a polished telephone persona will make the process move smoother.

* Keeping accurate records of your activities and detailed summaries of who said what and when could eliminate a future mess.

CHAPTER

5

ACCESSING THE INTERNET JOB MARKET

S urf's up! Web surfing, that is. Searching the World
Wide Web for the job you were born to do. Although
there are some 50,000 new web sites coming online every
day, all it takes is one job posting to make your employment
dreams come true. And if you're hesitant to spend time surfing, remember your odds of finding a job here are 50–50.
Only 10 percent of jobs are filled online, but 51 percent of
jobs are first found online, but then require additional work

in order to land it. And the siren call of fascinating sites filled with dozens of promising jobs compels the most stouthearted navigators.

Read on because this chapter will give you guidance in internet job searching so you:

1. know when job sites generate leads.
2. can make an e-newsletter flash and update hiring managers on your accomplishments.
3. can use e-mail express and compose messages that say "talk to me."
4. can create CD bios and picture your success story.

Just keep in mind that the internet job resource, like even the best, most-seasoned career advisors, can only point out job search techniques and opportunities. It's up to you to track down and capture the job on your own.

So what is the best use of the internet for job seekers? Well, with some savvy searching there's a clear path to be found through some very tangled overgrowth of job advice sites, resume boards, recruiter sites, and online networks.

Language lessons in web speak may come in handy. As you surf, be mindful that many sites, especially those serving the tech industry, indulge in internet buzzwords, jargon, slang, and acronyms aplenty. This insiders' lingo can be confusing at times or, worse, result in your saying the wrong thing to the right person when you share a cover letter with your online application. As part of your job search campaign, online or offline, you'll need to choose your words carefully. Just as web advertisers market their products with clear, powerful words that include a call to action, that is, a decision urged for the reader, so should your marketing message talk the talk of your customer, the hiring manager.

> **VIPP (Very Important Product Point)**
>
> Check for openings on the internet *first* and then lean on your network to see if someone has a contact name for a company that has an opening of interest. Dash off an e-mail or make a few phone calls before responding. That way you may be able to use a name in your cover letter reply.

In the end, once you've accepted your new job offer, you'll likely find that the time spent using the internet will be a bonus to your career. You'll have discovered many new and handy sites for future referral to get answers to employment issues, conduct industry research, and chat with others in your job network.

So, surf's up. Now catch the wave!

INTERNET VET: KNOWING WHEN JOB SITES GENERATE LEADS

If there's one aspect about the Web—in all its manifestations—that's a given, it's that there's a job search site (or two) offering the tailor-made position for you. The trick, of course, is finding it. The fervent search for a decent job site can be a little like clicking through matchmaker sites to find your best mate. You know that all it takes is finding the right one to make you happy.

There are plenty of search engines hoping you'll give them a try, so you have many options. You can Google it. Or Excite yourself. Maybe Ask Jeeves or hear it from Mamma. Let it roll with Lycos or start slowly with Metacrawler. Get the Big picture or enjoy the AltaVista. There are plenty of diving points into the internet's tide of job opportunities—you just have to log on and go for it.

You can streamline your search along the way to make the task a bit easier and faster. That means knowing important keywords to locate precisely the online job information you seek. Many of your keywords, of course, will derive from your preferred job title. Try inputting several variations. For example, if you are looking for job sites catering to web design professionals, you might enter web designer, web developer, web artist, web programmer, web graphics, etc. Or try any combination, including phrases such as web page design concepts for B2B (business-to-business), or B2C (business-to-consumer) sites, HTML coding for web design projects, or navigation protocols for web designers.

Another way to use job search engines effectively is to collect all the entries you have clicked on by bookmarking (saving) each into a folder for future reference. You might want to create several folders labeled by search engines or sites. That way you can quickly locate a search engine and, if applicable, use the search engine's log of your previous entries so you can pick up from the point where you left off.

A note of caution: don't become overly dependent on a search engine. Don't spend too much time "just looking." For one thing, after about the first eight to ten pages delivered to your desktop, the usefulness of the entries listed falls off greatly. The search starts to turn up fewer and fewer appropriate matches to the resources you seek. You may, however, find job board ads placed on the right navigation column of some pages helpful as you mine deeper in the category.

Also, many unwary job seekers have found the megasearch engines a big distraction after a while. Certainly, the search for appropriate and purposeful job posting sites is critical, but beyond making your initial selection of, say, up to a dozen key job sites, endlessly perusing new links can tease you away from your main search into pursuing sites with job-related products (resume preparations), services (bulk e-mailing), or just pure entertainment (famous bad job applications). Not to beat this into the ground, but less than 10 percent of jobs filled are landed through the internet. So it's great to use the web to research jobs that pay, but not to linger on sites for play.

CHECKING JOB POSTINGS

Of course, perusing job postings—every day—is the main reason anyone visits a job board site, though many such sites offer additional services (see below). But merely scanning line after line of job titles—some of which can be laughingly irrelevant on less effective search sites—won't help. Say you go to Jobs.com (yes, there really is a www.jobs.com; the site originators were obviously at the head of the line when the first URLs were handed out) and you type in: Software Marketing Manager. Now the page delivers 100 or so job postings covering that title or a close variation. Wow, you think, this is going to be easy pickings. The numbers are surely on your side. Just click on one posting after another, send off a resume via the poster's e-mail, and if even just 10 percent of the posters reply, you'll have your pick of ten interview invitations, right?

Well, not so fast. In Chapter 2, you learned not to count much on bombarding job listings with a blind resume mass-mailing campaign. Remember, it's all about your precision marketing to qualified target organizations. Just because trying the same method via the internet is five times faster, reaches far more recipients, and in most cases, is free, the results (sorry to report) are not proportionately much better. And keep in mind that others are thinking the same as you are about the ease of applying for jobs on the internet. That means that there are potentially tens of thousands of competitors around the region and country—or even the world. Sending reams of your resume into the Black Hole, that place where all good unsolicited resumes go to die, whether as a hard- or soft-copy document, is folly.

But do click on the links and read each listing carefully (and do keep copies of your preferred postings). Learn from them before jumping ahead with your application. See how different companies in your field describe their open positions. Consider these aspects:

- How are the descriptions similar? Different?
- What is the tone? Some postings want to screen out casual job seekers, so their copy can be downright intimidating or sound like a warning: "We work extra long hours and love it; so if you like to leave at 5:00, don't bother to apply!"
- Which indicate a salary?
- Explain the job thoroughly?
- Offer a company history or mission statement?
- Cite their customer base?
- Ask for immediate references?
- List job goals, responsibilities, and qualifications?
- Note any "definite plus" skills desired?
- Require a job test or work sample?
- Decline to include a company name or address? Watch out for these listings. Some recruiters, HR managers, or even other job seekers in your field post fake jobs just to see what talent will apply.
- Indicate when the job offer will be closed?

You need to distinguish not only the job titles that match your needs but also the specific roles offered. And note that many "new" jobs within a company, especially a start-up opportunity, are subject to changes in the job description and its tasks, even as soon as your first week on the job.

Here are some popular mainstream job posting sites (industry, career-specific, and company) you may find helpful.

- www.bigemployment.com
- www.careerbuilder.com
- www.careermarketplace.com
- www.craigslist.com
- www.directemployers.com
- www.employmentguide.com
- www.employment911.com

- www.get-a-job.com
- www.hotjobs.com
- www.jobbank.com
- www.jobfactory.com
- www.jobsonline.com
- www.monster.com
- www.6figurejobs.com
- www.usajoblink.com

E-NEWSLETTERS FLASH: UPDATING HIRING MANAGERS ON YOUR ACCOMPLISHMENTS

Once you have chosen some preferred job postings sites, you'll want to turn one or two into your online job search home base. Here is where you can set up a number of web tools customized to your job search methods and goals. One of the most effective tools is the e-newsletter.

E-Newsletters

Think of this format as the daily newspaper that's all about you, that is, your job skills. You can use many e-newsletter templates available as downloads online or for purchase as software packages. Let the various wizards, or instructions, show you how to assemble, display, refresh, and e-mail your personal e-newsletter.

If you have ever helped create a high school yearbook, college newspaper, or professional brochures, you may have a working idea of effective content and designs that maintain readers' interests. In the case of an e-newsletter, you have the added advantage that the issue can be sent instantly to hundreds of addresses, updated on the fly, and linked to as many other materials as you please for even more compelling news.

Today's standout e-newsletters are often simple, clear, and to the point. You don't want a lot of unnecessary and distracting bells and whistles that are fun for you to pile up in the pages but can distract a reader/hiring manager from your main message: "Hire me, I'll do a great job for you!"

You want to establish a clear hierarchy of your messages in the e-newsletter. At the top of the first, or cover, page (there should generally be about five to six linked pages for each edition of your e-newsletter), the headline should always emphasize—with genuine excitement—the breaking news about one of your latest success stories. Maybe include an interview with the spokesperson for a company that has lately benefited from your accomplishments. You can also include your value proposition, or at least the tag line that states your best skills.

Other stories to include are articles borrowed from your industry (cleverly organized by you for quick and easy reading), current field statistics that show how your skills rank high among your peers, or anything you think would be interesting for a hiring manager to read. Be sure to display your contact info prominently on the first page, too.

To fill out your e-newsletter, include an FAQs page about you, a portfolio page citing your satisfied clients, a Q&A column for reader e-mail feedback (hopefully, most of them will be hiring managers contacting you with job leads), and of course, a link to your downloadable resume.

As for images, it's always a good idea to present simple, bold, interesting, easy-to-follow photos or illustrations or charts/graphs reflecting your recent professional pursuits and achievements. Show photos of key people you've met at industry conferences, pictures of any awards or distinctions you've earned in the last few months, pie charts of added revenue you've generated for a business, or progress steps you've delivered for a volunteer organization, PDFs of training certificates you've obtained, and more. The e-newsletter is not the place, though, to post a photo gallery of your family or friends, but you can show images of any items related to your professional hobbies, such as pictures of products you've helped design in your spare time.

If you think it will help draw attention to your qualifications, you might even add a simple flash animation of scrolling or crawling text citing your most meaningful skills, much like financial sites use stock tickers to update their readers. But keep in mind that

> ## VIPP (Very Important Product Point)
>
> *Any* document you create for internet use—newsletter, personal web site, blog, CD-ROM, bios—needs to be of the highest caliber possible and as professional as you can make it. Using an amateurish and/or hokey piece will do much more damage than not having anything. Some senior staff hire a creative specialist to do the work. Test whatever you generate with various colleagues for honest input.

the e-newsletter should not be overloaded with slow or difficult graphics that can clog anyone's desktop e-mail.

You should plan on publishing a new e-newsletter issue each month, sending it first to those on your network e-mail list, while also testing some other professional group addresses and asking if these people would like to receive your issues. You will soon find that publishing an e-newsletter is a great way to promote your job-related activities and show you are still active and current in your field—and available to hiring managers.

RESUME BANK

A wonderful option/tool is to store your resume on one of the major internet sites. Most capable job posting sites include this feature. You can store as many as five resumes (and cover letters) at one time. Assign them unique titles for different applications. Then, when a posting appears on the base site (or any other), you can simply upload your targeted resume matching the job title or description.

Some career coaches, with good reason, warn you not to distribute more than one version of your resume. They fear that two differing versions of your resume might wind up on the same hiring manager's desk, which can be embarrassing and kill your job chances.

So, multiple resumes here means documents that emphasize different aspects of your skill set. For example, say you have an equal balance of both magazine and web site editing experience in your job history. If two job postings appear asking for an editor of either just magazines or just web sites, you can choose to send the version of your resume that highlights your print or your web skills. Either resume is equally accurate, but you have marketed your different skill sets to unique targets, increasing the chances your resume will be read with interest.

A resume bank can also log hits on your resume. You can select a program that allows various readers—recruiters, hiring managers, companies, other job seekers—to view your resume as posted on the site. Each time someone opens the link to your resume, you receive a hit and are notified of what type of reader viewed your page. This information can help you to track which of the five resumes in your bank gets the most attention and from whom, allowing you the option of refining and modeling the others to catch similar interest.

Some resume banks indicate that your resume will expire after a set number of days—from 30 to 90 days—usually meaning it will disappear from view, so you'll have to upload or simply refresh it often. But even in the best banks, your resume can be pushed down to the bottom of the resume postings list (that is, the reader may have to scroll down several pages or more to see your entry, because every day the site adds more resumes from your peers. The best approach is to check on your resume listing every week or two, go into the bank, and refresh the resume (simply changing a word in the title or rearranging items) so you can post it again and the site will read it as new and display it atop the listings.

SALARY CALCULATORS

Some job posting sites include handy benchmarking tools such as salary calculators (www.6figureJobs.com offers one example). These are a bit more sophisticated than the handheld calculator you may use to figure meal tips. Other sites that provide comparative salaries are listed in Chapter 2. You can use this tool to input your job skill set or history or goals and measure these criteria against the established salary parameters for similar jobs in your field. Say you are interested in a job posting, but either assume a certain salary, given the job description's requirements, or have no clue what pay level to expect or negotiate toward.

Using a salary calculator, you can apply for a job online already knowing what salary range to expect, and possibly other areas of compensation from perks to bonuses, and build on it in an interview process. Unlike candidates who use a personal network referral to find job openings, those who apply to postings via the web often report their biggest frustration is the lack of a specified salary. They go through elaborate steps and provide extensive information material

VIPP (Very Important Price Point)

Be mindful that all salary data are very dependent on current economic conditions and regional locations, which are often not easily accounted for in web sites where periodic updating is not systematic or difficult, so numbers can vary widely. Test by asking a local professional who has a similar job to balance the data you collect. *But remember*, there is a tendency for people to inflate their incomes when asked. The urban myth says that men are more likely to boost their salaries by 10 percent, while women more often tell the truth with an exact figure.

to the virtual poster only to learn much later that the job's low salary is unacceptable. Using a salary calculator can help avoid that mistake.

CAREER ADVICE

Many valuable job-posting sites build their fine reputations (and profit models) on the job seeker career advice they provide (free or for a fee). The better sites include lots of articles about online (and offline) job search techniques, dos and don'ts, and success stories. Some sites also publish downloadable tutorials and books to help your career moves. There are sites that also invite you to register for online virtual job fair events, interaction in real-time Q&A sessions with career coaches, and resume review and rewriting services. These services are a good draw and revenue generator for the sites, so you do want to be careful about the quality of the advice. Check out the professional backgrounds and credentials of the featured experts, any money-back guarantees, and other users' feedback.

DISCUSSION GROUPS

Sometimes the best advice you can get online is not from the teachers but from fellow students. That's where job-posting sites with active, robust, and easy-to-use discussion boards are a huge help. Trust the advisors to give you the best research and widest possible coverage of job search means, but also count on the job seekers—the site's users and customers—for the best possible inside advice on what works or doesn't work in a web job application.

VIPP (Very Important Promotion Point)

Be most discreet and appropriately businesslike when you participate in any internet job-related or networking/interactive discussion groups. This is not a segue to a dating service or an opportunity to screen for the love of your life. Stay strictly business at all times.

Many job-posting sites create discussion categories that suit various job titles for dedicated groups. You can read hot discussion topics and learn tips from your peers about interview tactics, salary negotiations, regional openings, industry trends, and the real-world job search skills that land new work. Better still, join the discussion, sharing your own thoughts and questions. You stand to gain much: a vast network of like-minded individuals, job leads, moral support, resume critiques, recruiter introductions, and more.

NICHE JOB BOARDS

The obvious strength of generalized job posting sites is their sheer reach and volume of coverage. But the best search is often the one most refined (or "getting granular" in your data mining, as webbies like to say). You can go from using a job search engine such as Google that yields hundreds of pages of results, to a generic job-posting site such as CareerBuilder with scores of pages, to a career-specific job board such as Dice.com (for the tech industry) to see tens of offerings. It may seem like you're limiting your options by digging this deep, but you're also hitting pay dirt. You'll find most jobs familiar to you and the most jobs you're likely to land.

Niche job boards are as numerous as there are job types. Beyond Quint Jobs.com, a portal or gateway site to lists of career-specific job boards, here are a few in various career areas:

- ih200.net (law enforcement)
- k12jobs.com (teaching)
- marketingjobs.com (marketing)
- nationjobs.com/medical (healthcare)
- salesjobs.com (sales)
- financial-jobs.com (financial)
- writejobs.com (writing)
- fashion-jobs.biz (fashion)

Once you identify a job board that suits your career interests, you can tap many of the offerings and tools available at the more generalized sites but with a few very key provisions as well. Many of these specialized sites include the following features:

- *Career newsletters.* Articles citing trade news, executive profiles, and job leads.

> **VIPP** (Very Important Product Point)
>
> If you choose to post your resume on a job board, be sure to find a few key words that you can religiously change every week or every other week. Most sites refresh and move new resumes to the top. Even that one-word shift will bring your paperwork forward.

- *Blogs*. User-supplied topics (and sometimes just outright gossip) that are invaluable for learning how your peers have fared in their jobs, or what they think about contacts at specific companies you may be applying.
- *Employer job postings*. These include some of the hidden jobs that are displayed here because they are composed in a job's particular jargon, have extra-fine task detail, require unique expertise, or are targeted to industry-only applicants.
- *Company announcements*. Links to various sites of companies known to be undergoing mergers, acquisitions, new product developments, reorganizations, relocations, new branch or division set-ups, etc. that note transitions and changes that may lead to fresh job openings.
- *Part-time or flexible work options*. Listings of opportunities other than full-time salaried jobs, including freelance assignments, investment aims, internships, training, or start-ups.

Another advantage of niche job boards similar in intent to discussion boards is the so-called peer-group job search. It's similar to a discussion board, but once you sign on, the commitment is more serious. You can join online groups with as few as five or as many as 25, but in any case, the plan is to work with your virtual peers to find jobs for one another. If you've ever played online poker with virtual competitors or shopped web auctions with other bargain-hunters, you have an idea of the communal approach to getting what you want from the internet.

This team approach can work wonders by extending your job search reach, varying the levels and selections of your research, and identifying more job opportunities. But the buddy system comes with clear obligations. Just as you have others using their online job search time and skills to locate the positions you want, so must you dedicate the same effort in seeking the jobs they desire, e-mailing them right away with links to anything you find that meets their job search criteria. And if you find an appropriate job opening for a friend that also suits your job interest, feel free to keep the lead for yourself. Your peers have already deemed this entirely ethical, because, yeah, you guessed it, they're doing the same. Most such teams set up the sharing parameters and quotas that work best for them or have policies in place for you to recognize before you join.

As these arrangements are free, if someone gives you a lead that eventually turns into a hire, there's no commission to pay. But you may wish to show your appreciation and respect by supporting your friend's continuing job search. You might, for example, be a fresh or unique resource by identifying for him any unannounced job openings in your new company and/or names of hiring managers in key divisions. Be a bit cautious, however, in making such recommendations when in your new job. Check carefully about the posting availability because you don't want to inadvertently divulge any internal-only job listings that may be improper or illegal to share outside the company.

And—oh happy day!—once you land a job, especially if it's a new role for the company or a new project division, your favorite niche site can turn around and become your best resource of talent and a means to post jobs for those you may be asked to hire quickly in staffing your team.

COMPANY JOB BOARDS

Sometimes, and this seems obvious, it's best to go right to the source. In the offline world, this might take the form of walking into a company's lobby and handing the receptionist your resume addressed directly to a hiring manager you know. On the web this means logging onto the site of a company in your target group, checking its job postings, and e-mailing your resume to the firm's specific employment code, or possibly e-mailing a resume to a company contact you met through networking.

The value of applying to a job description posted on a company site is at least threefold:

1. You can surmise that the posting is credible.
2. The job is clearly recent, relevant, and likely still available.
3. It is presented in the context of the company's corporate organizational structure and/or current employee needs.

Another advantage of dealing directly with a company site in applying online for a job is that you can readily see the firm's

> **VIPP** (Very Important Product Point)
>
> Before you press the send button, be sure everything you are transmitting is exactly the way you want it. *No mistakes whatsoever.* Retrieving a message with an incorrect first name or T letter or resume with a typo is nearly impossible, and the long-term error is something equally difficult to repair.

VIPP (Very Important Promotion Point)

Some company web sites might not be as polished as you'd expect. At this stage, keep an open mind and do not write off the position because the site, job description, or whatever does not meet your expectations. The reverse is also true. A company with the fantastically creative site and clever description and materials could be a jungle.

industry standing, mission, brand messaging, PR announcements, latest products and/or services, awards and distinctions, stock status, history, employee count, branches, affiliations, corporate and board officers' backgrounds, and often much more. Reading this information not only helps determine how you will compose your cover letter to emphasize your fit with their need but is knowledge you can use, if you study it well and have the facts straight, to drop into key points during a possible interview.

You might also compare the company's site to its competitors' sites, side by side on your computer screen, to differentiate its strengths and weaknesses. Such companies allow you opportunities to exclaim your value proposition in helping the company compete.

If the site has any products, tutorials, or other web-based tools or materials that are available on a trial subscription basis, you might take a tour to learn more about its business from the inside as a short-term customer, perhaps helping you better understand and appreciate the company's specific approach to its market.

E-MAIL EXPRESS: COMPOSING MESSAGES THAT SAY "TALK TO ME"

Probably the key component of any e-newsletter is your contact information that allows the reader to respond to your pitch. Your e-mail message campaign can be a great marketing tool in your job search for at least five reasons:

1. Hiring managers getting your e-mail can find you online.
2. You can e-mail images (or links) that display your accomplishments.
3. Client e-mail testimonials can enhance your credibility.
4. An e-mail blog can report on your latest professional efforts.
5. You can e-mail your custom value propositions.

Launching an effective e-mail campaign doesn't mean broadcasting your message everywhere. There are many companies that are happy to share your "shout out" for varying fees in e-mail blasts that can send your job seeker message to hundreds or thousands of addresses. But this may not be so valuable an enterprise if you're paying for poorly qualified lists, with your e-mail going to deadend boxes, URLs in triplicate, or broken addresses that result in bounce backs.

Still, with a focused e-mail launch, you can reach hiring managers, recruiters, company executives, and others who may have found in your unsolicited e-mail just the person they've been looking to hire, sometimes even before they have defined the job role they need to fill. Hint: If you don't have the e-mail address of a specific person you'd like to reach, log on to the company site, check out the e-mail addresses of key officers or others on the Contact Us page, then apply the name you have in the e-mail format shown and you'll be good to go. This is not foolproof.

You can also e-mail images or links that display your accomplishments. Consider sending a shorter, modified version of an e-newsletter by issuing a targeted e-card. Like a postcard, this e-format message is a brief, often event-focused, announcement. The e-card can help display a photo, map, or design drawing, or other illustration that promotes your job search. You might send an e-card notifying specific companies that you will be visiting in their area at a certain time and are available to meet for information or interview for work. You might also send an e-card with links to your former company web sites that have images of your products or projects.

Client e-mail testimonials can also enhance your credibility. You might ask your key references at select times, such as when you are scheduled to speak with someone in their network, to send an e-mail citing your relationship and endorsing your skills. These proactive e-mails are a great way for a mentor to introduce you to potential hiring managers who may be attending the same industry show and will be inclined to meet with you.

An e-mail blog—short for web log—can report on your latest professional efforts. This "open-letter" format is gaining popularity as a way to keep HR pros inside your target companies aware of your work and professional interests. Your blog can be an interesting running commentary or editorial reflecting your thoughts on trends in your field. As such, hiring managers may find your notes helpful in learning how you research and assess current issues also vital to their company. Make sure, however, that your blog is sensible and sincere; some are prone to ramble and exaggerate, and can create a disorganized, even juvenile impression. Remember that blogs can also be risky, as they are personal and may reveal information you may not want a future employer learning.

You can e-mail your custom value propositions as well. One step beyond a blog, this e-mail letter shows a hiring manager your specific observations about their company's products and services and, most importantly, your basic plan to help solve a problem or grow a business. This e-mail message can help differentiate your unique abilities and strategies. But be careful here to admit your evaluation is an educated opinion that you're glad to volunteer, not a thoroughly researched proposal that you're prepared to support. Also offer this proposition as merely a sample of your thinking so that once hired, you can provide the full objective—and receive pay for your quality ideas.

CD-ROM BIOS: PICTURING YOUR SUCCESS STORY

Not all of today's job search tools are on the internet. One of the best digital strategies beyond tapping job posting sites, e-newsletters, and e-mail campaigns involves sharing your bio on CD-ROM. As valuable—and practical—as a paper business card and resume can be, more and more job seekers are upgrading their contact information with the benefits of the CD medium. A CD bio, which is slightly more expensive to make and distribute than the paper versions and therefore best shared with those in your primary target group, offers a unique way to showcase qualifications and distinguish your credentials from competitors.

With many of the presentation advantages of an e-newsletter, the CD bio also allows you to control how your material is displayed but with more content and handy portability. For example, you can transfer content files (nonproprietary material and/or proprietary material with written permission from the publishers) from various computers as dozens of images and text files. Be sure to credit when appropriate. These may be loaded onto a CD as images of your activities with job presentations, community contributions, nonprofit work, and professional speaking engagements or as texts of your business forms, tables, white papers, performance awards, recognition articles, PowerPoints™, intranet announcements, and organization charts highlighting your career accomplishments.

The CD bio also makes a great item to hand out at networking events, provide in an interview as a sales demo, or include in a mailer. Unlike material sent electronically, it is less likely to be tampered with, corrupted, or deleted in the transmission process.

Once you have burned your files onto a CD, you have the further ability to catalog, store and save, and arrange the reams of documents for easy at-a-click user review. By comparison, accessing the same info through an e-newsletter

---

CEO (Consultant Examples and Opinions)

- If a cover letter is requested for an online job application, remember to fashion it as a T (or echo) letter, Your Requirements matched to My Qualifications (see Chapter 3). In addition to your opening paragraph comments, list in the left column several key requirements as identified by the job posting and in the right column the skills/accomplishments you have that match these. This way you can show how you are the candidate best aligned to the job needs.

- Make sure, at all points, that your internet job search is highly organized—preferably using Word Excel® spreadsheets and other files that are handy on your computer desktop. Because internet job postings, advice, and application options change so rapidly, you want to be sure that you log, track, and assess all the sites and resumes you're using and the jobs you've applied to clearly and regularly. You want to target the best jobs and avoid e-mailing to the same job twice; that's easier to do than you may think because companies sometimes revise a posting with a slightly different job title or description.

- Maintain your vast e-networking contacts, too. Send or reply often to e-mails from others in your job search support group, industry organization, references, or others who remain interested in your job search efforts.

- By all means, use multiple applications for your online job hunt and experiment with several combinations and proportions to see what proves the most successful set of tools: job search engines, job posting sites, personal web sites, or e-mail campaigns, e-newsletters.

---

might take many extra page views, and through an e-mail might take considerable time to download. Not all your targeted managers have computers that can handle opening the larger megabyte attachments.

In summary, the internet is a valuable tool among many in building a complete job search. It is not especially effective if used exclusively to land a new job. Here are some reminders of internet job search pros and cons:

Pro: It offers an enormous index of searchable job postings.
Con: It is so complex that it can lead to confusion and distraction.

Pro: It allows creative ways to contact employers, from e-newsletters, to e-mail campaigns to CD-ROM bios.
Con: It offers so many creative options that you may invest more time in designing more and more clever messages than in following up on job searches.

Pro: It offers many opportunities for online networking and job referrals.
Con: It substitutes for real-world meetings and neglects nurturing career relationships.

As mentioned before, the odds of finding a job through the internet have roughly a 50 percent success rate. So, flip a coin and hope it turns up a lucky job for you.

✳ *Summary* ✳

✳ Using the internet and remembering your activities there requires discipline and follow-through, similar to tracking your efforts in other areas.

✳ Remembering the response rate for cold replies should help your sanity and limit the time you spend alone at your computer.

✳ Creating your own internet tools can indeed distinguish you, but quality and professionalism must be top drawer or you will be remembered for the wrong reasons.

CHANNELS OF MARKETING

The Distribution Mix

Today it is a real challenge to get your product into the right hands, and in a pure marketing sense, an entire set of intermediaries is available to you now that wasn't 20 to 25 years ago. These channels of distribution ensure efficient communication flow and help deliver the right product as needed. For your job search success, use these channels to help.

REFERENCES AND REFERRALS

Generating and nurturing a list of appropriate references is a key part of your job search activity. And the list may be readily enriched and enhanced. While supplementary, your list is a powerful marketing pitch you should have ready before you begin to interview and are asked for such credentials. See Figure 6.1 for a sample reference sheet. The term "employee" is an alternative word for "subordinate." It could position you as more of a work-together kind of manager rather than a hierarchy type. "Colleague" or even co-worker is an alternative word for "peer." Either could position you as more of a collaborative team player.

Company applicant screening policies differ. Some employers request references even before the interview process. More typically, a company will ask for references only after an interview (or more); you can regard this as a sign the interview went well and you're still a prime candidate among the finalists. And if you're not asked for references, well, maybe you just have an honest face. But beware, just because you list your last boss, it doesn't mean that person will vouch much for you—many tight-lipped organizations now train staff to provide information only about the start and end dates of your employment and the job titles you held. And maybe if your last boss had a low opinion of you, that name-rank-and-serial-number information may be a good thing.

To form your list, you can start by brainstorming a list of those who would be willing to speak on your behalf. Leaving an organization is often the best time to collect references who are still familiar—and approving—of your recent work. Many bosses, co-workers, and friends will gladly volunteer help on your way out. Others may require more consideration.

The ideal list of references should include five to six individuals who know you and your positive work history. If you are leaving your first professional job or are new to the work force, the list may include those who speak more about your job potential. Your reference list should include:

- Your most recent boss or supervisor.
- Your previous boss or supervisor.
- Your professional colleagues or peers.
- Your customers, perhaps a vendor or an internal or external customer.

Figure 6.1: **Sample Reference Sheet**

WENDY WONDERFUL
300 Miracle Mile • Los Angeles, CA 91604
(213) 654-5689 • wwonderful@hotmail.com

Reference	**Relationship**

Name _____ Direct Report

Title _____

Company _____

Address _____

City, State, Zip _____

Telephone _____

Cell _____

E-mail_____

Name _____ Colleague/Peer

Title _____

Company _____

Address _____

City, State, Zip _____

Telephone _____

Cell _____

E-mail_____

Name _____ Key Internal Customer

Title _____

Company _____

Address _____

City, State, Zip _____

Figure 6.1: **Sample Reference Sheet,** continued

Telephone _____

Cell _____

E-mail_____

Name _____ Key External Customer

Title _____

Company _____

Address _____

City, State, Zip _____

Telephone _____

Cell _____

E-mail_____

Name _____ Employee

Title _____

Company _____

Address _____

City, State, Zip _____

Telephone _____

Cell _____

E-mail_____

Name _____ Manager

Title _____

Company _____

Address _____

City, State, Zip _____

Telephone _____

Cell _____

E-mail_____

- Your "champion," a leader in your field others respect who can cite the best qualities of your character, unique talent, or exceptional performance and provide more prestige for your candidacy.

Refine your list to the top five who will offer enthusiastic—and sincere—recommendations about your accomplishments and talents. See Figure 6.2. And by all means, make sure the contact information you have for each is the most recent and accurate. There are too many cases in which

VIPP **(Very Important Promotion Point)**

Create a single-sheet reference list that presents a 360-degree view of your work life. You are in the center of the baseball diamond, and your references support you: bosses employees, colleagues, customers, etc. At the same time, know that it's expected this group will praise you. A clever reference checker makes a phone call to someone he knows at your former organization and digs deep for the real skinny on you and your performance.

Figure 6.2: **Sample Reference Worksheet**

Individual	Relationship to You	Strengths to Highlight

job seekers got to the final round of consideration only to be undone by a reference person who when contacted had no recollection of the job seeker.

Next, you must be sure to find references willing to help you and also to learn how well they can assess you. Ask each potential reference if he or she is willing to endorse you for a new job. Listen carefully to the response to detect any hesitancy or unwillingness. You do want the other person to care about your success.

Question to learn how well he or she knows your career direction, strengths, and weaknesses. If at all possible, have an in-person discussion, as the face time underscores the importance of your relationship and lets you see reactions to your questions. If your reference is remote or you are pressed for time, a phone call works well. And remember, whoever finally agrees to speak for you, it is your responsibility to prepare him to say not only what is appropriate and consistent about your skills but also about your character. Consistency and congruency of reports among your references help build a hiring manager's trust. You can imagine how troubling it would be for a hiring manager to either hear your references present conflicting facts about you or, just as phony and embarrassing, repeat the same phrases as if they were reading from your prepared script.

Let your references know your career objectives, the kinds of companies you will be targeting, and which firms could be making contact. Refresh them on how your background supports your goals. Position your strengths and the skills you hope to sell during your interviews (see Chapter 7). Confirm your agreement. See Figure 6.3 for a summary sheet to help references.

Discuss your weaknesses or areas for improvement openly. Tell your references what you have been working to improve or particular development activities that have helped you. Be honest with them about how you will respond to the tried-and-true interview question, "What are your weaknesses?" (see Chapter 7) and test for reactions. Remember, the strongest employees are those who know their weaknesses well and can consistently overcome them.

The best way to prepare your references is to provide them with a list of questions most often asked by the hiring manager, the human resource staffer, or the contracted professional reference checker. Listen to their answers and determine if these are the responses you expect or desire. Rehearse with your

Figure 6.3: **Sample Supplementary Sheet for Reference Distribution**

Background information: _____

_____

_____

Reason for leaving Billme, Inc.: _____

_____

_____

Strengths: _____

_____

_____

Key results, successes, and accomplishments: _____

_____

_____

Areas for improvement (weaknesses): _____

_____

_____

reference, if you can. Sure, this can be a little awkward with some people, but think of the exchange as if you are preparing notes you might use for a speech or debate. Consider the following:

- How do you know the applicant?
- How long have you been associated, and what is your knowledge of the applicant's abilities?
- Tell me about the candidate's responsibilities when she worked for (or with) you?

- What specific accomplishments or results was she acknowledged for?
- What are the candidate's strengths or special talents?
- What are the applicant's weaknesses? Where is improvement needed?
- What has made the candidate particularly effective on the job?
- Why did the applicant leave the organization?
- Would you hire the candidate again if you had the opportunity? (The most skillful listener is alert to silence or even a hint of hesitation. Quick response to this question is especially telling.)
- Tell me about the applicant's strongest personal characteristics.
- How did the candidate interact with fellow team members?
- What were the overall perceptions of the candidate and how did most people respond to her?
- Who else can I talk to that knows this applicant's performance?
- Is there any other information you'd like to pass on that I haven't requested?
- Do you know anything that could disqualify this candidate from performing satisfactorily on the job?

Alert your reference immediately after a successful interview. Let your contact know how well the interview went—note specific highlights or qualifications you stressed—and that a referral inquiry might be coming. Make sure your reference knows the company name, job position, and interviewer.

Call particular attention to any unique skills the hiring manager or interviewer might require or ask about and suggest a reply: "He is looking for someone especially good at decoding; could you please mention my success with the Brannon Project?" "She needs an especially skillful people person—perhaps you can cite my Employee Cooperation Award." Here is another opportunity to provide your marketing channel with your key positioning information.

Reward your helpful references. A follow-up thank-you note and status report ("I start XYZ on Monday, February 2!") is what most people appreciate. You can distinguish yourself by hand delivering (or mailing) candy, flowers, wine, or even a gift certificate to a favorite restaurant. Recognize each person's help in proportion. Some might get a small gift; others you might treat to a meal. The point is to let your references know you care and appreciate the help and are available to reciprocate at any time and in any way you can.

Use an internet reference checking service (sites like jobreference.com or myreferences.com will confidentially contact your list) if you think you are being eliminated at the reference-checking stage or you are getting hints that your references aren't helping you. Fees can range from $60 to $100 and may be well worth the investment.

OTHER HELPFUL OPTIONS

There are opportunities for you to take advantage of services that are specifically designed for the job search. The following are a few of the options.

Outplacement Agents and Agencies

There are small specialty firms, large consulting conglomerates, and companies of all sizes that provide outplacement or transition services with a variety of options. Though the nature of this business is constantly changing and evolving due to economic shifts, many organizations experiencing a reduction in workforce or a layoff will still pay for their employees to receive outplacement services or counseling. You need to realize, however, that outplacement agencies are not in the business of finding you a job or making recruiting matches, but instead will provide the best tools for you to help yourself. Very few outplacement firms deliver services to individuals without a corporate affiliation, that is, a company footing the bill. Even though you are leaving, this company support can be generous and is an endorsement of the skills they believe you will continue developing elsewhere.

Outplacement or transition organizations also help a company's management prepare for the layoff by helping coordinate the announcement logistics, training managers how to explain the separation and benefits, and ensuring that counselors are on site to meet with departing employees to explain how the service will help them move on to a new position.

Typically, transition services are provided according to a client's seniority and job level. Management (that is, senior staff to first level supervisor), can receive as little as one month or as much as one year in a program, which often includes from 4 to 48 hours of one-on-one consultant time. Fees can range from $1,500 to $12,000, which tells you how much value a company places on its human resources, even when they are leaving. Executive programs at agencies can also include use of a private office space or a cubicle, regular networking and special-interest group meetings, administrative support, custom business cards and stationery, and access to the agency's own internet sites for job research.

Most often, the outplacement firm assigns a consultant or counselor to help you. Some agencies provide one who is the best fit, for a good chemistry personality match or related industry experience. Be comfortable with your consultant. Whatever hours are available, you should ask for a counselor of your choice. See the career coach section below for questions to ask about the outplacement consultant staff before you begin a program.

Senior level clients can receive this same range of service but many sponsoring organizations are now providing just a day or two of on-site seminars, with an optional hour of follow-up consultant time and unlimited access to the outplacement agency's internet site. These are cost-cutting measures. Fees for this coverage run about $400 to $500 per person. Today, because many people are able to work from home with the latest computers, agencies more and more rely on toll-free phone numbers and internet seminars to serve their clients, foregoing the traditional in-person training sessions.

Some common outplacement agencies provide the following:

1. *Self-assessment tools and analysis*
   - Discovery of skills, interests, and values
   - Recognition of motivation and needs
   - Clarity of ideal work environments and career objectives

2. *Career exploration*
   - Analysis of the employment market

3. *Research techniques*
   - Using the internet for data collection and research, postings, etc.
   - Relevant courses and development opportunities
   - Information interviewing and networking
   - Short- and long-term goal setting

4. *Job hunting*
   - Strategies and resources to obtain interviews
   - Resume building
   - Networking

5. *Interview techniques*, including mock video interviews and debriefings

6. *Making solid decisions*

7. *Negotiating successfully*

8. *Starting anew*

Here are some tips that can help you deal effectively with what outplacement agencies provide. It's important to know what services are included in the fee your company is paying.

> **VIPP** (Very Important Promotion Point)
>
> Always take full advantage, in any format, of your company-sponsored outplacement support or transition service. Never assume that you can go it alone and that you know all there is about getting a new job. You will benefit immeasurably and learn new things about the process and yourself. Besides, there is no real cost to you— someone else is paying for this valuable benefit.

- Ask what is not included in your service.

- Include your spouse or partner in supporting your goals.

- Commit to many key job search activities and plan a structured, active, and full calendar of job hunt actions.

- Complete all job search assignments and exercises. Don't waste your job consultant's time, or your own, by quitting projects that must be finished for you to get the full benefits.

- Trust your consultants. Disclose as much as you can and feel free to unburden yourself of your frustrations and negative concerns. They can provide professional empathy and support that relatives, friends, and colleagues may not offer.

- Be clear and specific. Speak up for what you want and need. Call regularly to keep your consultant informed on your progress.

- Honor your time and appointment commitments and meet frequently, perhaps an hour once a week in the beginning. Plan an agenda, too, and share questions. Make the most of your time together with productive issue solving and not mere rap-session ramblings.

- Strive to maintain optimism, keep a positive attitude, and take care of yourself.

Remember, do not:

- Expect anyone to do your work for you, especially not your counselor.

- Rush or skip major job search tasks, thus making careless mistakes.

- Give yourself too much free time. That can build up anxiety.
- Be too harsh with yourself. Try not to berate yourself when things go wrong. Mental anguish is counter-productive.
- Assume people know what you're seeking. Tell them.
- Panic. The outplacement process will work for you, too.

Skills Training: Upgrading Your Marketability

There are a variety of training programs or courses available that can help you fill a gap in your skill set (see Chapter 1). Some are free through the state employment development department (EDD) and include many of the instructions offered at an outplacement agency. Others vary in price, depending on where they are offered. Some examples of costs per course are: adult education through a local high school, $35 to $50; community college system, $100 to $200; university-level extension series, $300 to $500; for-profit training company, $1,000 to $3,000. Many people see the time between positions as a great opportunity to brush up on computer skills, enroll in certificate programs, learn better interviewing techniques, or refresh presentation skills.

Revisit your previous assessments and check to see where you can improve. Enrollments are especially high in computer courses that teach specific software programs, such as, Word, Java, and Acrobat, or provide technical skills in web design, code writing, or computer repair. Numbers enrolled in certificate programs are also increasing: project management, nurse practitioner, human resources, and executive coaching.

Private for-profit firms such as Toastmasters, Dale Carnegie, Karass Negotiations, Miller Hieman Sales Training, American Management Association, and Mandell Communications are proven business training organizations that have open-to-the-public seminars to improve your skill set and help increase your marketability. There are also organizations that specialize in helping you match your skills to job categories.

If the investment in a set of courses is great, be sure to do your research before agreeing on the fee:

1. Ask for a list of previous participants. Randomly call or e-mail a few to check on the value of the session. Ask them:

    - What did they learn?

- What are they doing now that they didn't do before completing the seminar?
- What did they like about the instructor or facilitator?
- What didn't they like?
- How much time was devoted to lecture? Interactive exercises? Group work?

2. Ask for the resume of your seminar leader. Confirm the leader possesses the expected level of education, qualifications, and accomplishments. Call to see if the course will cover the range of training you want. If possible, clarify how much coverage is based on lecture and how much on activities.

> **VIPP** (Very Important Promotion Point)
>
> Before spending any of your personal funds on seminars, coaches, or any other development activities, be sure you ask questions that give you the answers you need. You must be doubt free with your decision because you cannot afford to waste time or money on anything that is not just the right fit for you and your situation.

Career Coaches

The career management business is a growing industry because of the specialization required. Though there are more coaches than ever available, you're not guaranteed to always find the most well-qualified ones. A career coach provides many of the services of an outplacement/transition agent or agency. Some human resource departments provide in-house career counseling or career centers to help retain talent and link with their succession-planning programs. But often a career coach is hired privately to help people in their job searches. A career coach differs from an executive coach or life coach.

An executive coach focuses on modifying work behaviors that will help enhance the client's career development and professional profile. Work-style data, derived from the coach-client feedback exchange, exposes a client's rough spots that need to be polished. The client then draws up a specific work behavior adjustment plan and practices the new behaviors with the coach until the steps are ingrained. Organizations that underwrite this development coaching technique see it as a valuable executive development tool for top talent. (Typical fees paid by sponsoring organizations range from $3,000 for assessment and analysis only, to $7,500 for three months, and $15,000 for six months of training.)

A life coach often interacts with clients by phone or online contact and does not necessarily specialize in career, work, or job-related improvements. She gathers data about your former and current progress toward self-acclaimed life goals and helps you see where you are stuck in a rut. Helping motivate you to shift gears and work on your key issues, the life coach can get you back on track pursuing your meaningful long-term objectives. Typical fees range from $75 per hour for a phone consultation to $125 per hour for an in-person meeting.

Retaining or hiring a career coach and determining the level of engagement varies largely by personal choice. Some people like to set their own course. They know what they need to do, and are able to plan and manage their research and job search aids. Others like teaming with a coach who can help highlight their skills, interests, and values in the job search steps, select the best tools for the work, and keep them focused on the immediate tasks to accomplish.

Finding the right coach, however, is like finding the right attorney, psychotherapist, or surgeon: You must choose one carefully and wisely for a poor choice may do more harm than good. Although there are more coaches available these days, you're not guaranteed that all are qualified. Typical fees range from $125 to $200 per hour for independent sole practitioners.

Begin your search for a coach by asking for recommendations. Also network and check with your friends or colleagues for names of reputable professionals—either single practitioners or organizations with a career management/coaching practice and specialty. Settle on three to four contacts.

Then, you should review each biography and resume. Is gender important to you? Test for experience, credentials, and certifications. How many years has this person been a career counselor? What is his academic training, or additional sponsoring, and industry experience? How many assessment tools is he certified to administer? What is the fee structure and time frame for completion?

Finally, interview at least two counselors and revisit the questions above, if necessary. Also, use the list below (or create your own) to gather important information. Your goal in working with a career coach is to explore new job options and confer on compatible success schemes.

- What is your coaching philosophy?
- What does client confidentiality mean to you?
- What feedback opportunities are available?
- What former client(s) may I contact? How did you help them specifically?

- What do you consider failure in this process?

Mentors

A mentor is a friend or faithful counselor and confidant. No doubt one has already helped guide you in some significant, positive way and has understood and responded to your needs. Often this mentor appears in your career, social group, or volunteer organization. A mentor is principally one who sees and encourages your talent and potential—even when you don't. A senior co-worker, teacher, athletics coach, church group leader, or a summer camp head counselor may be a mentor.

A current mentor can reveal special insight now as you implement your marketing plan in pursuit of a new job. Some organizations have structured mentor programs that can match you with someone who will support your best career interests, pass on your ideas, get input on your written work, and report regularly on your progress. A mentor can serve as a career coach or outplacement agent, but with greater personal involvement and a 360-degree perspective.

Recruiters

Chapter 4 explained the importance of job recruiters, and here I again emphasize their value as partners in your marketing campaign. A good recruiter is like a reliable auto mechanic or electrician: a skilled professional who is worth her weight in gold. Retained recruiters are often especially well networked and know key people who may be able to hire you. Maintaining a positive and productive working relationship with your recruiter can open hiring doors otherwise closed. Be selective and forthcoming in your expectations, however, and remember recruiters have memories, too. A casual jibe or a dismissive or rude comment about a company member or recruiter can come back to haunt you. Maintain an assured stance and professional courtesy even if some recruiter behaviors are not always exemplary. Honor

> **VIPP** (Very Important Promotion Point)
>
> Know the difference between a coach and a mentor, subtle though it might be. A trained coach asks lots of questions and helps you see options and *helps* you make good decisions on your own. A mentor is often in a position to *tell* you what to do and has a career path similar enough to yours to pass on experiences and advice to directly help.

your appointments and time commitments and provide accurate follow up on your to-dos. Treat your recruiter with the same customer-focused skills as you would any channel partner. It will help in both the long and short run.

CEO (Consultant Examples and Opinions)

- Coach your references on the appropriate points, just as lawyers rehearse their witnesses, to be sure they present your case as positively as possible and to eliminate any chance of a surprise statement that could contradict your claims.

- Use any form of outplacement service your company provides. The service is sure to help your job search in several ways.

- Trust the transition process and let it work for you. All of the experiences, of struggle as well as success, condition you for the ups and downs of a long career.

- Even expensive career training experiences (pricey seminars, coaches, programs, etc.) are well worth your effort. Ask lots of questions of others to build awareness, knowledge, and confidence in your job search.

- If you confide in a mentor employed at your former organization or work with an internal employee relations specialist, be sure you have a precise and mutual agreement on confidentiality.

❋ *Summary* ❋

❋ Using the variety of resources available—outplacement support, coaches, seminars, and training—can only increase the probability of your success.

❋ Selecting, prepping, and nurturing the right references can turn a good interview into an offer.

❋ Working with a respected recruiter can open just the right doors. Trusting your recruiter is key.

SUCCESSFUL SALES

The Pitch to Succeed

You've arrived. You got the interview. It's the desired result of your efforts to date and certainly the most critical event in finally landing a job offer. The significance of this last key sales effort cannot be understated: It is the primary goal of your marketing plan, that includes knowing yourself and what's important to you.

There is a lot of hard work ahead and a lot riding on the quality of your presentation. Your goal is the offer. You need to focus on what the company wants and needs as you present your background and accomplishments. Also, what the individual you report to wants and needs, stated or unstated. At the same time, you must discover as much about the company and the position as you can and test-fit them with your criteria and career objective and your personality and values.

You want to do all you can to get a "yes" reply to the implied question, "Will I hire this applicant?" The decision to evaluate and accept a candidate comes after the interview. Despite these high stakes, you can still have fun in the experience and manage your stress effectively. Preparation and anticipation is the key to your interview success.

INTERVIEWING STYLES

Interviews take many shapes and forms, from the formal to the impromptu discussion. You need to be mindful of the various types only as a preparation option.

One-on-One Interview

The one-on-one interview is perhaps the most common version you can experience. It requires a relaxed, conversational approach (similar to a business meeting—not a martial-arts encounter) for you to be successful.

Screening Interview

A subset of the one-on-one interview includes the screening interview, often a phone contact, in which a trained personnel or HR staff representative tests for specific requirements such as certification musts, or exposure to certain tools, and eliminates noncontenders from a large number of candidates. Remember the phone tips from Chapter 4 (stand-up, smile, etc.), but be mindful that screeners often use a checklist. If at all possible, answer "yes" to everything asked first and then clarify and explain.

Human Resource Interview

The Human Resource (HR) interview searches for a proper corporate, executive, or cultural fit, and is often conducted by a trained HR professional seeking the right look, level of confidence, ease of conversation, or balance of drive and motivation. Most organizations want you to meet someone in HR before an offer is made, even if you enter with a CEO recommendation.

Hiring Manager Interview

The hiring manager interview is done by the would-be boss and emphasizes the job's specific tasks and the candidate's role on his team or department. It's a nuts-and-bolts interview, full of detailed questions about real job scenarios: what you can do and how you would do it. Though many organizations now provide their managers with sophisticated how-to interview training seminars with much emphasis on the legal dos and don'ts, the hiring manager is often solely focused on getting the work accomplished. (Think of anytime you have hired someone to do involved tasks for you; you wanted to be sure that even the kid you chose to shovel your snow could get the job done or else you might not get to work.)

Co-Worker Interview

The co-worker interview tests and evaluates to see if the interviewer likes you and sees you working compatibly, comfortably, and productively in her department/work group. She may not have much interview training but is certainly able to sense an arrogant tone or too casual behavior. In this case, act competent yet nonthreatening and be brief about your background statements, answers, and questions.

Group Interview

The group, or panel, interview has several people asking questions at the same time. This examination can be overwhelming, especially if you aren't expecting it. Make sure you know in advance if this approach is part of the interview. You don't want to find when you enter the interview room that there are five people seated on one side of a conference table and you on the other. You may feel you're before a congressional hearing.

Answering questions coming from many people's perspectives is difficult to master. Just remember that only one person can ask you a question at a time. Try to maintain sure eye contact and balance your responses to all interviewers.

Ignoring or isolating even one interviewer may lead to that person blackballing you. It's sort of like handing your treats out to most but not all takers and then getting a trick from an empty-handed, disgruntled person.

Remind yourself to look directly at the person when answering her question, then visit the others in the room, scanning the group and glancing at each person to check for their acknowledgment or understanding, that is, their "buy in." Be sure you close with a statement of your interest in the job.

Serial Interview

The round robin, or serial interview, is when you are moved from one interviewer to another. In this case, you get to meet and talk with your potential co-workers, employees, and other organizational team members, that is, those you will join in the office sports or lottery pools. For you to be successful here requires a combination of energy, patience, and enthusiasm. Sometimes there can be as many as six interviews in one day, often with you conducting a slide presentation or stand-up delivery as well.

Some pharmaceutical/scientific/biotech interviews require your presenting a paper or delivering a seminar topic. Marketing, library science, or training and organizational development interviews might also insist you provide a performance sample showcasing your real skills in action. Although these presentations represent a lot more preparation and work, don't begrudge the interviewers this extended look-see. Think of it as your first day on the job, knowing that if things don't go well or as planned in the exercise, you've had a chance to see how your would-be peers respond and can gain confidence right away in the new position or bow out gracefully without breaking a commitment.

Be sure your serial interview answers are consistent (often, group members meet to critique and assess your replies) and your tone is pleasantly upbeat, not fatigued from repetition. Indeed, you may be drained, but you should not express boredom or exhaustion. Rather, if you must cite similar statements to one interviewer after another, use the repetition to further fortify your experience or even add effective new selling points that will occur to you as you proceed and become more comfortable talking about your value to others.

Simulation Interview

The experiential exercise or simulation interview is often part of a corporate-sponsored assessment used to predict success in groups. You and other applicants work together on a simulated group project and are observed by the trained evaluating staff. Follow directions carefully and participate warmly, knowing your ability to solve problems and collaborate are key success indicators.

INTERVIEW FORMATS

Interviews also come in various formats. Knowing the various combinations and understanding the approaches in your exchange can tell you something about the interviewer and the organization.

Structured Interview

The structured interview typically allows you about 65 percent and the interviewer 35 percent of the talk time. Questions, prepared and scripted in advance, are adapted to meet the specific criteria of the position, and the interviewer tries to determine your competencies in meeting the job responsibilities. There is a time limit and a logical flow to the process. Watch the interviewer; he may also be taking notes on your replies to the questions while you are speaking. Remember not to embellish thoughts or ask questions if you see the interviewer jotting down her thoughts or circling ranking numbers on a structured list of questions. These notes may be crucial to the hiring process, especially if they're positive marks. They may be gathered later and studied to distinguish your responses from competitors' comments.

Unstructured Interview

The unstructured interview is not the opposite of a structured interview. The goals are the same, but the process is much less formal. More conversational and open in tone and approach, here the interviewer asks questions that get you talking, hopefully not rambling. A skillful interviewer using this "just talk between pals" technique can get you to let down your professional stance and blab negatives about former work and other inappropriate topics, and then probe deep into the replies to discover and raise red flag issues. Some applicants see the unstructured interview as a poker game with bluffs or aces up one's sleeve, but if you regard the proceedings as a competition with the interviewer, you'll be the one folding your cards in the job game.

Behavioral Interview

The behavioral interview looks to your past experiences as indicators of your future success on the job. Interviewers prepare questions that will test what you have done and how you have succeeded with what the position requires. A typical behavioral question begins as, "Tell me about a time when you . . . ."

Free-Form Interview

A free-form interview is filled with questions that seem unrelated and unfocused. Random and unpredictable, it often reflects the interviewer's lack of experience rather than a strategy or purposeful approach to garnering candidate information. Quite often the interviewer does not take notes and does most of the talking. With this freewheeling dialogue, your goal is to connect positively right away and to work stories and experiences that highlight your accomplishments into the conversation. Smile a lot, be warm and natural, nod when you acknowledge your empathy, and cite your success stories as examples that identify with similar circumstances expressed by your interviewer.

Even in the most casual work environments, there are common assumptions and activities for interviewees to keep in mind:

- The interviewer should have your resume and/or application and some idea of what to ask you.
- You should have prior knowledge of the company, the interviewer, and the position.
- The interviewer will try to welcome you graciously and attempt to establish a relaxed atmosphere by initiating small talk about directions or offering you something to eat or drink, etc. Smile and repeat the name of everyone you meet initially, including the receptionist, as you may one day soon be working with them.
- Greet others with a professional handshake and be sociable, at ease, and forthcoming.

- The interviewer poses the questions; you provide the answers.
- The interviewer asks for questions, you pose issues that are important to you other than salary terms, which will probably be raised only after you have been selected as the preferred candidate.
- The interviewer closes the discussion, sells the job and organization if appropriate, and sets the next step's discussion. Never close the interview at your convenience, or you will have closed the door on your chances.
- You thank everyone for their time, get follow-up agreements, shake hands, and part company.

> ## VIPP (Very Important Promotion Point)
>
> Remember information and preparation are the two key words for a successful interview. The more your *know*—from the best route there, to the dress code, type of interview, and environment—and the more you can *practice*—from a sample phone screening to a mock videotaping—the greater your real-time success will be. Leave as little to chance as possible, *never arrive late, eat, or chew anything*, and assume the interview will be conducted by a professional who has also prepared and trained for your being there.

GETTING READY

As you learned in Chapter 2, Research and Development, and Chapter 3, Packaging, part of your preparation is thoroughly understanding the organization and your interviewer and effectively presenting yourself. You should learn as much about the company and the people who will be interviewing you as you can. Use your network and make some calls for tips about the people you will meet. Be sure you know the exact spelling and pronunciation of each person's name, especially the hiring manager. If you're in doubt, the receptionist will usually clarify this for you.

If possible, visit the company's location. There you can pick up an annual report, corporate newsletter, product brochures/data sheets, or other information-rich literature. You can test the drive time, check out the office ambiance and work tempo, and see employee dress as well. Although it's not quite research for landing on the Moon, you can never have too much information for landing a job.

Dress comfortably, especially if you have a six- to eight-hour day of interviewing planned, and act naturally. It may be helpful to look and feel like you fit in, but it is essential to present your true self for long-term success. You need to look current and at ease, not trendy or pushy. Good grooming is a must: clean and trimmed nails and hair—and mustaches and beards as well.

Seasoned professionals (over age 55) might consider toning up at a gym and/or coloring gray hair to look younger and more marketable. Think carefully about this; it can backfire if not done professionally and not something you would normally do. Still, a great energy level, fresh ideas, and enthusiasm for the job are the most powerful ways to present a vibrant and youthful work appearance.

Despite more office examples of business-casual dress codes and even laid-back work environments that allow flip-flops, hip huggers, and T-shirts, it is best for men to wear a silk tie (color coded to an outfit) and jacket. If the office attire is especially casual, men can always take off their ties. Be sure, though, to wear a button-down shirt so the collar and jacket ensemble will still be consistent. Women should wear a suit and dress blouse for the first interview. Shoes should be polished and on the conservative side. Men's socks should match and cover the ankle skin, and women should wear stockings without runs. You want your common-sense professional personality to be noticed, not your latest fashion-sense creativity.

You should avoid loud colors and bold prints for scarves, handkerchiefs, other accessories, and even outlandish manicures, and inappropriate-for-your-age styles. Appearing vigorous for a job does not involve dressing young like your Gen-Y son or daughter, or your co-worker for that matter. Statement jewelry—huge stones in rings, bracelets or cufflinks, dangling sparkler earrings, or gold chains—is better for glamorous occasions than jobs. Tattoos, body piercings, and earrings for men are still a very high risk look in many work settings, and that includes an arm tattoo with your new would-be boss's name. Also try not to use too much perfume or after-shave. If someone who isn't hugging you can smell it, it's too much. Those with allergies will also be negatively impacted.

> ## VIPP (Very Important Product/Package Point)
>
> Test your interview outfit, accessories, and overall appearance with someone who cares about you. Be sure there is a high trust level and lots of opportunity for honest feedback and suggestions for improvement. Better yet, create two equally appropriate ensembles for approval, just in case you are asked back the next day or the same week.

Another way to prepare is to revisit and practice your OARs—Opportunities (problems), Activities, Results—those accomplishments you generated in Chapter 1 to build your resume and to include in your 60-second infomercial or elevator speech. Once more, you need to be sure you are prepped to explain these success stories succinctly and to present the measurable achievements and results that not only benefited the company but also met and exceeded the requirements of your job.

Think of the qualities the position requires, which are sometimes named directly in the job description or posting, or the hiring manager seeks. Then craft the questions you think he might ask. Better yet, craft questions you would ask if roles were reversed. See Figure 7.1.

Figure 7.1: **Sample Preparation Question and Answer Sheet**

1. **Quality**: Good customer service skills

   Possible Question: "Tell me about the toughest customer you had and what you did to win him/her to your side."

   OAR Story Answer
   I was hoping that I'd get a chance to talk about H.B. I inherited an influential and large customer account that consistently had mistakes in both its shipping and billing, and the client was constantly badgering the staff to fix these fast. The customer was ready to take his business elsewhere, too. I researched the problems, then drove three hours to the company's location for a personal meeting and explained the causes of the errors. I made time-based commitments for improvement and positive change on our side with the condition that he would pledge to treat our staff cordially on his requests. The volume of his business increased 25 percent over the next three months, and our mistakes and his behavior improved substantially. I was seen as a sort of miracle worker after that solution—and when the customer moved on to another company, he even renewed his business with us.

2. **Quality**: Ability to multitask

   Possible Question: "What is a busy day for you? How do you handle it, and how do you know you were successful?"

   OAR Story Answer
   I'm pleased you inquired. Jumble's reception desk was always a bevy of activity, even on so-called quiet days. On Tuesday mornings from about 8:00 to 10:30 A.M., I would greet and sign

Figure 7.1: **Sample Preparation Question and Answer Sheet,** continued

in the recruits from around the world there for sales training—badges, packets, etc. —distribute the mail into our boxes, answer and transfer all incoming calls, including occasional pages, and check in the string of FedEx and UPS morning deliveries. I just kept my composure, smiled and chuckled a lot, and knew all had gone well when a visiting consultant waiting in the lobby to coach our CEO passed on a compliment on my lack of mistakes and unflappable style. He even told the CEO, and last October I won the Employee of the Month award.

3. **Quality:** Team player/collaborative

Possible Question: "How do you define a team player? Provide a personal example that illustrates your definition."

OAR Story Answer

There are probably lots of acceptable definitions here, but since you asked, for me a team player is someone who knows his or her role and the responsibility that goes with it. In my world, a team player is someone able to see beyond personal gain for the success of the team and/or task at hand.

At CCC we rotated our presentation responsibilities, and I was next in the queue to present our creative campaign to a relatively new but potentially big-spending client. I agreed to break order and give up that opportunity when we learned that another artist on our team went to grad school with the new client. All of us were confident that the client relationship would be solidified and made much stronger with a more familiar face at the PowerPoint.

This was not easy, to say the least. I had not made a presentation in a while, and it was a favorite part of my job. All worked out. That client spent a fortune, and my next presentation yielded the biggest print campaign spending in the agency's history—about $5,000 per month.

Now you build a sample question sheet.

1. **Quality:** _____   **Possible Question**: _____

_____   _____

_____   _____

OAR Story Answer

_____

_____

_____

_____

_____

_____

_____

2. **Quality:** _____   **Possible Question:** _____

_____   _____

_____   _____

OAR Story Answer

_____

_____

_____

_____

_____

_____

_____

3. **Quality:** _____   **Possible Question:** _____

_____   _____

_____   _____

OAR Story Answer

_____

_____

_____

_____

_____

_____

_____

FIRST IMPRESSIONS: BREAKING THE ICE, TWICE

Quite often, all candidates who are called for an interview have the baseline qualifications to do the work. The offer, however, generally goes to the applicant who will be the best fit, easy to work with, quick to learn, and low maintenance to manage and integrate into the organization.

You have just a few moments to make a positive first impression. Some interviewers make up their minds about you with the initial contact or a few minutes into the interview. You need to sell your fit immediately.

Your goal is to generate an equal mix of sociability and competence—right away as well as throughout the interview. If you are too nice, you will most likely appear to be insincere and overwhelm the interviewer. If you are too task- and business-results focused, you will most likely seem arrogant and pushy and also overpower the interviewer. Present yourself as a confident, self-assured professional, gracious yet capable. Appearance is your frame. What you say and how you say it is your picture.

When the interviewer arrives, introduce yourself and offer a firm but not bone-crunching handshake. "Hello—I'm Shanda Lear," you might say. "I'm pleased to meet you." (Try to arrive five to ten minutes early, so you can acclimate to the surroundings and relax a bit. If the reception area has any company literature or framed awards, you might stand and "look interested," examining these at the time your interviewer arrives.)

Walk and position yourself confidently, with good posture and energy, which can illustrate both interest and enthusiasm. Wait until you're offered a seat or the interviewer is seated before you sit down. Try to be seated at the same eye level or directly across from her. When sitting, you might lean slightly forward from time to time because this signals particular interest. Leaning back a bit at times, especially after the halfway point of the interview, can show you are relaxed and comfortable with the interviewer. Shuffling, slouching, and stiffening up, however, can convey boredom, fatigue, or nervousness.

Open the dialogue by thanking the interviewer for calling you in. Choose from some of the topics below to break the ice and to make the transition to the more formal part of the interview easy for both of you:

- Convenient site location
- Ease of traffic or commute

- Office décor or art collection

- Contact/referral connection
- Weekend recap, such as a local sports team win
- Positive publicity reference

Note: This opening exercise has little or no bearing on the interview that follows, BUT it does give you a chance to relax and to connect positively with the interviewer in those important minutes of evaluation. It also gives you a chance to assess the type of person the interviewer is and what's important to him/her.

Because body language communicates 60 percent of what people want to say, maintain an open posture. Never cross your hands over your chest. Crossed hands can signal a closed approach or unwillingness to listen. Look directly at the interviewer, maintaining positive eye contact. Looking away can suggest anything from shyness and dislike to dishonesty and lack of interest. If you need practice, try a staring contest with your dog; it will seem to go on forever.

You need to speak clearly and succinctly. With moderate volume, use a tone that modulates both in pitch and inflection. You'll know this is working when your voice rises with passionate topics or lowers with more factual subjects. Remember not to speak too slowly or too fast: Slow speech hints at hesitation or lack of knowledge, and fast speech sometimes reflects the shallow salesperson's style. You will want to generate warmth and an upbeat manner. Warmth is not easy to convey if doesn't come naturally. Smiling helps, but not that constant, pasted-on, silly grin. Referencing the person by name occasionally also helps. Most often people who appropriately reveal something about themselves through stories or anecdotes appear warmer than those who never share anything. Whispering or bellowing in either a monotone or sing-song style could bore the interviewer or present you as cold, with a flat affect.

You must monitor your gesturing. Pointing and shaking a finger have judgmental connotations, but natural hand motions to pantomime an object or event can actually help the interviewer "see" what you're describing. Test to see if your movements are congruent with what you are saying and remember not to fiddle with your pencil, much less chew it, or scratch, rub, or shift your position unnecessarily. Your gestures need to reinforce your message and communicate both confidence and competence rather than distract, interrupt, or signal anxiety.

Your language should be conversational and easy to understand. It's OK to use the buzz words or jargon of your profession moderately, but don't talk down to an interviewer if you know they haven't heard the terms you use. Also, avoid overly familiar lingo that might suggest an intimacy not yet earned. You do not want to seem stilted or arrogant in your delivery. And don't finish your interviewer's sentences. What you assume is about to be said may turn out to be something entirely different, so save yourself the embarrassment.

Finally, you always show respect and courtesy and establish a rapport with the interviewer as you would a peer or close associate. Remember: Be polite, do not patronize, and do not be overly familiar. Even if you think the conversation has gone very well, it's bad form to ask the interviewer out for a date.

ACTIVE LISTENING: HEARING WHAT THE COMPANY NEEDS

You cannot sell yourself if you cannot hear what your customer wants and needs. Listening, in the context of a job interview, can be your key to success. Every job requires good listening skills, and even the most unsophisticated or untrained interviewer is testing for them. You need to answer the questions posed to you. You need to listen before you respond. You need to check, if you can, to hear what is behind the query to be sure your answer meets either the hidden or expressed need.

Remember not to interrupt, rush to finish an inarticulate or incomplete question for the interviewer, or forget the question asked. These are the most obvious indicators that you are not listening. In multitasking efforts these days, people have become ingrained selective listeners, but concentrate on this talk as you might to hear your baby's first words.

A pen and pad, or Personal Digital Assistant (PDA) if you want to appear up-to-date with technology, are essential for you to jot down a complicated or multipart question. You can keep both in an attractive folio with extra copies of your resume and your reference sheets, but avoid lugging in a briefcase, looking like you own the place. Ask if it's OK for you to take notes during the discussion.

Paraphrase or restate questions as a way to frame or position them before answering. This tells the interviewer you

VIPP (Very Important Promotion Point)

Midway through the interview, check to see how you're doing and ask the interviewer: "Are these answers giving you what you need?" "What else can I bring to the table that will help you make the decision?" Also, remember to avoid repeating any inflammatory word that can perpetuate negativity—failure, regret, conflict, etc.

are clear about what she wants and may also give you a moment to craft what you will say. Do this only after the interviewer has completed her thought and the complete question is presented. Typically, the voice goes down a bit when the thought is completed, and even though it might be very frustrating, always let the interviewer finish those incomplete sentences and in-process queries. Some people may see you as quick and clever if you guess the right word correctly or complete the thought appropriately, but the risk in seeming pedantic is too great. A larger majority will view this behavior as anywhere from impatient and controlling to not listening and pushy. And never correct an interviewer unless it's to repeat a key fact. Any simple misunderstanding can be amended in your follow-up thank-you letter.

Remember that this interview is not about you. Listening for needs means you reply in ways that show how you will generate revenues, increase market share, bring back a lost customer, or better yet, make your future boss look like a star.

The preparation mentioned above is the best way to refine your listening skills. You gather background information about the organization and the position, so you can form hypotheses about needs. Typical organizational needs are skills for increased productivity, waste reduction, retaining reliable/loyal talent, generating creative ideas, and solving problems. You then match your skills, interests, special talents, and ideas to these hypotheses. Practice, then, by describing your past successes and how you can add fresh value to meet present needs. If you are ready with your answers, you are most likely able to hear the questions and answer the needs with greater focus.

The steps below provide a guideline:

- *Step 1*. Ponder a moment before answering. Jumping right in and answering too quickly might seem too slick and smooth, and a bit over-rehearsed. If possible, answer the question referring to the company's own situation. For example, if you have a success story about how you sold a slow moving line of clothing, adapt your solution by substituting the car company's products and how you would market their overstock of parts.
- *Step 2*. Frame or position your answer before you reply. You can do this by paraphrasing the question, "So you want to know my decision-making

style—is that right?" or by commenting and reflecting on it, "I was hoping you would ask about the way I manage my staff."

- *Step 3.* Provide a direct answer. "Yes, I met my sales numbers three quarters in a row," "I am fast on the keyboard—almost 90 words a minute now."
- *Step 4.* Close with your metric result or accomplishment. "The person I had to let go was so touched by my handling of the situation that she closed a big $200,000 deal before leaving. She did not have to do that. We then were able to make our budget number."
- *Step 5.* Test for reaction clues, if necessary, before you proceed very far with an answer. Watch for facial expressions, such as raised eyebrows, open-mouth, or rolling eyes: "How close are my answers to what you wanted or expected?" "Are my responses to these questions giving you the answers you need?"

Practice alone with a tape recorder both the questions and answers that you think will come up and those that do the best job of showcasing your skills and talents. Your comfort level at listening should increase with your confidence in answering.

You should then practice with a trusted colleague, spouse, partner, or coach, and videotape this rehearsal. Select those questions you might find sensitive or difficult. Once more, you will be able to test your listening skills and overall ability to answer effectively. Critique the video honestly. Resolve to improve both the content, that is, what you say, the text of your answers, and the process, that is, how you say them—tone, nonverbals.

SHORT STORIES: SCENARIOS THAT SELL YOUR SKILLS

Use your OAR stories to sell. Certainly humility and modesty are virtues but not during the interview. This is your chance to shine and cite your strengths in ways others might not. If for whatever reason you think it is bad luck, too pushy, or self-serving to talk about your talents, just realize that you have been specially invited to do so and your competitors are also blowing their own horns.

Remember that your hire will be based on:

- Your competence in and skill for handling the job responsibilities. This accounts for 30 percent of the hiring decision.

- Your potential value and the potential scope of your contribution to the organization.
- Your chemistry, and your fit with the environment and culture. Your match in values, personality, and work ethic accounts for another 50 percent of the hiring decision.
- Your interest in taking the job and your enthusiasm about the assignment accounts for the final 20 percent of the hiring decision.

Review and retell your success stories in terms of the value you can add to this position. Work with Figure 7.2 to highlight your added value.

Figure 7.2: **Added Value Worksheet**

My top three professional achievements are: _____

_____

_____

_____

_____

My strong knowledge areas are: _____

_____

_____

_____

_____

My key marketable skills are: _____

_____

_____

_____

_____

Figure 7.2: **Added Value Worksheet,** continued

My distinction from other candidates is: _____

_____

_____

My unique added value for the organization is: _____

_____

_____

_____

Achievement #1: _____

_____

_____

_____

Achievement #2: _____

_____

_____

_____

Achievement #3: _____

_____

_____

_____

Achievement #4: _____

_____

_____

_____

Remember in retelling your stories to present or describe the Opportunity or situation you faced. Be specific and provide enough detail—names, dates, places, numbers—for the interviewer to understand or for him to see the future application. The experience can come from a previous work assignment, a volunteer project, or any relevant event. Also, explain what you did—your Action to solve the problem, remove the roadblock or eliminate the conflict or whatever. Describe the activity, even if you were a member of a team or special project task force. Use "I" did, or managed, or created, at least as much or more than "we" did, or managed, or created. It's good to be a team player, but the interviewer is looking to hire you, not them. Finally, accentuate the Result. What was accomplished? What did you learn? How did your group benefit? Again, be specific and provide as much metric data as you can (30 percent increase in sales or 20 percent decrease in shipping mistakes, etc.).

A quick summary at the end of the interview helps sell your point:

> "This example illustrates my ability to organize efficiently with outside vendors and to proactively look for ways to save money."

> "This story shows how I can create experiences that help change behavior and improve the bottom line at the same time."

> "Here my solid communication skills at all levels motivated the team to win the competition and bring in the new business."

POINT AND COUNTERPOINT: WINNING THE DEBATE BUT LOSING THE JOB

Besides giving the correct answers to questions, there are many other elements to an interview. You and the interviewer should be working together to check the fit or

VIPP (Very Important Promotion Point)

Err on the side of brevity. That all-inclusive and achievement-positive answer might just be *too long* to retain the interest of your interviewer. When you practice, test to see if you can crisp up your replies in either the pacing or provided information. Look for facial expressions, yawns, or fiddling to be sure you are not getting bored messages from the interviewer. It's a fine line between giving the complete answer and missing some important signals. Besides, what you think is thorough and data-packed could be perceived as pedantic and obsessive or, worse yet, an indication that you know more than your interviewer or hiring manager.

future match. The content part of your exchange is the area you can prep for most.

Some professional service organizations, such as international consulting firms, and high tech companies hoping to cull for creative, innovative, and out-of-the-box thinkers, make it a policy to ask problem set questions to applicants. They also pose puzzles or brain teaser queries that test your thinking and problem-solving abilities. For example, in his article "Cognitive Reflection and Decision Making" (*Journal of Economic Perspectives*, Volume 19, Number 4, Fall 2005, 25–42), Shane Frederick creates three questions he calls a Cognitive Reflection Test. Here are the questions:

1. A bat and a ball cost $1.10 in total. The bat costs $1.00 more than the ball. How much does the ball cost?

2. If it takes 5 machines 5 minutes to make 5 widgets, how long would it take 100 machines to make 100 widgets?

3. In a lake, there is a patch of lily pads. Every day, the patch doubles in size. If it takes 48 days for the patch to cover the entire lake, how long would it take for the patch to cover half the lake?

"The three items on this CRT are 'easy' in the sense that their solution is not hard to understand when explained, yet reaching the correct answer often requires the suppression of an erroneous answer that springs 'impulsively' to mind." Yet, the average correct score for members of the Harvard student choir group, which was primarily female, was only 1.43, significantly lower than the 2.18 average correct score for MIT but significantly higher than the 0.57 recorded at the University of Toledo.

William Poundstone, in *How Would You Move Mount Fuji?* (Little Brown, 2003) poses questions such as:

- How many times a day do a clock's hands overlap?
- How would you weigh a jet plane without using scales?
- Why are beer cans tapered at the top and bottom?

Interviews with problem set questions are harder to prepare for and might require special drilling. The hypothetical case problem is something else that can be a surprise question: "What would you do with a client who . . ." "Read this scenario and tell me how you would handle it." These questions, like hands-on challenges such as diagramming a solution on an office white board or fixing broken equipment on the spot, require on-demand skills that are hard to prep for at any time. If the test proves especially tricky, you may offer to perform the task as homework by offering to add more details to the solution. Read as much as you can about the company's plans or products and try to stay current in your skills.

VIPP (Very Important Promotion Point)

Some professions, bench scientists and stand-up trainers in particular, may require a group presentation on your research or a seminar on "communication" as part of your interview process. Remember to do as much generic preparation as you can in advance, using Power-Point, hand-outs, etc. Have the shell of what you need ready. You should be alert and energetic, not exhausted from a last-minute all nighter at the computer.

Check out the questions in Figure 7.3 and see if you can come up with answers that will work for you. The next section of this chapter will help you with answers to some of the tougher questions.

Figure 7.3: **Test Questions**

About Yourself
- Describe yourself.
- Why did you leave your last job?
- Cite your strengths.
- Share some of your accomplishments.
- What are your weaknesses?
- Why should we hire you?
- What negatives would your last boss have to say about you?
- What would your subordinates say about you?
- What will your boss say about you in six months?
- What is your most underutilized skill?
- Where have you had the greatest impact? Describe your role in that achievement.

Figure 7.3: **Test Questions,** continued

- What areas of personal performance gain you compliments? What areas of personal performance are noted for improvement?
- What is the most recent frustration you had on the job?
- If I asked your spouse, manager, or coworker to describe you, what five adjectives would he or she use?

Your Professional Goals

- What position are you seeking?
- What are your career plans or ultimate goals?
- What are your salary expectations?
- What did you like about your last job?
- If you could have made improvements in your last job, what would they have been?
- What assistance would you need from us to help you achieve a good start?
- How do you show your anger and frustration?
- Have you made any mistakes during your career? If so, what were they? How did you fix them?
- Let's talk about set-backs. How have they affected you and your family?
- Is there any pattern to critical feedback on you?
- What is the best career decision you have ever made? The worst?
- With the benefit of hindsight, what would you have done differently with your career?
- What three things could you do to improve your overall effectiveness?
- Where have you had the greatest impact? Describe your role in that achievement.
- What was the most important business lesson you learned in the last five years?
- If there were some responsibilities you could have skipped over the past few years, what would these have been?

Your Relationships

- What kind of personalities annoy you the most?
- Cite a co-worker or boss you respect. Describe him or her.
- What has been your biggest regret in your relationships with other people?
- Who was the most interesting customer or client you dealt with in your last job?

Figure 7.3: **Test Questions,** continued

- Describe the best person who ever worked for or with you.
- How do you stay current in your professional life?
- Why would you change jobs?
- If you were speaking tonight to the National Association of Manufacturers, which subject would reveal your specialty as a businessperson?
- What is the difference between a good position and an excellent one?
- If we hired you next week, what unfinished business would remain in your current work?
- After being with one organization for such a long time, won't it be difficult for you to adjust to another?
- What do you want to be doing five years from now?
- Do you feel you have been successful in your current role? What accounts for your success?
- In your career, have you ever experienced a serious conflict of goals? How did you resolve the issue? How did you decide which goal was the more important one?
- What is your ideal job?
- Why do you want to work for our company?
- What direction do you see this industry headed in the next five years, and where do you see (name of company) in this progress?

Your Management/Work Style
- If we could talk to your previous supervisor, what would he or she say about you?
- How did you prepare for this interview?
- How do you handle difficult personalities?
- Dealing skillfully with others on the job is important in being productive. Describe a time when you were successful in dealing with another because you built a trusting and harmonious relationship.
- Describe a high-pressure situation you have had to handle at work. Note what happened, who was involved, and what you did for problem solving.
- Give an example of having to devote extra hours to your job, when it was necessary to take work home, work on weekends, or work extended consecutive hours. Be specific.
- Many times it is important to be hardheaded about a decision you make, particularly when others don't like it. Give an example of a time when you stuck to a decision even though it was under attack by others.

Figure 7.3: **Test Questions,** continued

- Describe emergencies or unexpected assignments that forced you to reschedule your work time.
- How are you best managed?
- How do you evaluate the performance of your subordinates?
- When and why have you fired people?
- What is the most adverse situation you had to handle in your personal or professional life? How did you deal with it? What was the outcome?
- Relate the events surrounding firing someone or severely reprimanding someone. How did you feel about it?
- Note how your approach to managing an organization has changed in the last ten years.
- How do you stand on the issue of training people vs. getting the immediate job done?
- Compare and contrast the options for improving results through a salary reduction vs. reducing staff.
- What will you do the first month on the job?
- Have you ever had to implement a radical new idea? What was your success?
- Describe your experience in coaching others.
- Explain how you incorporate quality tools and best practices with your employees.
- What would you tell your boss is the most important thing he or she could say or do to support you?
- Give an example of a situation where a peer, boss, or subordinate stalled your progress and you felt ready to quit. What was the problem and how did you resolve it?
- Describe a situation that revealed you are a thorough analyzer and decision-maker.
- Note a situation where you had to defend a position even though it reflected poorly on you.
- What would be the best way to motivate you for better performance?
- How do you turn around the bottom line of P&L?
- How do feel about downsizing staff? How would you implement this?
- How do you keep your boss informed?
- How much work structure do you need?
- What would you change about your last or most recent boss? Your last company?

Figure 7.3: **Test Questions,** continued

Your Insight

- How do you respond to criticism?
- What was the most valuable criticism you have received in your career?
- What have you learned from your job search?
- What is the greatest risk you've undertaken?
- What was your greatest failure?
- What has been your experience in working with conflicting, delayed, or ambiguous information? What did you do to make the most of the situation?
- What relationships do you prefer: those at a higher or lower rank?
- Explain a disagreement with a former boss. What was the outcome?
- Describe a time when your understanding of the political dynamics at work was put to good use.

Your Values

- What qualities have you liked/disliked in your bosses? Why?
- How do you balance your personal and business lives?
- According to your definition of success, how successful have you been?
- What was the most difficult ethical decision you have had to make and what was the outcome?
- What was your most creative work situation? Did it provide financial reward, recognition, and personal satisfaction?

Your Leadership

- How do you build a team?
- In your last job, what was your business strategy, your vision?
- What does "leadership" mean to you?

Talk your responses to the questions in Figure 7.3 over with a trusted second party and be sure the information is both honest and reflects who you are and how you want to be perceived. There are no right answers, yet you can provide all the right information and still not get what you want. Here are some additional tips that might help make a difference in how your responses are received:

- Use short, pithy sentences that focus on your results and accomplishments and can bring benefit to the organization. Remember not to overtalk or explain too much. Make your set up crisp enough so the interviewer can ask follow-up questions for details.

- Use language that will connect you to your interviewer. Listen to see if he is using certain words (think vs. feel or see vs. hear) and then integrate these same words into your answers. Mirror also, if you can, the pace of delivery and energy level. Also, remember not to use "we" in referring to your former organization because it might obscure what you did to help your former employer succeed. Instead, use "we" when referring to what you plan to do on the new job (this is leverage designed to help the interviewer see you as already part of the team) and to strengthen your personal involvement and successes.

- Use your time wisely. Remember not to ramble, pontificate, or reminisce. Get to your point quickly. But there's no need to remind the interviewer of the time, especially in a serial interview session, because the courtesy you extend may cut short a good interview or imply that you and not the interviewer are controlling the clock.

- Use discretion at all times. Remember not to gossip or to speak negatively about your former boss or organization.

Often, the biggest chance to win over your interviewer comes at the start of your time together, with the lead question, "Tell me about yourself." Here is an opportunity to illustrate both your sociability and competency components. Be careful not to fluster, filibuster, or familiarize. If you are not prepared, talk too long, or get too personal, you will lose the interviewer's interest early and the substance of your following replies—however purposeful—will be lost to deaf ears.

You can use the ingredients of your infomercial here, but start with a clarification:

"Let me begin by telling you about my professional self."

You can steer the interviewer to your resume next.

"As you can see from my resume . . . ."

You can then explain your education and describe your best work from position to position:

"I got my B.S. in Business from Bryant and then went directly to _____ (FACT) where I _____. One year after I was promoted, my former boss recruited me to _____ (INSIGHT), where I _____, etc."

Once again, use action words to describe what you did and strong descriptors to describe how you did it.

You can finish by emphasizing a winning accomplishment from your last position:

"I'm most proud of the XY project I set up at Signal. Here I _____."

You can summarize and close with your interest to continue the relationship:

"So that's me at work. Later, I'd enjoy telling you about how my job pursuits are also reflected in my personal interests."

An alternate format appears is:

Tell Me About Yourself

I thought you'd want to know about this, so let me highlight my resume and tell you about my work experience first. I have _____ years' professional experience as a _____ in the _____ industry, specializing in _____ and _____.

One accomplishment that makes me proud was completed just recently at _____. My _____ resulted in (increased or decreased percent; number of hours, days, times, rank, products, accounts, items, customers, sales, reliability, durability, accuracy, repeat business, etc.).

In addition, I'm a New England native and have a (AA, BS MA Ph.D., certificate, license, degree) in _____ from the College of _____ in _____.

There's more of my work interest also expressed in my personal life; if you'd like, I can share more about this at a later time.

COMMON AND POTENTIALLY DAMAGING QUESTIONS

Even the most positive (and skillful) interviewer is searching for red flags, any misstatements, contradictions, or extreme views that would disqualify you right away. She knows more about the position, the cast of characters, and the organization than you do, so the questions, if crafted properly, are used to see how you match the requirements and environment. You must be honest and forthcoming. You cannot lie or misrepresent yourself. No, even a white lie, the kind many use to rename position titles, dates of employment, or grade point averages, is a false pretense with troublesome consequences. The risks of dismissal are too great. You can trigger a negative reaction. You can inadvertently wreck your chances. You can lose the offer or fail miserably at the position if you are lucky enough to land it. Even high-profile, professional sports coaches, banking executives, and well-backed politicians may not be long into their careers when lies on their resumes are discovered and they are fired in humiliating fashion, which also makes it that much harder to gain the trust of another hiring manager.

A comprehensive interview can include 40 to 50 questions. There is no list that can anticipate every possible query or reply, but check out the lineup of questions and answers in Figure 7.4 as a guide to some of the more common interrogations.

> **VIPP (Very Important Promotion Point)**
>
> Remember, a job interview is not confession. You are not on a one-on-one with your religious leader. Reveal and report what puts you in a positive light: only appropriate information and data that is requested, not unsolicited or volunteered information that could ultimately lose you an offer. The interview is not a time for disclosing your dirty laundry.

Figure 7.4: **Questions and Answers**

1. *Why did you leave your last position?*
   Feel free to rely on the public statement you crafted in Chapter 1. Be positive. Be brief. Remember there's no need to provide too many details or to dwell on sensitive or emotional issues. The country music hit song lyric says it well, "That's my story and I'm stickin' to it!"

   "Our entire group was eliminated when the organization restructured. It was purely a business decision where many of the company's top employees were impacted."

2. *Why should we hire you?*
   Be clear that not only can you do the job but you also want to do it. There's no need to be coy or humble.

   "I'm pleased you included that question. I'm encouraged by the near-ideal fit for what you need done and what I'm successful doing. This match motivates me to apply my proven skills to achieving the tasks you have in mind for the role here."

3. *What are your strengths?*
   In your self-assessment exercises, you have spent lots of effort preparing for this question. Try to select a work-related positive that is of particular value to the position, team, or organization.

   "My people skills are always singled out at review time. I try to treat people respectfully, no matter where they fit into the organization and resolve issues directly before they fester. That style probably saves a lot of churning of decisions and downtime when problems come up. At Hightop's sales convention a year ago, I even won the most cooperative engineer award."

4. *What are your weaknesses?*
   Try to admit a weakness that's not directly related to a core competency. But be mindful that many interviewers are now tuned in to the weakness-that-some-consider-a-strength approach: "I work too hard." "I'm too much of a perfectionist."

   You're probably safe noting a weakness related to your work style (or one not connected to the job role you're seeking, that is, a software engineer or a bench chemist might disclose that she is not a terrific public speaker and needs work there, a shortcoming you were told about early in your career and have now mastered, or a generic glitch that everyone can work harder to overcome, such as with more computer or technical training or enhanced presentation skills).

Figure 7.4: **Questions and Answers,** continued

"No one is perfect, of course. Everyone can get better at something—I certainly know that. Early in my career as a manager, I was told I needed improvement in delegating assignments. I kept on loading not-so-challenging work on only those who asked or volunteered for it. I took an in-house training course called the 'Art of Delegation' and focused on asking better questions and matching skills to interests more. It must have worked. Now I usually get super ratings when employees are surveyed on how well their manager delegates."

5. *What negatives would your last boss have to say about you?*
This can be a tricky question (one with a trap for you to fall into), especially if you were asked for additional weaknesses or areas for improvement earlier in the interview. Again, use the same guidelines presented above, but remember that only two or three weaknesses should surface for the entire interview. An artful interviewer will ask for improvement areas in many different ways, hoping you will pile up a list.

"My boss would have mostly nice things to say about me; but if pressed, she might say I short-shrifted myself in professional development. I applied for at least two seminars each year, but cancelled all of them at the last minute when my work got extra busy. She urges personal growth and wanted me to find a way to attend the seminars. I'm sure I disappointed her."

6. *What are your salary expectations?*
Tossing out a salary number without knowing the industry wage range or what the organization pays for that role can put you in either the overqualified or bargain-basement candidate category. If you've ever purchased a new car, you know the salesperson often asks, "What do you want to pay?" which is like asking, "How much do you have in your bank account?" In short, if you know the fair market value for the role, you can negotiate prudently and in good faith. See if you can determine the compensation range of the position beforehand. Many web sites in your industry can give you this value range, such as www.sixfigurejobs.com, www.wageweb.com, www jobstar.org, www.salarysource.com, and www.salary.com, and then give your acceptable range, if pressed further for a reply. If you ask, some interviewers will tell you the range then, and you can verbalize if it's acceptable. Finally, you need to be honest and straight-talking if the interviewer asks you directly for an earnings history or for the exact dollar amount of your base pay, bonus, or total compensation where you worked most recently.

Remember also to avoid statements in the interview that can come back to haunt you when you start salary negotiations.

Figure 7.4: **Questions and Answers,** continued

"Money isn't important to me right now." "I really don't need very much to live on." You're independently wealthy and would perform this job for free as a public service?

A better approach would be:

"My expectations right now are open, and I certainly take into consideration the entire compensation package, not just base pay. I did do some research on salary ranges and what Springfield companies are now paying for this work. You have a strong reputation, and I'm sure you, too, are paying fairly for the position. How have you set the range?"

7. *What do you know about this company?*

Now is your chance to draw on the research you did to prepare and wow the interviewer with the data you were able to uncover and inside information you learned. If this question does not come up, try to weave some of this knowledge into your other answers. Let the interviewer know you did you homework—and that the dog didn't eat it this time.

"Thanks for raising that now, because it reminds me of a question I have for you later. I did spend quite a bit of time reading on your web site and was especially interested by . . . ."

8. *Have you made any mistakes in your career? If so, what were they and how did you fix them?*

This is an opportunity to test your honesty and your goals.

"Mistake" may be too strong a word for any adjustments in my work because I have tried to live my life fairly regret-free. Nevertheless, as I look back, I think I stayed at Agoria about 18 months longer than necessary. I was bored and ready to do more meaningful work. But my boss wasn't due to move up or ready to move on anywhere, either. So, I learned a lesson about being proactive for my own career progress and am now much more suited to positive change."

9. *What did you like most about your previous job?*

List as many factors as you can that match the job you're seeking.

"Hopscotch involved a fast-paced environment when I worked there. I especially enjoyed the company dynamic and my co-workers, too. I also had a chance to experiment with some new technology and to work on the cutting edge of industry progress. Basically, I'd say it was a fun place with smart people and challenging work."

Figure 7.4: **Questions and Answers,** continued

---

10. *What do you want to be doing at work in the next five years?*
Try to present a flexible and open view of the future. This question comes up a lot for those either at the start or near-end of their careers and is usually asked to test your commitment, work energy level, or goal-setting ability.

"Wow, that question hasn't come up in a while. Five years seems like a long time in my work world, but I do hope to still be in HR and to continue to learn my craft. I wouldn't mind having a role with a bigger scope or more people to manage, either. The big progress in five years would be how much more I could know, and how much greater impact I could have in my job contributions."

THE IMPROPER QUESTION

VIPP (Very Important Price Point)

Listen carefully to the wording of the salary question. There is a difference between "What are your salary expectations?" and "What was your base pay at Hopscotch?" The first gives you a chance to position or to ferret out the existing range before providing an acceptable number. The second deserves a direct response. In each case, you do have the option, however, of adding any money made via an incentive bonus, sign-on fee, freelance pay, or consulting compensation for your complete salary. Note that most company HR reps now, if asked for your salary figure, are required to withhold the information, confirming only your dates of employment and job titles.

Many organizations spend time and money training managers on the legal implications of the job interview and tell them what questions should never come up—questions that are illegal, and if asked, can cause both short- and long-term damage. Any queries *dealing with age* (i.e., When were you born?), *martial status* (i.e., Do you have children?), *ethnic origin* (i.e., Where are your parents from?), *religious preferences* (i.e., What church are you affiliated with?), *females* (i.e., Can you make plans for child care?), *sexual preference* (i.e., Do you have a wife?), and *disabilities* (i.e., What health problems do you have that we should know about?) are suspect and subject to challenge. You are protected from ever being asked a question from one of the seven categories.

Should any of these questions surface, you need to decide how to handle them. If you choose not to answer, let the person know in a nice, nontesty, nongotcha kind of way (i.e., "I'm surprised that came up. How relevant is this to the position?").

Your goal is not to alienate the interviewer or to show him up, especially if you really want the job. Remember not be lulled into a false sense of complacency either. You may be correct, but you can also be taken out of the running.

If you have established some kind of positive rapport and are really OK with

answering—not offended or wounded or see the question as just a way to get to know you or to connect—then do so.

This is, indeed, a signal or red flag but not necessarily an indication the person is a bigot, racist, or sexist. The interviewer could just be uninformed or not properly trained. Once you're on the job, you might meet with the person who posed the question and let him know the legal implications. This heads-up discussion will be invaluable, but is not a first-day (or before-hire) encounter.

HANDLING OBJECTIONS

Most professional salespeople claim that this is the toughest part of their job, and a large segment of a sales training seminar is spent rehearsing selling techniques, including 1) clarify the objection, doubt or skepticism; 2) provide proof; 3) overcome with benefits; and 4) probe for acceptance.

In the context of a job interview, this may be difficult to do. The key here is to respond without being defensive. Take whatever objection or concern surfaces in the most open-minded way. Stay relaxed, try not to sit up straight abruptly or cross your hands in a flight-or-fight stance, and acknowledge the statement: "I can see how you'd think that." "I would probably feel the same way if I were you." Then, address the objection directly for clarification, and sell your benefits and get acceptance.

Some interviewers throw in an objection just to see how you handle it. This is especially true for sales, marketing, or customer service job openings, but most likely the interviewer's legitimate concern stems from the thought that you might not be able to succeed at the job.

The question of a job candidate's overqualification surfaces a lot, especially in a tight job market. The interviewer may see you as overpriced (the compensation would never meet your expectations), overeager/desperate (the minute a better offer comes in, you'll leave), overskilled (the job isn't challenging enough to retain your interest), overexperienced (you have more working knowledge than the staff or the interviewer and may be difficult to manage), or just over the top (your fit seems too good to be true). Remember never to mention money, and try to focus on what you can still learn and how you can make your boss or your team look good with your contributions.

"I was pretty sure you would get to that issue eventually. Indeed, when I was hiring top talent, I was always on the alert for the consequences of bringing someone on board who had exceptional experience. In my case, I am still motivated by what I can learn (at GoGo I picked up on three new programs) and really believe all these working years make me a proven plug-and-play job performer—I can make a difference from the get-go. At Spring, I improved sales revenue 15 percent over my first three months on the job. Besides, I tend to create my own challenges and excitement. GoGo's shipping costs were reduced by 20 percent when I found a more efficient packing system."

In response to the interviewer identifying you as underqualified, you need to ask "In what way?" which is a clarifying attempt, and then try to respond directly to the objection that has surfaced. Some objections raised, for example, "I don't think you have the right educational background" — are vague and offered as an excuse not to hire you. Again, do your best to clarify. "What about my educational background concerns you?" "Tell me, please, where my education falls short in meeting your needs?" Proceed to provide proof, sell benefits, and probe for acceptance.

"That may not be an issue, though I can certainly see your concern and reason for surfacing it. At HeeHah, a business known only to hire top-tier school MBAs in its Finance group, I was put in charge of revamping all of the accounting systems and procedures. My recommendations brought in about $100,000 in savings and were implemented on time and within budget. I got lots of accolades from the work group, and that meant much, too. I trust that resolves your initial concern about my credibility and my ability to work within your management hierarchy."

APPROPRIATE QUESTIONS TO ASK: BEGINNING YOUR OWN DUE-DILIGENCE

What you ask is almost as important as what you answer in gaining the most desirable job. Here is another opportunity to balance your sociability and competency. If you're naïve about this side of the conversation, certain questions you ask will put you in a poor "me first" light, for example, pushing too hard too early for details about promotions, benefits, vacation, job security, etc.

Choose from the questions in Figure 7.5—perhaps one or two from each category—to create your own list of major questions to include in your interview. The order here helps show you as both strategic and tactical in your approach to the position.

Figure 7.5: **Questions to Ask at a Job Interview**

Business/Company/Industry/Trends

- How is your company reacting to "X" trend? (Be sure to do research on the company and industry prior to the interview.)
- How is the company (budgets, etc.) affected by the state of the economy?
- What has the company done to strengthen itself in the prevailing economy?
- How is outsourcing overseas expected to impact the company?
- My research tells me that Company X is one of your major competitors. Do you agree, and whom else do you see as your major competitors?
- What differentiates you from the competition?
- What is a major company problem that you have yet to answer?

Figure 7.5: **Questions to Ask at a Job Interview,** continued

- Tell me your major challenges. What causes you greatest concern?
- What is the source of your company's name?
- What are the driving factors that protect your market share?
- What product or service do you think has the best potential to grow the business?
- Give me a view of a structure of your company.
- What are the business challenges for the next year?
- Where do you see your company's progress over the next five years?
- Tell me where XXX stands against YYY.
- What is the biggest challenge XXX faces today?
- Where is the industry going and how will your company fare?

Boss

- What work do you see yourself doing in five years?
- How do you reward employees that do well?
- How do you like to communicate with your employees?
- How is your success measured here?
- What kind of person do you work with best?
- Tell me about the confidence level in your department.
- How do you handle goal setting/objectives and track them?
- What would you do if your team was behind in a project? How would you motivate them?
- Tell me about your management style.
- What are the two areas here where you need the most help?
- Tell me about your relationship with your boss.
- How do new employees get management feedback?
- Tell me what a busy day looks like for you.
- Why do people like working for you?
- Who else is involved in making this hiring decision?
- What part of this company do you like or dislike?
- What would your staff tell me about you?
- What are your goals for this department?

Figure 7.5: **Questions to Ask at a Job Interview,** continued

- How do you grow employee competencies and educate staff? (Listen for mentoring options here.)
- Tell me about employees in your department who have done well and how they have progressed.
- Tell me about position advancement in your department.

Staff/Department
- Why is this job available? Is it newly created or did the person in this role leave?
- What are the skills and experience level of the staff?
- Tell me about the team dynamics.
- How long have the most senior and junior persons been with the company?
- How is your department viewed in this organization?
- How big is your group as a percentage of the company workforce?
- What are some of the team development activities in the department?
- What are some of the results of the work done?
- Who internally (if anyone) has applied for this position?
- What are the immediate deliverables for this group?
- What is the reporting structure?
- What is the predominant means of communication?
- How do you measure success for individuals, staff, and the organization?
- How much does the political organizational chart agree with the administrative organizational chart?
- What is communication like within the group?
- How well does your group's skill set contribute to the company's objectives?

Environment/Culture
- How do you see this position relating to various internal teams?
- What do people like about working here?
- What do people dislike about working here?
- How do you celebrate successes at your company?

Figure 7.5: **Questions to Ask at a Job Interview,** continued

- Your company's vision statement says "you're flexible" or "you're customer-focused." How are these qualities fulfilled by your group?
- How do people here handle difficult circumstances?
- Give me an example of your group structure. What systems are in place?
- What's the typical turnover per year in the organization?
- What do people do for fun here?
- How often does the team get together after work?
- How important is a college degree here?
- What's the team spirit like here on a Friday afternoon?
- How does teamwork show itself?
- What is the office dress code?
- How would you describe a week's workload and how would your staff describe it?
- What work ethics (values) exist here?
- How open is management about sharing employee ideas/information?
- How much input do employees have on influencing the company culture?

Self

- Are there any obstacles I would need to overcome to succeed in this job?
- What opportunities for growth exist in this position?
- Given my background, are there any concerns you have about my ability to succeed in this position?
- What additional tasks are part of the position that do not appear in the job description?
- How does my background in X or Y fit your needs?
- How do I compare to the ideal candidate and which of my skills match this best?
- What do you need to know about me that will assure you I can do this job?
- Tell me what your nonnegotiable, your must haves, are for this position.
- What credentials inspired you to grant me this interview? Given what you've learned so far, what do you see as my greatest strength and why?
- What in my qualifications concerns you?
- How do I compare with the previous person who held the job?

Figure 7.5: **Questions to Ask at a Job Interview,** continued

---

- I've always been interested in _____. How can the company help me to stay current?
- What are the critical success factors for this position?
- What are the training opportunities for new employees?
- What is your experience with assigning mentors, and who would that be?
- If I'm hired, what would you expect me to achieve in the next three to six months? In the first year?

Future Plans/Next Steps
- When would you want the hire to be on the job and productive?
- When do you expect to make a hiring decision?
- When can I expect to hear feedback from you?
- If I don't hear from you by X, can I call you by Y?
- Who else is involved in this hiring decision? How can I convince them I am right for the job?
- Is there anything else you need from me at this point?
- Where are you in this hiring process? How many other candidates are you considering?
- How many people have you interviewed?
- How many candidates will be called back for a second interview?
- What is your process of candidate selection?
- What is the percentage of my chance to be hired?
- What is the next step in filling this position? How do you want me to interact during the interview process?
- How long has this position remained open?
- What aspects about the organization should I consider prior to the next interview?

If some answers you receive raise red flags of concern for you, try to remain open-minded at this point and concentrate on continuing to sell your strong points. Try not to rule out the position, even if something surfaces that can be a

VIPP (Very Important Promotion Point)

Very often there isn't enough interview time to get the questions you need and want answered. It is certainly acceptable and within range to ask the interviewer what to do or how to resolve some of the unanswered questions that are important to you. Take your cues from him but remember to select questions to ask that fit your audience; some queries might trigger politically sensitive hot buttons or telegraph a personal sophistication level that could be threatening.

deal breaker. Play it out until an offer comes. Then you'll be in the decision-maker's role.

ROUND TWO: ASSURING A SECOND INTERVIEW

No sales or marketing process is complete without "going for the close" or "asking for the order." Remember finding the right moment to ask for a big date? Or prompting your professor for your term paper grade? Closing a job interview involves just the same tact and timing. For you, it means ending the interview with information you need to move forward and following up in a way that ensures that either an offer or a call back for more interview time will come soon.

Before you leave, be sure to tell the interviewer you are still very much interested in the position, and now that you've met and spoken, you are even more confident that the fit of your skill and their job is an ideal one. You should resolve any objections that surfaced and end by emphasizing your strengths and ability to perform the job successfully. Ask about the next steps if they are not clearly outlined, and be sure you have permission to call within the next week or so if you've had no contact from the interviewer.

After the interview be sure to write a thank-you letter similar to that in Figure 7.6 and those in the Appendix. E-mail seems to be the medium of choice nowadays, especially if the company is more high tech than high touch in the business—but consider that a typed or handwritten note on classy stationery, of course, not cutesy notepaper from your kids' pad, might distinguish you. If you live near the office, you might drop by and leave your letter with the receptionist the next day, adding another personal touch to your profile. But be careful. Anytime you are in the office, you are subject to others' opinions. So if you make a visit, wear business casual clothes, not your old sweatshirt, and be prepared to chat with potential co-workers.

Letter topics should include citing your appreciation for the interviewer's time, recounting key points of conversation, offering ideas still to be discussed,

Figure 7.6: **Sample Interview Thank-You Letter**

William Warrior
Senior Vice President, Human Resources
AZA
1300 Fraternity Row
High Desert, Utah 03476

Dear Mr. Warrior:

I trust yesterday's meeting was as valuable for you as it was for me. Thanks so much for your time and for the thorough explanation of your HR training position and life at AZA.

I was especially pleased that you appreciated the new benefits orientation I developed and delivered at BBG, and hope I can create something similar for your staff. AZA's mission and growth plans are exciting and motivating.

Thanks again, and please call with any questions or concerns. I look forward to hearing from you soon.

Regards,

John Youth

---

or clarifying any fuzzy facts. But keep the letter short and direct. This is a thank-you note, not a format to resell your abilities.

Try to send a similar note, personalized in any way you can, to every person you spoke with in your interview. If you only have the key person's e-mail address, you can encourage her to forward the thank-you note to the others.

Follow-up with a telephone call to show you are taking initiative and interest and to further distinguish yourself among the many applicants. Be sure to remind the interviewer of your name, ask for a search status report, and reiterate your intention in moving forward and staying in touch. There is a fine line between being an eager beaver and a pest. Keep your calls brief, and check if it's OK to call back again. Limit your calls to just one or two in a week; more than that will make you look desperate for feedback, ignorant, or insensitive to the interviewer's other work obligations or travel time. Think about how you feel when your mom calls more than three times a week to remind you about making a decision.

Finally, review your interview and evaluate the results. Interviewing is like taking an exam: Sometimes you may have a gut feeling that you aced it or flunked it, but be objective, perhaps by sharing the story with a trusted friend for another perspective, and work on improvements for the next interview, if there are any. A note of caution: The interviewer's reaction might be hard to assess, unless you read minds or have lots of interviewing experience. Many are simply eager to please, fearful of legal retribution, or so reticent about discouragement that you may hold a false sense of success and never know what they truly thought of you. So it's extra important for you to compare various interviews and gauge your tactics and consistency:

- How much did I learn about:
  - The job responsibilities?
  - The reporting relationships/subordinate issues?
  - The success factors for the first 30, 60, 90 days?
  - The make or break skills that would ensure productivity?
- How effective was I at:
  - Expressing interest and enthusiasm about the work, the company, the team?
  - Providing specific examples?
  - Keeping my questions direct and clear?
  - Shaking hands warmly?
  - Speaking in a natural, upbeat, and well-modulated voice, that is, articulating professionally?
  - Appearing confident and decisive?
  - Emphasizing results that can contribute to the organization's needs?
  - Posing good questions?
  - Establishing a next-steps time frame or action items?

- How do I really feel about:
  - The interviewer and future colleagues?
  - The work environment and culture?
  - The ethical stance and business values?

WHEN YOU DON'T GET THE OFFER

Sometimes the offer does not come, despite positive signals from the interview process. If you are working with a recruiter, now is the time to get as much feedback as you can on what really happened. Sometimes the job was put on hold; other times an internal candidate was selected. There are also the possibilities that your references didn't click or the final interviews were not as powerful as you thought. See if you can get some corrective input from the recruiter that could help you in the future.

If you did not use a recruiter, try to make contact with the hiring manager yourself to learn why you were not selected. Many employers are reluctant to pass on any substantive information, sometimes fearing a discrimination lawsuit, yet any feedback you can get will help you in the future. Comments like, "You came off a bit cocky" or "You were a bit too aggressive with the VP," deal with behaviors that are readily modified for the next interview. Emphasize that you value the insight and can use suggestions that will help you secure a similar position elsewhere.

Some professionals recommend that you follow up the rejection with a quick letter to the HR contact or the hiring manager, letting him know you were disappointed but hope to be considered for other work at the organization in the future. Leave the door open to fresh contact because sometimes if you call back in a few months, the selected candidate has left and you can revive the company's interest in your skills.

CEO (Consultant Examples and Opinions)

- Come a few minutes early for an interview. Remember not to cut it too close or be a little late. Even if you arrive at the building on time, if the receptionist is slow and it takes awhile to locate your contact, you could be judged late. Give yourself enough time to dry off or freshen up if coming into the office from a downpour or snowstorm.

- At meeting and departure contact, be sure to shake hands with each person in your panel or group interview and get a business card from each person, if you can.

- Bring along some energy bar snacks for boosts during an all-day interview when there might not be breaks to eat.

- At minimum, know the company's stock price, key competitors, and latest public policies or issues. You might also learn the credentials of those interviewing you. You might discover a network peer.

- Bring a PDA with you to the interview. It can suggest you're computer-savvy and comfortable with technology, and perhaps dispel an older image.

- Try to schedule your interviews in the morning, when most people are fresh and alert. Avoid Mondays and Fridays, if at all possible, and book your spot at the end of the candidate cue, last if you can. Those interviewed last (56 percent) vs. first (14 percent) obtained the most job offers, perhaps an indication that busy interviewers tend to remember those most immediate in their thoughts.

- Soften negative or inflammatory words by recrafting them in a positive tone. Remember not to repeat a negative term to the interviewer. Turn "weakness" into "area of improvement" or "something to master"; "failure" to "things could have turned out differently"; "regret" to "I wish it had turned out better"; or "conflict" to "issues" or "challenges."

✳ *Summary* ✳

✳ Doing your homework for a job interview is exponentially more important than doing your homework ever was for school. Product, place, price, and promotion aptly apply here as well.

✳ Creating a positive first impression is paramount, especially when some theorists think the like/dislike decision is made after just a few seconds.

✳ Answering the questions appropriately requires the ability to understand, to listen, to look, and to balance what's going on at the moment. Practice, practice, practice.

✳ Asking thoughtful questions can not only position you positively but can also help you make an informed decision later on. Practice, practice, practice.

✳ Following up appropriately is a key step no matter what the result.

PRODUCT IMPLEMENTATION

Landing Your New Job

Take a bow. The job is yours! The job offer is an especially satisfying reward that comes from all of your hard work and careful strategy. It validates that the company sees value in your strengths and wants you to be a part of its organization. You should enjoy the thrill of making the sale.

Nevertheless, your ultimate goal is the right job, not just any job, and you must evaluate your offer in the context of your short- and long-term career aspirations. It is your choice. Certainly, the number of offers—perhaps this is the only one so far—and the time you have been looking are practical and key issues to consider.

GET IT IN WRITING: THE BONA FIDE JOB OFFER

Your job offer is typically made over the phone first. You should not be too surprised. Most companies like to check in before creating and delivering the more formal offer letter and want to be sure you're still interested in the position. Avoid evaluating the job and your responsibilities or money and benefits negotiation until you have your offer letter in hand. Many deals have been lost at this "I'm-preparing-an-offer-and-want-to-know-what-you-think" stage. You don't want to create doubts where there were none or suggest lofty job expectations or personal needs that show you as a poor team player. Besides, you need to be sure you are getting everything you want. A letter can give you that specific assurance. And, don't feel guilty if the letter needs to be revised. It is in your mutual best interests to clarify and confirm all the particulars of your hire. Think of any negotiation as your way of again demonstrating your attention to details, which is valuable to the company in many ways once you finally come on board.

There are a number of tasks for you when your letter does arrive. First, give yourself some time so you have the opportunity to fully ponder the offer. It's OK to ask for the time. The extra few days will help you make the right decision and should not cause HR havoc at the organization. State your interest in and appreciation of the proposal and explain that this consideration time reflects your business sincerity. Suitable replies to the offer, if pressed, include: "I need to talk it over with my family." "I am waiting for an offer from another company, and want to decide what's the best one for me." You can play this delaying tactic as a bluff, counting on the company to get nervous and sweeten its offer, but you also risk losing the genuine offer you have. So, this is perhaps a ploy best left to poker players and frequent car buyers.

You should also get some closure. Be sure to call the other organizations interested in your candidacy and let them know you have an offer in hand and are eager to hear from them. Craft your words carefully, and ask for the status of the process. See if you can create a sense of urgency in moving forward, without threatening, bragging, or offending. You might say, "We agreed I'd let you know if another offer came through, and, well, one has, this morning. I was hoping you'd let me know how close you are to making a decision. I'm still very interested." It is probably best not to go into the particulars or name names and figures. Build a little mystery and competitive spirit at the same time, if you are pressed to do so. Try this: "I don't think it's appropriate at this stage to give details, but the firm is also a non-profit and has a competitive compensation range."

Finally, you need to get an objective perspective. Before deciding to take the job, carefully recall the preferred job criteria and career direction you established at the start of your search. And be sure to involve and assess both your reason and feelings in the decision. One way to proceed is to complete a list focussing on the pros and cons of the position.

> ## VIPP (Very Important Product Point)
>
> Look to see how you made other key decisions in your life. What was your process? Keep this same pattern, if you can, and try to apply both logic and instinct to a series of exercises and activities. Get your left and right brain working together, but remember to *save this energy until after you have your offer letter in hand*. Hold yourself back from what ifs. Too often people expend effort on situations that never materialize.

Pros and Cons of the Position

Pros

_____

_____

_____

Cons

_____

_____

_____

A more comprehensive approach is to re-evaluate the job criteria you established in Chapter 1 and look at your career interests, work values, and personality to again envision the ideal job. See Figure 8.1 for help doing this. There may be additional specifics to consider, and many of the same, if you are looking at a position at a start-up organization.

Figure 8.1: **Offer Evaluation**

Weigh the importance of the various characteristics in your next job, and compare them to the offers at hand. Compensation analysis comes later.

Criteria Characteristics	Weighted Importance 1 to 10 Ranking	Offer Details	Points to Negotiate/Consider
I. Criteria Analysis			
Position Title			
Daily Tasks—Variety of projects			
—Tapping talent potential			
—Scope of responsibility			
—Autonomy			
Performance review cycle			
Compensation discussion			
Professional development/training			
Boss relationship—compatibility			
Collegial or employee relationships			
Work environment			
Advancement potential			
Flexibility			
Exposure/decision-making authority			
Travel commitment			
Commute to work			
Lifestyle shift			
Work values			
Company image and reputation			
Company product and service reputation			

Figure 8.1: **Offer Evaluation,** continued

Criteria Characteristics	Weighted Importance 1 to 10 Ranking	Offer Details	Points to Negotiate/Consider
Company financial future / stability			
Compensation analysis			
II. COMPENSATION			
Base salary			
Bonus (frequency/percentage of payout in last 3 years?)			
Personal performance			
Department and/or company performance			
Commission criteria			
Profit sharing			
Sign-on bonus			
Lump-sum distribution			
Earned equity			
Immediate stock options			
Earned equity			
Benefits			
Insurance percent of employee participation?			
Health (Dental? Eye? Drug? Annual medical exams?)			
Cafeteria/flex plan			
Long-term disability			
Term life			
Matching funds			

Figure 8.1: **Offer Evaluation,** continued

Criteria Characteristics	Weighted Importance 1 to 10 Ranking	Offer Details	Points to Negotiate/Consider
Keogh plan			
Child care			
Sabbatical program			
Vacation			
Relocation			
Moving expenses assistance			
Temporary housing expenses assistance			
Mortgage assistance			
Spousal outplacement assistance			
Retirement			
Continuation of health benefits			
Pension			
401K			
Annuity			
Stock options			
Savings plan			
Position Pluses: Rug Ranking			
Office location, size, décor			
Telecommuting, work-at-home options			
Car allowance, mileage reimbursement			
Monthly parking space and/or reimbursement			
Upgrade travel			
Association/club memberships			

Figure 8.1: **Offer Evaluation,** continued

Criteria Characteristics	Weighted Importance 1 to 10 Ranking	Offer Details	Points to Negotiate/Consider
Laptop/cell phone reimbursement			
Severance package (Executive Protection Plan)			
Company product discounts			
CPA and/or legal assistance			
Other			
III. START-UP ANALYSIS			
Risk			
Product differentiators			
Resume reputation (avoid adding another failed business?)			
Market size			
Experience of the team/track record of success			
Personal fit			
Finances			
Funding			
Stage			
Run rate (spending philosophy)			
Travel requirements			
Title/scope of responsibilities			
Location			
Compensation			
Stock participation (change of control protection?)			
Base salary vs. bonus ratio			

There are also some other questions you might want to consider in making your final decision:

- How excited am I about the opportunity?
- How does the position lead to my long-term career goals and match my skills, interests, and values?
- How will my work priorities be established? Is there more than one person I will report to?
- What are the skill sets of my employees? Education and range of experience?
- How does the position fit into the overall organization?
- What is the success or failure rate of others who have held the same position?
- What obstacles might prevent me from being successful?
- How does the company deal with its employees' performance problems?
- Is there a printed and posted mission statement? How is it being fulfilled?
- How would accepting or rejecting the job impact my financial situation?
- Does the total compensation meet or exceed my minimum requirement?
- What are the current opportunities in my job market and the job economy in general?

If you have multiple offers or the position presents a radical career shift or lifestyle change, the strain of making the right decision may continue. You can ease that stress with talk and imagination.

Talk over the issues with a confidant, partner, or professional. Sometimes hearing your descriptions of the various opportunities can be telling, and she can pick up your enthusiasm or fears easier than you can and help you see that. You can also imagine the role. Once you're comfortable with a decision, daydream the outcome. See if you can imagine yourself in each situation and play it out in your mind. Very often the right decision will be confirmed for you.

If you decide a job offer is not the best career move and/or the position is not right for you at this time, let your contacts at the organization know as soon as you can. Call and explain your reasons and regret, especially to anyone with whom you connected well. Cite differing personal career needs and long-term goals rather than problems with the organization or its personnel. If you are still interested in the organization, though not the particular job, emphasize your faith in the company and its goals or how you were impressed with the team. Reaffirm that you wish to be considered for other openings that are a better fit. Often an especially effective recruiter, HR talent scout, or hiring manager will remember you and call you again for another opportunity. Besides, you may meet some of the company's people again at an industry function and your last impression with them can leave as much impact as your first.

BIG GOALS AND BENEFITS: NEGOTIATING THE NEW DEAL

You are in the driver's seat once you have the offer letter in hand. You have effectively sold yourself and are now in the power position. You are in control. You can head wherever you want to go. No matter how sweet the offer might be, you can negotiate. You should negotiate. You need not accept the conditions of employment until your short- and long-term career needs are met. Today, most employers expect some negotiation over the job terms. This is not the same as haggling over the price/value of a product, such as a car, but setting proper terms early to establish your stance and leverage in future salary discussions with your management.

Negotiation should not be confrontational, rushed, or completed to only one side's satisfaction. In certain jobs, sales and purchasing, for example, negotiation skills are key to success, and you may still be evaluated on your approach. See the experience as the ultimate win-win engagement for you and the organization by establishing your individual worth and productive value to the organization. Below are some more specific negotiables and/or reference points for your analysis sheets:

- Annual bonus plans and sign-up
- Annual physical
- Base pay
- Day care facilities or reimbursement
- Deferred compensation
- Dependent tuition
- Disability

> ## VIPP (Very Important Price Point)
>
> Remember everything is negotiable. Most employers expect a counter and factor that in for a discussion. Pick something to negotiate—perhaps an item that has a certain amount of flexibility or no direct out-of-pocket expense. Asking is always OK. No need to be sensitive about it. How you ask and how you deal with the answer is worthy of some practice.

- Enhanced insurance packages
- Executive "protection package" (severance/outplacement monies)
- Incentives and stock options
- Insurances—term life, medical, dental
- Keogh
- Memberships/dues
- Pension, 401K
- Performance/salary reviews (time frame)
- Personal professional development
- Professional conference costs
- Relocation costs—present and future
- Sales commissions
- Scope of responsibility
- Spouse outplacement
- Staff professional development
- Start date
- Stock options
- Travel upgrade
- Tuition reimbursement
- Use of company facilities
- Vacation, sick days, sabbaticals

The base salary is probably your first point of negotiation. It's important to do some homework before you begin this part of your discussion. If you are changing jobs, you may know a current salary range for your role in the industry and have a fair, set market value in mind. If you are new to the workforce or if you are starting a new career, you might want to talk to a professional in the field to check for typical salary ranges for your position and to gather some baseline figures. You can also look to salary guides or the internet, such as www.salary.com, to pinpoint appropriate ranges.

Here are some tips that might help in your negotiations:

- Talk to industry professionals about their views on your salary range and compensation guidelines.
- Scan ranges listed in classified advertisements for similar openings.
- Call recruiters or industry associates and inquire about typical base salary ranges.

- Visit the library for additional reference materials listing job titles and pay scales, with recent wage and salary surveys, for example.
- Search the internet for sites that provide the data (see Chapter 6).
- Remember, several factors influence the salary range—the job's location, company size, other benefits provided—so you should not restrict your figure to simple dollar-for-dollar comparisons.
- Note some key economic realities:
  - The cost of labor cannot be precisely determined.
  - The level of compensation rises with the level of contribution and responsibility.
  - The employee exists to make a profit for the organization.
- Be sure you understand the company's perspective and the information it has at hand, including:
  - How much you were earning at your previous position.
  - How long the search has been going and how difficult it has been to find the ideal candidate.
  - How long you have been on the market.
  - How many other candidates are suitable and available.
  - How much financial flexibility the company has. Larger organizations, with strictly defined and well-researched ranges and honored corporate compensation philosophies are often bound by precedence and have internal equity issues as well. They instruct their managers to bring new hires into the lower part of a three-part range. Smaller, less-structured firms might have more room to work with candidates on a case-by-case basis.

The negotiation is a balancing act. Again, your goal is to create a win-win situation where you and the organization both benefit and each is satisfied. If you choose to accept the job, begin the new association on a positive note. Be sure to begin enthusiastically. Try saying: "I'm really very interested in pursuing this opportunity and am eager to talk about a few issues." "I'm really excited about the offer, though I do want to talk about a few issues or particulars that need some clarification." "I'm looking forward to getting started, and your offer is a solid one, but I do have a few concerns we need to talk about."

When discussing salary, you ought to counter with a question: "How have you ranged this position?" "Where is this figure in the range?" "How much movement is there in this figure?" Keep your tone upbeat and positive. But as a matter of course, ask for 10 to 15 percent more than the minimum salary you will accept. Everything may be adjusted, not just base pay; you can negotiate bonus, relocation, stock options, etc. Once a figure is identified, it is unlikely to increase beyond this discussion stage. Make sure your stock reflects a percentage in the company rather than a set number of shares, and that you can secure a change of control clause, a severance package, or executive protection plan as additional protection.

Ask for a sign-on bonus and all of the perks that come with this title or organizational level. You don't want to learn on your first week of work that every other Senior VP has a Country Club membership, but you don't.

Present your requirements in ranges, and organize your target salary into various increments. For example, $75,000 per year reduces to $6,250 per month or $1,562.50 per week. These figures will help you plot the financial means to meet your expenses, savings, and entertainment funding.

Be prepared to justify your base salary request, perhaps citing your industry research and using words such as "value," "contribution," "value-added," "ability" to succeed, or "experience" to apply skills immediately. Avoid offering reasons like your huge debts or extensive living expenses. Express any disappointment in the salary offer by citing other expectations, saying: "Well, my expectations were in the _____ range." "My professional need is for a higher base."

Remember to apply the assumptive sales technique, and use "we," "our company," and "our goals" to reinforce your commitment and eagerness to work for the organization.

If you are unsuccessful in gaining your preferred compensation, you can ask for an early compensation discussion/review, perhaps in about the first four to six months on the job. Be careful, however, as a mere performance review may not include the incentive of a raise.

Remember to judge how the total compensation impacts your long-term career goals. Even if you are unsuccessful in any of your negotiated items, you have not lost anything by asking.

Below are some frequently asked questions and answers that can help:

Q: What if the first figure presented is more than I wanted? Should I still negotiate for more?

A: Maybe. Accept the figure, but don't underestimate your market value and be sure the amount is in the top of your expected scale. Let your data guide you here.

Q: What can I do if the organization refuses to increase the base salary?

A: Be as creative as you can. See if you can expand the role's responsibilities and influence to gain an upgraded job description. Or obtain a sign-on bonus, commission plan, or an early compensation review.

Q: How much leverage can I use by mentioning that I have another offer?

A: You can mention that other organizations are interested, but be careful. Make it clear that your preference is this package and organization, and you hope a compromise is available. If you are overassertive or demanding, you could disqualify yourself.

Q: What is my option if the compensation offer is firm and significantly less than I was making before?

A: It depends. Consider what the position offers you long term and what you can learn from the experience. Perhaps the role can provide a positive change of work environment for you, including a more supportive boss or growth-oriented team. If you are promised other benefits in lieu of a higher base pay, make sure these are explained in writing in the event the person giving you his verbal assurance later leaves the organization.

Q: How can I say "no" to the salary presented without nixing the offer?

A: Establish your genuine interest in the position and your commitment and confidence to bring value by saying, "I'm still unsettled with the base pay. Can we structure this for our mutual satisfaction? I'm determined to work with you and make the job rewarding for both of us."

Q: If I'm working with a recruiter or search firm, who should do the negotiation?

A: It is the responsibility of the recruiter to convey your requirements for the

> **VIPP** **(Very Important Price Point)**
>
> If at all possible, try to arrange for your partner or spouse to join you on the look-at-the-new-location-area expedition. Some companies will pay for someone to join you. Use your own resources if that does not happen. Moving is a tough transition, and making decisions without your partner is too risky.

position. If everything is in place, then she did a fine job. If the proposal package is less than you expected, it is OK to request a meeting to finalize the negotiations and to let your contact know you are not completely satisfied.

Q: Should I apologize for any difficulty in the negotiation?

A: Not at all. You shouldn't regret trying to get the best or most appropriate salary for your services. In fact, you can emphasize that this is how you do business in driving a hard bargain with clients, customers, and vendors to get the best value for the organization.

Q: If my start date is sooner than I expect, can I extend it?

A: Let your contact know when you planned to begin work. Explain that you have set vacation plans, family commitments, or key projects to complete before leaving your present organization. Mention your standards of excellence and desire to honor all involved in this transition.

Q: How is the agreement finalized?

A: When the offer letter is revised to your satisfaction and signed by you and the organization.

Sometimes relocation is involved in accepting a new job. This may require a special negotiation. You may ask for a lump sum to cover moving costs you have researched and arranged. Share any relevant expense documents and estimates from your moving company, storage facility, and/or temporary housing rental. Some firms prefer to assign a relocation firm to work with you. Try establishing the following details:

- Who will pay for your trips to look for a new home? Will the same expenses be covered for your spouse or partner as well?
- Who will pay for you to commute to the job or pay for temporary housing until you get settled?
- Who will cover any losses in selling your present home?
- Who will cover taxes, interest, even utilities, on your present home until it sells?
- Who will pay for points and closing costs or provide additional help with a down payment or special loan?

- Who will pay for outplacement or career counseling for your spouse or partner?
- Who will arrange for renting or leasing your present home if it doesn't sell quickly?
- Who will pay for the boats and cars to be shipped?

Although employment contracts are used less frequently in today's job market, you may want to retain an attorney to oversee the terms. Make sure the terms are clear on the bonus plan, termination clause, and proprietary information requirements before you sign. These three criteria are typically the most crucial in finalizing a contract.

GOOD NEWS ANNOUNCEMENTS

Once you have successfully negotiated the terms of your new position, signed your offer letter, and confirmed a start date, you can close your job search. Remember to inform contacts at prospect companies, hiring managers you've met, recruiters and other job search professionals, your family, and friends/colleagues, that is, your entire network if possible, that you have landed a new job. Send them your thanks and a new business card as soon as you have a direct telephone line and corporate e-mail. See Figure 8.2 for three examples of the announcement.

Another good news announcement to be involved in is the e-mail or formal announcement that your boss sends to introduce you to your new organization. If at all possible, work with your new boss to craft this letter. You want to be sure your arrival is positioned in the most positive way possible. Provide background information and a photo, but make sure you save final approval before the letter is distributed. This is another marketing tool and can often set the tone for your acceptance, credibility, and future success.

A Ph.D. researcher took her first industry position as a member of the staff of a training and development organization

VIPP (Very Important Promotion Point)

Too many things can happen between when you get your offer and when you sit at your desk on that first day of work. Hold back your thank-you and good news announcements until you are on the job and settled in. It can be embarrassing to have to contact everyone to let them know the position fell through at the last minute.

Figure 8.2: **Sample Good News Announcements**

Example 1

Date: July 15, 2006
From: Lucky Lu
To: Harry Simmons
Subject: Good News

Dear friends and colleagues,

I'm pleased and excited to inform you that I have joined PAS—the world's largest supplier of computer software—as an Organization Development Manager as of June 4.

I will be working on management skill training, a new manager survival/orientation guide, and as a faculty presenter at PAS University. As you know, these are all tasks I enjoy, and I'm looking forward to making a significant contribution.

I want to thank everyone who helped in my career transition, and I hope to stay in touch through our thriving network.

My new work contact information:
    E-mail: Lu@PASinternational.com
    Phone: (610) 661-3096
    Fax: (610) 661-3097

Thanks again,

Lucky Lu

Example 2

From: Sonny Day
Sent: Monday, August 27, 2006
To: List
Subject: New Position at Metrinet

Dear friends,

Here's some good news! I joined Metrinet as Vice President of Information Technology in mid-August to help transition wireless internet service into reality for the next decade. Metrinet provides data communication from Los Feliz, CA. In my new role, I will work to optimize the current system design and initiate new plans for higher speed applications. I'm looking forward to the challenge.

Figure 8.2: **Sample Good News Announcements,** continued

I want to thank you and the many people who have supported me during my job search and to give everyone my new contact information.

I can be reached by phone at (408) 399-8410 and via e-mail at sonnyd@metrinet.com. I look forward to keeping in touch with each of you.

Best wishes,

Sonny Day
Vice President, Information technology
Metrinet, Inc.

Example 3

From: Jill Job-Satisfac
Sent: Monday, September 16, 2006
To: List
Subject: CareerMate's New Marketing Manager

Family and friends.

Thank you. Thank you.

Effective September 3, I joined CareerMate in San Francisco as its new Marketing Manager. CareerMate, for those who might not know, is a start-up organization that provides both individual and group career development services, and I will be responsible for introducing the company's offerings to the marketplace.

I also hope to do some direct service seminar delivery and one-on-one counseling. This is the ideal job for me right now, and I am thrilled at the opportunity.

I would not have obtained this role without your support and encouragement, and I am most appreciative.

Feel free to contact me, and know that I will do whatever I can to stay in touch and help you however you'd like.

My best,

Jill Job-Satisfac
Marketing Manager
CareerMate, Inc.
Phone and Fax (415) 637-3000
E-mail: JJobsatis@CareerMate.net

committed to validating the effectiveness of its programs. Her announcement highlighted her thesis topic, *Study of Inter-Cultural Aspects of the Sri Lankan Fourth Generation and its Impact on the 3–6 Grade School Curricula*—which did nothing to establish her credibility as a business professional who would be interacting with peers to validate key behavior changes from training. For years, this presentation was a laughingstock throughout the organization. Take care that your first steps or reports are relevant to your new organization's business.

YOUR FIRST 90 DAYS*

Starting a new job is like many new experiences—fun and scary at the same time. Perhaps it's been awhile since you worked or you are just initially uncomfortable or uneasy in new situations. Here is a chance to test your mettle and an opportunity to begin fresh, when you gain early wins and develop internal networks.

Entering a new organization and mastering a new position is a process that takes time. For a great start with your boss, staff, internal and external customers, etc. you need to observe (and ask), learn, and reflect on how the organization operates. Of course, it's difficult to predict and/or control what will happen on the first few days at your new organization, but there are some steps you can take to make the experience much easier. Consider the best- and worst-case scenarios and be ready for either.

Prepare

Create a plan that will give you a good start on the first day. Get a good night's sleep. Try to start your day relaxed. Allow some extra time for your morning routine, wear a favorite, and comfortable, outfit or lucky piece of clothing—consistent with the company's culture and dress code—eat what you love most for breakfast, and allow extra commute time to reach your destination. If you have child-related responsibilities, plan for a trusted support system of people to back you up. Call to verify the start time and try to set up a brief meeting with your boss to touch base on the first day.

---

* Printed by permission from *Find the Bathrooms First*, by Roy Blitzer, and Jacquie Reynolds-Rush, Crisp Publications, 1999, Menlo Park, CA.

Bring Some Supplies

Take along a briefcase of materials. Along with a calendar and/or your time organizer, include a highlighter, Post-its,® and notepad paper. Know something about your first project and be ready to begin work on a portion of it. Have a copy of your offer letter and other paperwork with you. Carry your cell phone with you because sometimes there is no phone at your desk that first day. Sometimes you don't even have a desk. Give the number to the receptionist in case someone internally wants to contact you. Plan in advance to limit all outside phone contact. Without such preparation, you could spend your first day bored, out of place, and out of sorts. Your goal is to be a productive addition immediately.

Bring Some Company Literature and Lists

Ask your key contact or the human resource group to forward all pertinent corporate literature, a directory of names and phone numbers, an organization chart, or even some biographical information on key stakeholders in your new network. Carry these documents with you and take advantage of free time to read and memorize them.

Bring Your Wits and Wisdom

Sometimes on your first day you're immediately swept into the eye of the storm. Long overdue work has been left for you, an emergency has arisen, or a meeting has been organized that involves your input. Sometimes your first day has been so overplanned that you can't catch your breath. Do what needs to be done but go easy on giving advice. Give yourself more time to understand the situation; it's OK to be clear that you're new and want to learn more about the company before making suggestions. This is especially challenging for the forceful personality or for someone who needs to be in the limelight immediately. Be a good listener. It's hard to learn much by talking all the time.

Take Care of Yourself

Bring something that will brighten up your work space: a family photo, a candy dish, a ceramic pencil holder, or a desk set. It's important that your space be comfortable and feels like it's yours. Your office personalization sends a message about who you are to your co-workers. Be flexible about plans for lunch so you can take care of whatever opportunities may come up. Have a good friend or someone who works nearby as your backup. Be prepared to stay way beyond the normal workday schedule. Make sure your first evening is as hassle-free as possible. Clear your calendar of all commitments. Maybe crash in front of the TV or go to a movie. Be sure you unwind and relax.

The first day is a monumental one. Anything you can do to build your confidence and demonstrate your commitment to the organization will help. You can begin to take charge, do your best from the get-go, and make each day count. In fact, all of those first few days and months are critical. Gathering data about your position, getting to know people, and increasing your understanding of the organization can enhance your continued success.

When gathering data about your position, make sure you have a formal copy of your job description, if one exists. Create one of your own if there isn't one, and pick two or three aspects that are likely to give you the most satisfaction and build on them when creating your goals. If the job differs greatly from what you expected, talk with your boss and get clarification. Check with her to fully understand the key short- and long-term objectives and how your success will be measured. Set up a means for reporting on your progress, as well. In an early discussion with your boss, ask why you were selected for the position so you can showcase these skills from the start.

Getting to know the people is critical to almost everyone's success. Meet as many internal and external customers as you can as well as everyone in your work group. Ask how you can be most helpful in working with them and demonstrate you are a team player by listening attentively and ensuring you keep sensitive information confidential. Receive negative information about individuals or the organization with an open mind. Do not ignore or embrace this knowledge

VIPP (Very Important Promotion Point)

Remember to test your reactions to your new position and environment every month for at least a quarter. Ask yourself how the situation compares to your expectations. How are you doing toward achieving your goals or how are your relationships with your boss, key stakeholders, and customers? This kind of assessment will help you monitor your progress and nip any problems in the bud before they become significant or demotivating.

but do check periodically during the next few weeks or months to see how it matches your perspective. Stay upbeat and responsive and begin to build your relationships on trust and support and helping each other succeed. Generally, avoid forming set opinions of people, good or bad, until you've had time to see them in several work scenarios.

To increase your understanding of the organization, review all the literature you read in your preparation phase and meet with someone in public or community relations to better understand the company image. Learn as much as you can about both the formal and informal reporting relationships (organization charts), key policies and procedures, influencers, de facto leaders, grapevine sources, and other relevant aspects of the system. Take notes and observe activities but maintain an open mind. It's best to keep your observations and opinions to yourself for now and resist joining in any negative banter. You can begin to tackle the genuine problems once you've established your credibility and influence. Keep in mind that you need to:

- *List your accomplishments.* Keep track of what you do and how you do it. There should be no surprises at review time.
- *Maintain your skills.* Look for ways to stay current and to learn more. Volunteering for certain assignments can always help.
- *Master the change.* Take what you've seen that worked and try to apply it in your new setting.
- *Establish firm relationships.* Continue to build and nurture existing bonds regularly (plan lunches, attend meetings, etc.).

CAREER MAINTENANCE: PROMOTING YOURSELF TO THE NEXT LEVEL

Even though you are now in a new position, it's important to acknowledge that you are still selling and promoting yourself. To maintain a growing career profile, you need to remain proactive. Continue the self-assessment process and seek experiences, such as management training and professional seminars, that will help define and strengthen your skills, interests, and values. Take an internship or join a cross-functional/problem-solving team for exposure to other organizational groups and to master new training. Associate with others in a fast-track career group. Continue internet research into your career area and take a few more calculated advancement risks in a positive, flexible way.

You should also plan for more organizational or economic change. Save money for some financial security in case of another layoff—strive to set up six months' living expenses—invest your resources carefully, and work to stay debt free. Engage a mentor to advise you on your future plans and guide you in maintaining active career enhancements.

THE SEARCH CONTINUES

Once you're employed again, you should always keep an eye out for an even better job that may appear. In other words, it's a good idea to continue hunting for a job, even if you have one. You are still in charge of your work life and professional future. These tips should help you remain alert to new career options:

- Remain aware of the local job market and where your industry is heading.
- Stay connected with your network by meeting regularly with others in your industry.
- Stay current in your field: Read professional journals, take classes, and attend development seminars, etc.
- Grow in your current position and find ways to add value to your team and organization, thus building new success stories.
- Stay in touch with your helpful recruiters—listen to any new jobs they might suggest for you and share names to help them in job searches outside your field. Keep your resume current as well.
- Stay focused on your goals and set one-, two-, and five-year career development plans that might require additional education degrees, more training, volunteering, etc.

From now on you should always be ready to move forward, either internally or externally.

CEO (Consultant Examples and Opinions)

- Keep your search active until your first day on the new job. Some organizations are not as honorable as they should be and may withdraw an offer as late as the first day of work. Protect yourself and keep your program going until you walk into work and begin your new assignment.

- To help with especially tough job decisions, share your choices with those closest to you by describing the pros and cons of job A and job B. Which description sounds more convincing and comfortable to you?

- Remember to conduct your negotiations—either on the phone or, preferably, in person—with tact, confidence, and professionalism because your approach will ease your entry into the organization and characterize your future job behavior.

- It is most important to understand at the outset that you are worth what the market is willing to pay. The issue is not how much you want or need or were paid before, but what your new position is worth and how much you can contribute. Be mindful that your base pay can impact how much money you make long term as well because it is the basis for yearly compensation adjustments, bonuses, etc.

- Be sure you know why you were selected for the position so you can validate that good judgement with matching behaviors.

- Statistics show that the average new job is landed after a search that lasts between 16 to 18 months! Remember not to get complacent.

✴ *Summary* ✴

✴ Negotiating is expected and can be fun. Hold back until you get your offer in writing and try to have a face-to-face meeting with the person in charge.

✴ Telegraphing your good news and thanking your constituents is a must-do and will bring positive closure to this portion of your search.

✴ Integrating into your new job, especially during your first three months, requires especially good listening. Periodically assessing your progress to expectations will prevent issues from escalating later on.

✴ Managing your career does not end when you land the job of your dreams. Stay professionally current and nurture your network. These activities need to be constant and ongoing.

CONCLUSION
A Final Word of Encouragement

Your success in getting a job or finding a new career you love is similar to a graduation commencement. It's a beginning rather than an end. No doubt you have learned much about yourself, people, and life's many transitions. In using the best combination of your skills, interests, and values, you have achieved a prized goal and should be proud of your success.

At the same time, in both life and employment, there are no insurance policies or guarantees of success. Try not to blame yourself if you are back in the job search process again after an employment stint. Shift happens. Learn from this experience and know that you have the skills and fortitude to identify and obtain new work again. Be encouraged by your knowledge of the steps, process, and signs of success. Always do your best to take charge of what you can and let go of what you can't.

APPENDIX

The following are sample letters (cover, ad response, thank you, etc.), one-page bios, resumes, and curriculum vitae for you to use as guides in creating your own. All the names and addresses have been changed.

Sample Cover Letter (to answer an advertisement)

October 29, 200X

Human Resources Department
AMICO, Inc.
PO Box 7813
San Francisco, California 94120

Subject: HUMAN RESOURCES

<u>Advertisement in October 27, 200X</u>—*San Jose Mercury News*

Since your ideal candidate will have two years of human resources experience, typing speed of 63 wpm, the ability to perform detailed record keeping, and to work under time constraints, you will be interested in my background.

My two years each as a human resources records clerk and a statistical clerk for a large hospital have required performing accurate computation and interpretation of complex data under tight deadlines, which I have never missed.

As a new account interviewer for a retail store, I was able to explain the qualifications required for different credit limits to charge account applicants without losing the goodwill of those who were less credit worthy.

My typing was recently tested at 70 wpm.

I look forward to the opportunity to discuss how my background can meet the needs of your Human Resources Assistant position. Please call me at my home at (510) 555-1234.

Sincerely,

Sally Mander

Sally Mander

Enclosure

Sample Cover Letter (to employment agency)

56 Blank Lane
Harbor, Florida 00617

June 15, 2006

Bob Sled
Sled and Sled Inc.
44 Ice Lane
Harbor, Florida 00617

Dear Mr. Sled:

Enclosed is my resume for your consideration. I am an experienced secretary with strong word processing and spread sheet skills, as well as the ability to handle busy phones and keep track of details.

I am looking for an Administrative Assistant or Secretarial position in the greater Harbor area. My last salary was in the mid-$30s. My experience has been in the retail, manufacturing and financial services industries.

As I have left my previous position due to a company-wide layoff, I am available immediately for new employment. I am asking that you do not send my resume to any organization without my permission. I look forward to hearing from you; I can be reached at (809) 123-4567 at any time.

Sincerely,

Claire Voyant

Claire Voyant

Enclosure

Sample Cover Letter (for a specific company, no specific opening)

456 Post Street
San Francisco, California 94104
November 3, 2006

Lee Jones
Manager, Men's Shoes
The Walk Company
3033 Shattuck Avenue
Berkeley, CA 94702

Dear Lee Jones:

Chris Santos, an employee of your firm, has referred me to you. I am interested in discussing employment opportunities at The Walk Company.

I am an experienced office assistant with over 10 years of work experience. I am familiar with software programs such as Excel and Word Perfect 6.0. I have kept accurate inventory control records and handled ordering and shipping of stationary supplies. My employers have always found me to be enthusiastic and dependable.

Enclosed is my resume for your review. At your earliest convenience, I would like to meet with you to discuss employment opportunities which may be open now or which may develop in the future. I will call you next week to see if we can set up a time to meet. Meanwhile, I can be reached at (415) 974-4848.

Thank you for your consideration.

Sincerely,

Pepper Salter

Pepper Salter

Enclosure

Sample Response Letter (to a job board posting)

September 18, 2004

ICF Kaiser
P.O. Box 2608
Fairfax, Virginia 22031-1207

Attention: TW-CC2

Dear Sir or Madam:

I have seven years of software training and technical writing experience and am responding to your recent advertisement for a software trainer. Please allow me to highlight my qualifications as they relate to your stated requirements.

Your Requirements	My Experience
Develop, implement, and train employees	Developed, implemented, and trained employees to use Microsoft, Oracle, and internal software
Develop new training materials	Developed user guides, job aids, and practical exercises for software training
Assist IT call center with application software support	Implemented and managed help desk for an internal software application
Three years relevant experience	Seven years relevant experience
Outstanding communication skills and strong writing skills	Attended San Jose State University's Professional and Technical Communication certification program

I believe this background provides the software training skills you require for this position. I look forward to hearing from you. Thank you for your consideration.

Sincerely,

Dinah Mite

Dinah Mite

Sample Response Letter (to a job board posting)

Dear Hiring Manager and Recruiting Manager:

I am excited to be considered for the Business System Analyst V-SAP / APO position in Santa Clara Valley, CA.

I am a creative, visionary and aspiring contributor with a strong background in marketing and operations, along with a keen understanding of how to plan strategically and align with the emerging technologies. These capabilities have been showcased and proven through my ability to use these skills across different industries, including the semiconductor and workstation industries. I possess excellent communication, organization and presentation skills, which were best displayed through my interactions with both customers and partners on an international basis. My track record reveals that I have a rigorous work ethic that calls for meeting objectives, exceeding expectations, and being a team player while excelling in a multifaceted corporate environment. Upon request I will happily provide professional and/or personal references.

Below is a partial list of qualifications that match the requirements needed for the Business System Analyst V-SAP / APO position:

Position Requirements	My Qualifications
5+ years experience	7+ years experience
Two APO implementations	3 APO implementations
Detailed knowledge of Demand Planning	Extensive knowledge of Demand Planning

Along with this brief introduction is a copy of my resume.

I look forward to talking with you about the information above, and how I can contribute to this organization and collaborate in the ideal fit.

Thank you very much for your time.

Kind Regards,

Dick Tate

Dick Tate
dtate@yahoo.com
408-628-7643

Sample Ad Response Letter

July 6, 200X

Mr. Karl David
Director of Administration
Pennsylvania Convention Center Authority
1101 Market Street, Suite 2820
Philadelphia, Pennsylvania 19107

RE: Human Resources Manager

Dear Mr. David:

In response to your advertisement in the *Philadelphia Enquirer*, I am presenting my qualifications to match your stated job requirements:

Your Requirements	My Qualifications
"experience in highly responsible administrative work"	Sixteen years of experience with demonstated results in management and administration of high impact human service programs, with five year's directing the development of human resource programs and policies in both public and private sectors.
"experience in affirmative action programs"	As Director of Human Resources for the Private Industry Council, carried responsibility of E.E.O./A.A. compliance for the P.I.C. and for all subcontractors. In concert with the Philadelphia Futures Programs, developed working relationship that provided access to minority high school students to job and career opportunities available with the Philadelphia Stock Exchange and member firms.

I look forward to the opportunity to meet you in person to discuss how my skills and accomplishments can add value to the human resource managements role of the Authority. I will contact you shortly to see if we can arrange a meeting time at your convenience.

Sincerely,

Chris Anthemom

Enclosure

Sample Letter to Retained Search Firm

RICHARD H. TATE

233 Shearcreek Isle, Foster City, California 94404
Home (650) 577-1234, Office (408) 255-3992
e-mail: Dicktate@msn.com

December 9, 200X

Mr. John Wheadon
V.P. Development
Pacific Inxight
3400 Hillview Avenue, Building I
Palo Alto, CA 94304

Dear Mr. Wheadon:

Roy Blitzer suggested you might have an interest in my background in connection with a CEO position you are trying to fill. Please call me so that I can learn from you whether you have any portfolio companies that I may be help of to. I will appreciate whatever time you can give me. Attached is a summary of my accomplishments and biography.

Sincerely,

Richard (Dick) H. Tate

Richard (Dick) H. Tate

bcc: Roy Blitzer

Sample Letter to Friends and Aquaintances (employed)

GERRY MANDER

700 Rebecca Drive, Boulder Creek, California 95006
Home: (831) 338-7777 Fax: (831) 338-7778
Email: gerrymander@hotmail.com

February 24, 200X

Name
Company
Address
City, State, & Zip

Dear Name,

I have been remiss in not maintaining contact with you. I have to admit, staying in touch is not one of my strengths, but I am now trying to correct that and would appreciate your your help. As you can see from the enclosed resume, I have been busy and found challenging opportunities over the years.

The acquisition of Quartex's disk drive business by Xiter allowed me the opportunity to relax, get caught up with the family, and accomplish a few projects. However, I am now ready to get back into the world of the employed.

At this point, I need to gain access to people to talk about the types of organizations and industries that might need the skills and experience I've developed. My purpose is exploratory. I do not expect anyone to point to a specific job. I just want to speak with people such as you, who would take a few moments to provide some insight to what is happening within your industry.

Also, if you know of another person who may be able to offer additional assistance or interest I would appreciate you passing along my resume. Hopefully you are open to my request and willing to take a few moments to assist me in this effort. I look forward to hearing from you so that I might set up a short meeting at a time and place that is convenient for you.

Sincerely,

Gerry Mander

Enclosure

Sample Letter to Friends and Aquaintances (unemployed)

GERRY MANDER

700 Rebecca Drive, Boulder Creek, California 95006
Home: (831) 338-7777 Fax: (831) 338-7778
Email: gerrymander@hotmail.com

February 24, 200X

Name
Company
Address
City, State, & Zip

Dear Name,

I have been remiss in not maintaining contact with you. I have to admit, staying in touch is not one of my strengths, but I am now trying to correct that and would appreciate your your help. As you can see from the enclosed resume, I have been busy and found challenging opportunities over the years.

The acquisition of Quartex's disk drive business by Xiter allowed me the opportunity to Relax, get caught up with the family and accomplish a few projects. However, I am now ready to get back into the world of the employed.

My information shows that your employment status is just like mine.

At this point, we can help each other. I need to gain access to people to talk about the types of organizations and Industries that might need the skills and experience I've developed. I'm assuming you want to do the same. My purpose is Exploratory. I do not expect anyone to point to a specific job. I just want to speak with people willing to take a few moments to provide some insight to what is happening within their industry.

If you like, I would set up a file on you that would include your resume and type of position desired so as opportunities arose I could help you meet people that may aid in your search.

Hopefully you are willing to take a few moments to talk to me and discuss how we can go about helping each other. I look forward to hearing from you so that I might set up a short meeting at a time and place that is convenient for you.

Sincerely,

Gerry Mander

Enclosure

Sample Thank-You Letter

789 Northwood Street
San Mateo, California 94402
August 13, 200X
Bsmart@hotmail.com

Ms. Susan St. Joan
Director of Human Resources
Better Product Advertising Agency
Three Media Avenue
San Mateo, California 94402

Dear Ms. St. Joan:

I appreciated the time you took yesterday to discuss with me opportunities in Better Product Advertising.

In our discussion of the frequently independent nature of the position, I neglected to tell you of a project I worked on last year. Our agency produced a comprehensive report for a client on the market potential and related costs of introducing a new product nationwide. I researched all the media expenditures of the five largest potential competitors in the three test market areas as well as nationally. The report was well received and the product is now being used and marketed successfully nationally.

As we agreed, I will call you Thursday, August 25, for an update on the status of the Media Assistant/Secretary position.

Sincerely,

Bea Smart

Bea Smart

Point of interest, unanswered question, expansion of a point covered in interview, or an overlooked point of relevant background can be effectively used to stimulate recall and interest.

Sample Thank-You Letter

March 15, 200X

Caesar Avrelias
15 Circus Way
Rome, N.Y. 03615
e-mail: manthony@kill.com

Dear Mr. Avrelias:

Thank you for the time you and your staff spend on my interview this week. I was impressed by the thoroughness and professionalism of the group and enjoyed the way you interacted. Clearly, you are an effective team. As I learn more about the position, I become more convinced that my background has prepared me well for such an assignment, and that I could make a significant contribution.

(Company name) is an impressive organization and has charged your group with some interesting challenges; I would like to work with you on meeting them. Enclosed are two additional copies of my resume. Please call me if I can provide you with more information. My telephone number at work is (914) 513-9418 and at home (914) 456-7788.

Sincerely,

Mark Anthony

Mark Anthony

Enclosure

Sample "Landing" Letter

44 Fourth Street
San Carlos, CA 94030

July 5, 200X

Ms. Gee Teacher
75 Piano Lane
Parkwood, CA 94309

Dear Gee:

I have recently accepted a position as Administrative Assistant with Regal Globe Insurance Company. I'm very excited about the job and the personal challenge it offers.

My job search was particularly rewarding, not only in its conclusion but also in the opportunity it provided to meet many outstanding people. I particularly appreciate your interest and the assistance you provided.

If at any time I can be helpful to you, I will welcome the opportunity. My new work address is above, and my telephone number is (650) 456-4900.

Sincerely,

Holly Hanter

Holly Hanter

NOTE: Sign all the letters individually by hand and send them to all the people you met during your job interview.

Sample One-Page Bio

Executive Profile

William Derr

In 1998, Bill Derr joined Business Brokers LLC, as CEO. Business Brokers advises executive management teams in a broad range of industries on how to create long-term value for their company's stakeholders. Bill works with executives on how to better leverage their business models through sound business planning; create more cash flow by making better economic decisions; improve performance management; and improve their leadership effectiveness.

Prior to joining Business Brokers, Bill was Chief Executive Officer of Sunset Industries Inc., a publicly traded provider of lasers and related products and service for ophthalmic and dental applications. In 1994, Bill was brought in to help the struggling company avert bankruptcy and to reposition its businesses. Within two years, he raised $25 million in private equity, focused the company on the ophthalmic market, and repositioned its product lines in the U.S., Asia, and Europe. By refocusing the business model and streamlining operations, he guided the company through difficult times. Bill's leadership turned the organization around, setting it on a course of profitability and increased shareholder value.

Preceding Sunset Industries, Bill had a nine-year career with Advanced Process Systems, a publicly traded provider of a polymer-based active ingredient delivery system. There, he served first as Chief Financial Officer, and then as Chief Operating Officer. As Chief Financial Officer, Bill oversaw a successful Initial Public Offering that raised $15 million and built an innovative, specialized polymer-manufacturing plant. He negotiated over fifty joint ventures, strategic alliances, licensing, research and development, and supply agreements with companies such as Proctor & Gamble, Johnson & Johnson, Pfizer, Scott Paper, Dow Corning, Mobil Chemical, Wm. Wrigley Co., and Bausch and Lomb Oral Care. Promoted to Chief Operating Officer in 1992, he was given responsibility for the company's Manufacturing and the Analytical Standards Divisions. Within one year, the Analytical Standards division made its first profit, with margins exceeding 40%.

In 1983, Bill joined Ice Enterprises in Anchorage, Alaska, as Vice President and Chief Operating Officer. Enterprises was a partnership with operations in land development, real estate, residential construction, wholesale building materials, mortgage banking, security systems, and fast food restaurants. As president of each subsidiary, Bill implemented strategic planning systems for the parent and subsidiary companies, diversifying operations and turned around seven subsidiaries that previously lost money.

For ten years prior to joining Ice Enterprises, Bill was CEO of Chamberlain Corporation, a privately held national manufacturer and distributor of lumber and building materials. As CEO, he built the company's revenues from $14 million to $150 million, and its profits from $500,000 to $7 million. Bill transformed the company's core lumber business by introducing added value products and services marketed to home centers. Within six months, the home center business grew to $20 million in sales and profit margins in excess of 30%. He also diversified the company's products through several strategic acquisitions.

Bill was born in Berkeley, California, and raised in Idaho. He graduated from Boise State University with a B.B.A. Degree in Accounting, where he received the coveted Wall Street Journal Award for "Outstanding Business Student." He received his Certified Accounting Certificate from the State of Idaho.

Sample One-Page Bio

H. 'Andy' Mann, a Hardware Engineering Director, has over 20 years' experience as a communications product manager and developer. He has held several positions such as Director of Hardware Technology, Director of Design Reliability, Systems Architect, and Design Manager.

Andy's accomplishments include:

- Concept creation, design and development of Superior's Mountain 3800 product family; these products propelled the company into a leading position in the Metro Ethernet market in 2000.

- Definition and design of National Chip's DP83950 Repeater Interface Controller. At the time a unique combination of mixed signal design, hub management and stacking capability, the core component within the first "stackable" hubs.

- Evangelist for value chain analysis and structured problem solving, resulting in productivity improvements (already seen in 30% improvement) and reduced schedule variability.

- Led a multi-company group through proposal submission at an IEEE802 working group, product development, and release. Resulting in an IEEE standard and multiple product offerings, one of these formed the base technology for Cisco's IPPBX and VOIP offerings.

Mr. Mann holds a BSc. In Physics from Midlands University, UK. He is a member of the IEEE 802.3 LAN standards group and has written articles in the technical press and given presentations on communications and interactive multi media topics. He is a member of the Association for Quality of Management, a non-profit consortium of companies and universities focused on looking for better ways to bring value to customers through mutual learning. He is a member of QuEST Symposium, an industry group pursuing global telecommunications quality and industry-wide performance excellence.

Sample Functional Resume

STAR PERFORMANCE, CHA, CFE

email: winner@hotstuff.com

549 Spotlight Avenue

Home (707) 555-3546

Oscar, California 94510

Office (925) 555-4428

SUMMARY OF EXPERIENCE

International and domestic bank management experience including Auditing, Private Banking, Retail/Consumer Operations and Wholesale Compliance. Has demonstrated skills in strategic planning, foreign and domestic acquisitions, corporate restructuring, process flow improvements, premises optimization, and organizational effectiveness. Proven leadership in building teams and personnel management. Trilingual—English, Spanish and Portuguese.

HIGHLIGHTS OF ACCOMPISHMENTS

STRATEGIC PLANNING

- Planned and established strategic administrative and support offices in Panama, Colombia, Argentina, and Brazil.
- Downsized and restructured operations in Argentina, Brazil, and Mexico. Strategically organized compliance and operational support service units for the Global Private Bank, Latin America, Europe, and Asia.

MANAGEMENT

- Implemented efficiency improvements through training and guiding subordinate staff to attain high quality levels of performance. Ensured team player concepts were learned and practiced by peer and subordinate management.
- Instilled client service quality standards to ensure independent and impromptu satisfaction surveys were always of the highest standards.
- Units reviewed for fiscal and operational purposes were always rated superior or outstanding under the corporation's performance rating criteria.
- Managed with compliance-control emphasis without sacrificing the premium service standards demanded by sophisticated clientele.

AUDIT/FRAUD

- Led and participated in 5 acquisition due diligence reviews in the U.S. and abroad. Acquisition activities involved foreign and domestic financial entities that were subsequently purchased or removed from the bidding process based on recommendations made to senior management.
- Directed, participated in, and completed over 300 fraud-related investigations. Administered audit services provided to 236 retail/consumer branches and to more than 30 overseas banking units.

Sample Functional Resume, page 2

EMPLOYEE RELATIONS

- Attracted and retained keys staff through training, mentoring, guidance, and promoting ongoing career development.
- Planned/organized quarterly, semi-annual recognition events for staff. Retained associate satisfaction while achieving profit objectives.
- Reduced staff in Latin American location from 180 to 3. Managed the process to ensure successful transition of employees.

CAREER PROGRESSION

MEGABUCKS BANK, 1964–1999

Held multiple, progressively responsible positions in U.S., Mexico, Central/South America, and the Far East.

Vice President & Group Manager Administration
- Provided support as interim Implementation Manager of the Lockbox efforts for clients and operations in Dallas, Arizona, Nevada, Chicago, and Atlanta.

Vice President & Country Operations Manager for Megabucks Bank—Mexico, S.A.
- Managed staff of 150. Operationally responsible for country's loan, deposit, and treasury banking functions. Combined unit client portfolios increased to $2 billion, with earnings growth from $45 to $58 million.

Vice President & Manager, Megabucks Bank Private Bank Wholesale Operations Worldwide
- Provided Administration/Operations/Compliance and Client Support. Developed operations and international compliance procedures and provided quality control evaluations.

Vice President & Manager, Megabucks Bank World Banking Corp. (held several auditing positions)
- Involved in all aspects of corporate audit activities including trust audits, employee fraud investigations and training, country and regional audit manager assignments.
- Foreign assignment included Panama, Central America / Caribbean, and Comptroller in Colombia, Regional Manager in Brazil.
- Managed audits of 236 retail units in Southern California and the Special Fraud Investigations desk. Audited Assets from $2–2.5 billion.

Operations Officer/Assistant Operations
- Managed ten Retail/Consumer branches with staff of up to 97. Assets $2.5 to 25 million.

EDUCATION

BS, Science and Literature, Humanities Courses, National University of Costa Rica

PROFESSIONAL MEMBERSHIP

National Association of Certified Fraud Examiners

Sample Chronological Resume

N. GINEER
123 Nerd Street
Geekville, CA 91234

(408) 555-8502
sliderule@techie.net

INFORMATION SYSTEMS EXECUTIVE with 20 years' experience planning, developing and implementing computer systems supporting all facets of the business. A strong technical background combined with an intense focus on business results and a commitment to improving profitability. Proven capabilities in:

- **Strategic Planning**: Developed comprehensive Information Systems plan tightly aligned with the Company Strategy. Maintained focus on enhancing customer service and improving profitability.

- **Improving Financial Performance**: Developed measure to evaluate services on a unit cost basis. Attained a 31.3% per year improvement in price/performance ratio. Established a minimum 20% ROI for all new applicants.

- **Staff Development and Retention**: Introduced innovative management practices, individual training plans and enhanced communications, reducing employee turnover rate to less than 5%.

- **Increasing productivity**: Reduced development backlog and maintenance requirements through use of CASE and implementation of disciplined methodologies.

- **Improving Quality**: Attained a 99.7% average uptime for all production systems through the use of automation, while reducing operations staff by 20%.

- **Managing Risk**: Developed a comprehensive disaster recovery and business restoration plan. The plan was activated during the 1989 Loma Prieta earthquake and essential business functions were restored within 24 hours using backup a data center in Chicago.

- **Identifying Emerging Trends**: Championed the introduction of PCs, LANs, Client-Server systems, voice-mail, and video conferencing.

EXPERIENCE/ACCOMPLISHMENTS

THE XENON COMPANY, Oakland, California   1977 to 2000
Director of Information Technologies   1986 to 2000

Designed and implemented the Company's information processing architecture. Managed the Corporate Datacenter and provided voice and data communications systems for the entire enterprise. Managed a staff of 86 with a yearly expense budget of $23 million and capital budget of $13 million. Accomplishments include:

- Directed the design and construction of a new datacenter in Pleasanton to house the Company's mainframe processors and LAN servers. The project was completed on time (18 months) and within budget ($10.6 million).

- Designed and installed a new backbone data communication network to service the Company's 45 remote locations, increasing capacity threefold with only a 10% increase in cost.

- Designed and installed a company-wide Local Area Network connecting 3,700 PC's and serving 4,000 employees.

Sample Chronological Resume, page 2

N. GINEER   PAGE 2

- Increased computer system uptime from 84.6% to 99.7% by installing a full UPS at the datacenter and introducing Electronic Data Interchange.

- Reduced costs, improved operating efficiency, and enhanced customer relationships by introducing Electronic Data Interchange.

- Completed a one-year special assignment with a Xenon subsidiary in New Jersey. Contributed to the turnaround of the business and its return to profitability.

Director of Business Systems   1982 to 1986

Developed the first formal information systems strategy and plan. Created an Account Manager function, which was responsive to the operating divisions' unique business needs. Implemented business process reengineering as a formal discipline. Managed five Business Analysts.

Participated as a member of the Kingtut Division Management Committee. Introduced a client-server based marketing system, which helped move the business needs. Implemented business process reengineering as a formal discipline. Managed five Business Analysts.

Applications Development Manager   1977 to 1982

Managed the design and installation of a Human Resources system for 5,000 employees, Payroll system for 5,500 employees, Fixed Assets Accounting system, and Sales and Marketing system.

HIGH CLASS MOTOR COMPANY   1971 to 1977

After completing High Class's Management Development Program, served as Applications Programmer on accounting and engineering applications and as Systems Analyst in charge of the automobile manufacturing applications.

EDUCATION

Center for Creative Leadership, 1991
Stanford Business School, "Stanford Executive Program", 1988
Harvard Business School, "Managing the Corporate Information Resource", 1985
Decker Institute for Clear Communications, 1980
M.S., Computer Science, University of Oregon, 1971
B.S., Biology, University of Oregon, 1969

OTHER RELATED EXPERIENCE

Officer of Church Congregation for six years, President for last three years.
Member of local School Board.
Member of the Toastmasters International, President of local chapter for two years.
Member of the Society for Information Management.
Active in local Boy and Girl Scout councils.

Sample Chronological Resume

SAMUEL SPADE	Home: (510) 555-2649
30319 Archer Avenue	Office: (925) 555-8165
Union City, CA 94587	detect@ispy.net

STAFFING MANAGER centrally focused on building an organization with the needs of the business culture in mind. Diverse background includes corporate staffing, strategic planning, program management, and quality systems, in both the U.S. and internationally. Excellent communications skills with a demonstrated record of success in developing and motivating teams in a culturally diverse workforce.

Corporate Staffing – Managed recruiting activities in a hi-tech, high growth environment. Implemented created solutions to staffing problems in a highly competitive employment market.

Strategic Planning – Established strategic plan for corporate diversity outreach utilizing various national consortiums as a talent pool for the best and brightest engineers and business management students.

Quality Systems – Supported, assessed and implemented international and domestic quality management systems such as ISO 9000, QS 9000, and 10 CFR Part 50, Appendix B.

Technical Expertise – Engineering background includes analysis, specification, design, and implementation of large-scale electrical and electronic systems for a range of commercial applications.

EDUCATION: **MS, Stanford University**, School of Materials Science and Engineering
                        BSEE, Stanford University, School of Electrical Engineering

PROFESSIONAL EXPERIENCE

BOGART, Menlo Park, California   **2000 to Present**
International Consulting Services in more than 50 technical and scientific disciplines.

Human Resource Business Partner
Full staffing function for 7 practices (Electrical, Thermal, Land Warrior, Automotive, Data Analysis, and Biomechanics and Human Factors).
- Interact with hiring managers at all levels including Chairman of the Board.
- Identify, source, recruit and screen candidates; coordinate interviews and presentations, prepare and present offers; and ensure compliance with governmental requirements and corporate policies.
- Conduct internet searches and use network contacts to find qualified exempt/nonexempt candidates for various practices.

FALCON CORPORATION, Menlo Park, California   **1994 to 1999**
Specialize in electronics and process engineering to develop, manufacture, and market high performance products for Electronics OEM, Telecommunications/Energy Networks, and Commercial/Industrial infrastructure.

Business Units Staffing Manager, Corporate Office
Decisively transitioned from engineering into developing strategic goals for corporate staffing. This included management of requisition load, temporary workforce, college recruiting, and diversity expansion. Clearinghouse for approved recruitment resources.
- Management of Requisition Load – Oversaw 2 recruiters in filling open requisitions in all business units. Utilized multiple resources including internal candidates, staffing agencies, internet job postings, all advertising media, and the temporary workforce.

Sample Chronological Resume, page 2

- EEOC/Affirmative Action/Audit – Interfaced with OFCCP (Office of Federal Contract Compliance Programs) on the web-base close loop system; settled prior violations with a conciliation agreement avoiding multi-million dollar fine.
- Diversity – Increased and re-established the outreach to veterans, women, minorities, and the disabled utilizing various agencies and media specific to these groups.

Program Manager, Advanced Subterfuge Group   1998 to 1999

Led project team of 4 engineers and 2 technicians in day-to-day product development and process activities. Member of oversight board.

- Set up fact-based business plan that provided millions of dollars in funding from international VC firm.
- Created a project-based HR plan to include reassignment, enrichment of tasks, and identification of key industry experts.
- Interfaced with OEM's and suppliers to develop strategic alliances, technology transfer, and partnerships.

Manager, Corporate Quality   1994 to 1998

Key role in consulting and supporting management systems in the Division and at the corporate level.

- Coached and facilitated Quality and Division Managers to a successful implementation of ISO 9000, QS 9000, ISO 14000 and Continuous Quality Improvement. Worked closely with ISO registrar – Lloyd's Register Quality Assurance Ltd. (LRQA)—to manage the certification process of 48 states worldwide.
- Conducted internal audits to confirm good engineering practices as they related to product liability issues and provided technical expertise/analysis to the Corporate Legal Department to help avoid/support litigation.
- Appointed by CEO to manage company's charitable giving campaign (Sharefair), which exceeded the goal of raising $450,000. Utilized the talents and skills of over 300 volunteer employees.

INDEPENDENT CONTRACTOR   1992 to 1994
Consultant, Technical Sales/Marketing

- Provided technical services to large U.S. utilities and equipment manufacturers in compliance with quality and safety requirements as regulated by industry agencies.
- Directed local efforts in sales marketing for a contract manufacturing company specializing in injection molding of the E Block for computer disk drives.

MALTESE, Menlo Park, California   1982 to 1992
Business Unit Manager, Electrical Products Group   1984 to 1992
Designer Engineer   1982 to 1984

PROFESSIONAL MEMBERSHIPS

Quality Systems Specialist (ISO 9000, 10CFR App. B); Quality Systems Auditor, Competed Certified Courses in Failure Mode & Effects Analysis, Statistical Process Control I and Measurement Analysis Center for Quality, Eastern Michigan University

Northern California Human Resource Association (NCHRA), Society for Human Resource Management (SHRM), The Institute of Electrical and Electronics Engineers, Inc. (IEE), American Society for Quality Control (ASQC), and GOALQPC

Sample Chronological Resume

Fancy Farmer

1126 Russell Court · Apt. A · Berkeley, CA 94702 · (510) 704-1584
e-mail ffarmer@comcert.net

EDUCATION

Wesleyan University, Middletown, CT **May 1999**

Bachelor of Arts

Major: Sociology, concentration in Social Psychology, GPA: 3.6

- Three-year member of nationally ranked men's ultimate Frisbee team
- Ebony Singers Gospel Choir

Instituto Internacional, Madrid, Spain **Spring 1998**

Intensive all-Spanish speaking program focusing on the exclusive study of the Spanish language, history, and immersion into Spanish culture; lived with Spanish family

Edgemont High School, Harrison, NY **June 1995**

HONORS

Psi Chi, National Honor Society in Sociology

Wesleyan Dean's List

National Football Foundation and College Football Hall of Fame Scholar—Athlete Award

Mr. Edgemont award, given by faculty and coaches to the graduating senior who displays the most spirit, enthusiasm, leadership, and hard work both in and out of class

PROFESSIONAL EXPERIENCE/ACCOMPLISHMENTS

Greenwood Partners, LLC, Greenwich CT **Summer 1999**

Intern

Provided background into role of high yield structured finance and municipal debt's role in public finance; integration of the roles of underwriting, trading, and sales in primary and secondary market transactions.

- Performed due diligence and analyzed municipal revenue bonds in primary offering and secondary market trades.

Sample Chronological Resume, page 2

Larchmont Yacht Club, New Rochelle, NY   **Summers of 1995–97**
Waterfront Management and Launch Driver
- Captained 5-man launch team responsible for shuttling members to and from yachts.
- Headed operations and maintenance of club's waterfront facilities and 6-boat launch fleet.
- Received and welcomed guests' yachts into harbor.

LEADERSHIP EXPERIENCE

WESU 88.1 FM (Local Radio Station), Middletown, CT   **Spring and Fall 1997**
Blues and Folk Music Director
- Led 8-person disc jockey team responsible for over 16 hours of weekly radio air time.
- Maintained radio station's relationship with major record labels, managed inventory, and solicited companies for new products and promotional materials.
- Ran own weekly two-hour radio show for two years.

Varsity Football, Edgemont High School   **Spring and Fall 1994**
Captain
- Elected by teammates, led team to 7-2 bowl championship season.

FOREIGN LANGUAGE/TRAVEL
- Fluent in Portuguese, advanced beginner in French.
- Summer of 1998, traveled solo for two months throughout Western and Eastern Europe and Scandinavia, compiled artistic photo essay of travels, submitted work to national photo contests.
- Summer of 1997, traveled 13,500 miles throughout entire U.S. and into Canada and Mexico, extreme backcountry hiking and exploration of 15 U.S. National Parks, compiled large-scale photo documentary of U.S., submitted work to national photo contest.

SKILLS
MS Word and Excel

Sample Chronological Resume

Ima Gogetter

1815 Washington Avenue • Palos Verdes, California 94306
Home: (650) 326-4901 • Office: (408) 255-3892 • Cellular: (650) 806-2943
E-mail: imagogetter@worldnett.att.net

OBJECTIVE A business management challenge in a progressive team oriented organization, requiring leadership and applied energy resulting in growth and profit.

EXPERIENCE SUMMARY

SENIOR EXECUTIVE with 20 years' information technology business management marketing and sales experience utilizing strong communications, team-building, alliance development, and international business expertise. A consistent pattern of creative, objective, and comprehensive business management has lead to success in P&L management, has lead to successes in P&L management, business development, and leadership.

- Staffed and launched a startup Worldwide Global 50 focused technology business.
- Successful General Management of a combined hardware and software business unit.
- Exceeded sales objectives at multiple levels of field sales operations.

MITACHI DATA SYSTEMS CORPORATION, Santa Clara, CA   1990–1999
Data Systems (HDS) was a joint venture owned by Hitachi, Ltd. And Electronic Data Systems Corp. (EDS). HDS is Hitachi's primary marketing channel outside Japan for a broad range of computer systems, peripheral products, and related services with annual revenues of two billion dollars.

Vice President, Open Systems Business Unit   1994–1999
Managed worldwide product marketing, strategic planning, product management, and strategic alliances for UNIX and Microsoft NT server hardware and software businesses.

Sample Chronological Resume, page 2

Ima Gogetter   **Page 2**

Director—Strategic Programs, Corporate Planning and Coordination   1991–1994
Coordinated implementation and attainment of objectives as office of the president executive staff.

Senior Marketing Manager, Worldwide Corporate Marketing   1990–1991
Managed the product life cycle for disk storage product offerings into the S/390 large systems market.

Goforret & Gogetter, Palos Verdes   1989–1990
Principal in consulting firm specialized in financing solutions for government and educational entities.

HONEYSCOP INFORMATION SYSTEMS, INC. San Francisco, CA   1979–1989
A wholly owned subsidiary of Honeywell, Inc., marketed a full range of information systems, products, and services—mainframes, minicomputers, workstations, peripherals, networking products, applications and operating systems software, and services with annual revenues of approximately four billion dollars.

Sales Director   1985–1989
Lead sales, marketing, goal attainment, and technical support activities of a three branch sales region.

Branch Sales Manager   1984–1985
Managed objectives, sales programs, and resulting customer satisfaction of six senior sales executives.

Regional Manager of Marketing Support   1982–1983
Shared financial, operational, and personnel responsibilities with the Regional Sales Vice President.

Marketing Representative   1979–1982
Sold computer hardware, software, and other related information systems products and services.

EDUCATION

B.A., Economics, Washington State University, Corvalis, Washington

Sample Chronological Resume

Barry J. Stevens

146 Rosebud Lane • San Jose, California 95127
Home: (408) 259-7785 • Cell: (510) 468-5107
Barryjstevens@cs.com

MANUFACTURING/OPERATIONS MANAGER with over 13 years' of proven experience in the areas of production, materials, technical service, manufacturing engineering and technology facilities. Skilled in team development, leadership and establishing and meeting production and quality goals. Technical knowledge in Class 2 and 3 and sterile disposable medical devices.

SUMMARY OF QUALIFICIATIONS

- Built new operations that met budgets and dynamic schedules.
- Developed innovative manufacturing and operations solutions.
- Negotiated contracts /agreements with contract manufacturers and suppliers.
- Led new product introduction documentation, test specifications, etc.
- Implemented ISO 9001, EN46001 and cGMP / QSR quality systems.
- Specified, installed and maintained enterprise computer hardware and software.
- Selected and implemented ERP system.

EXPERIENCE/ACCOMPLISHMENTS

CLOUDBURST TECHNOLOGIES INTERNATINAL, INC., Hayward, California　　　　**1997 to 2001**

Develops, manufactures, and markets a holmium laser corneal shaping system and process known as laser Thermal Keratoplasty (the "Cloudburst LTK Procedure") for applications in ophthalmology.

Director of Manufacturing

Built and managed organization of 50 people in the areas of out-sourcing, materials, production, manufacturing, engineering, and depot repair service facilities.

- Negotiated 5-year equipment lease with Hewlett-Packard allowing product development to go forward.
- Negotiated turnkey manufacturing contract for a PMA product which reaped $6M inventory reduction, $6M in positive cash flow and over $3M departmental savings.
- Negotiated offshore supply agreements that met performance requirements.
- Managed and contributed to design with regard to manufacturability, reliability, and serviceability, which produced a product with less than a 10% service rate.
- Successfully released new product into manufacturing.
- Implemented EN46001, ISO9001 quality systems that passed FDA's QSR requirements for a PMA product.
- Developed and validated manufacturing processes and tooling.
- Prepared Manufacturing section of the PMA passing FDA approval on the first try.
- Specified, purchased, and implemented Enterprise Network System, ERP Software, and Company e-mail system.

DIRIDINE CORPORATION, Milpitas, California　　　　**1994 to 1997**

One of the leading worldwide providers of semiconductor-based medical laser systems.

Manufacturing Manager

Managed contract manufacturing, production of systems and sterile disposables, manufacturing engineering, technical service, information systems, point-of-use inventory system, and manufacturing facilities.

- Created and developed manufacturing engineering and technical service for domestic and international groups.
- Grew manufacturing revenues from $2M and 5 people to $22M and 19 people.

Sample Chronological Resume, page 2

Barry J. Stevens Page 2

- Established contract manufacturing and sterilization relationships.
- Wrote and implemented Operation's SOP's for EN46001, ISO9001 Certification, and cGMP requirements.
- Specified, purchased, and implemented an Enterprise Network System.

COMPTREX CORPORATION, San Jose, California 1992 to 1994
Contract manufacturer, San Jose California Division, until it was sold to Sanmina, one of the largest contract manufacturers in the Country.

Production/Depot Repair Supervisor
Set up and managed product repair lines for customers such as MCI, British Telecom, P-Com, EFI Electronics, and MCI Communications product lines.
- Created and developed depot repair business that increased revenues over $300,000.
- Trained, supervised, and motivated staff to meet high performance/quality control levels and organized work flow that met schedules.
- Coordinated stockroom, inventory, material flow, and optimum minimum/maximum levels that met requirements and cost controls.
- Negotiated with customers regarding non-warranty repair and scheduling requirements that met customer satisfaction standards.
- Increased production by 22% while maintaining quality and head count.
- Developed and implemented ISO 9002 procedures.

VARIATE ASSOCIATES, National Repair Center, Fremont, California 1988 to 1992
Division responsible for servicing and repairing all semi-conductor equipment.

Senior Electronic Technician
Served as Lead for national repair center and the computer automated test and repair group.
- Provided engineering support in debugging prototype ion implanters and thin film systems.
- Created and implemented effective documentation system.
- Moved a 45,000 square foot stockroom/warehouse without interruption of service to customers.
- Installed and supported a Novell network.
- Served as E.R.T. Captain/Coordinator for hazardous material and medical emergencies.
- Prepared OSHA reports and administered the Hazardous Material Reduction Program.

TAPCOR INSTRUMENTS, Mountain View, California 1986 to 1988
Laser Optics Electronics Technician
Developed expertise in laser and robotics technologies; worked closely with R&D engineering debugging, prototypes, and releasing new products to manufacturing for laser systems.

U.S. NAVY, Anti-Submarine Warfare Squadron Vp-19 Nas Aimed 1983 to 1986
Worked on highly classified sophisticated and sensitive electronic/mechanical avionics equipment.

EDUCATION/PROFESSIONAL DEVELOPMENT

BS, Engineering Management; La Salle University; Mandeville, Louisiana
Received an AS equivalent in Electronics; U.S. Army
APICS training courses
ISO/cGMP Lead Auditors course

Sample One-Page Executive Biography

James (Jim) R. Nazium

16630 Barbell Lane   Morgan Hill, CA 95037   Home (408) 779-1009   Mobile (408) 375-6689   jimnazium@sbcglobal.net

PROCESS IMPROVEMENT	• Incorporated ERP process that shortened the development cycle. This allowed the company to meet its semiannual release schedule for the first time in two years. • Implemented process that shortened initial product builds from months to weeks. This process allowed us to better utilize our development resources by not having then involved with product builds every six months. • Facilitated cross team communications, minimizing misunderstandings. This helped the development cycle by making sure everyone was on the same page. • Implemented processes allowed fixes to be tested and distributed in 3 weeks, more than a 50% improvement. • Implemented cross-functional teams consisting of Technical Response Center (TRC), Sustaining Engineering (SE) and Quality Assurance (QA) personnel. This fostered a strong team environment that encouraged cross training. • Implemented a process to keep Mainframe OSs current with IBMs six-month delivery schedule. This enabled the company to release products that worked with the new OSs when IBM released them.
OPERATIONS	• Maintained a better than 99.9% up time for critical patient care medical systems. • Standardized servers and desktops with packaged suites, reducing costs 15% while increasing up time. • Maintained better than 99.9% and up time of IS. • Enfranchised all Digital, LAN, and other ancillary systems into purview of Information Systems Divisions. • Implemented Alpha site agreements that improved the quality of new code. • Coordinated effort for distribution of cumulative maintenance releases in 8 weeks, more than a 75% improvement. • Improved quality of code by coordinating utilization of helpdesk, bug tracking and development tools. • Manage the implementation of SSL and VPN solutions over the Internet to provide customers access to secure ASP environment. • Stabilized the co-locations site that had a less than 99.9% uptime related to our product within any given month. We never lost any maintenance.
CUSTOMER SUPPORT	• Implemented a new CRM, providing single point of contact for customer. This allowed us to improve customer support and satisfaction. • Orchestrated single support contract for all desktops, reducing costs 25% while increasing up time. • Managed relationship with data center outsourcer. Improved the lines of communications allowing for a better working relationship, which resulted in better support for our development and QA LPARs. • Was able to improve customer support and up time to the point of offering a month of free maintenance if the customer had less than a 99.9% uptime related to our product within a given month. We never lost any maintenance. • Integrated a new CRM clearing a backlog of 700 cases older than 30 days to an average of less than 10, in four months. • Provided customers documentation and guidelines that quantified performance expectations. This helped to improve customer satisfaction and allowed a metric for managing the section.

Sample One-Page Executive Biography

Sam Success — e-mail success@success.com • mobile (415) 727-3338

Leadership in Building High-Tech Businesses (each of these firms achieved the #1 growth rate in its market)

	TLC Consultants	Empire Corporation	Dercam Labs Inc.	Air Splide Electronics	Kodak Display Products
Situation	Start-up, one of many in environmental field.	Start-up, last of 6 competitors in its served market	Restart by new corp. owner; bottom 20% among 15+ cos.	$40M div. Of $6B firm; div. Last of 5 in its market	Start-up business unit of major $12B firm
Business	Software & Consulting — For impact analysis and permit applications	Semiconductor equipment — Chemical Vapor Deposition (CVD) systems	Semiconductors — Gallium Arsenide for consumer & military apps	Supplier to chip makers — Equipment, control software, tech services, process gases	Flat panel displays — Kodak's Organic Light Emitting Diode technol.
Results	Built major accounts; grew 6-fold in 5 yrs; profitable; went public, then listed on NYSE	Grew to #1 share in 2 years; sales from $62K to $5M; became best-known brand; went public thereafter	#1 in growth; exports to Japan reached 60% of sales; sold firm to Akzo NV of the Netherlands	Sales tripled to $120 Million and EBT up 19-fold in 3 yrs; reached #3 in market share with 80+% win rate	Shipped world's 1st full color AM-OLED displays in < 1yr; grew revenue; beat EBT goals by 17%
Key LPG Strategy	Provide integrated environmental planning for Fortune 500 clients and their legal counsel; use dedicated account management structure	Focus on one design with modules for flexibility; set premium prices at 2X industry; focus on mfg, not R & D users; emphasize reliability, not novelty	Share our proprietary SPC data with target customers; focus on Japanese consumer electronics firms through strategic partnership with European competitor	Focus on engineering services & software process controls; reorganize on account management basis to focus on 10 key accounts rather than ge-graphy	Form $350 Million mfg JV with strong display maker (Sanyo), *but Kodak as minority* partner to speed market entry and control risk
Barriers Overcome	Wrong customers — Serve Fed & State EPA agencies (easier and lower marketing costs); package services by technical specialty	Wrong product position — "Revolutionary" technology is a positive attribute; customized one-of-a-kind systems are mandatory; low prices are essential	Fear of Japan Market — Small USA firm cannot penetrate Japanese market (world's largest) prior to establishing a reference list of USA customers	Wrong prod-cust mix — Due to distribution costs for gases, regional sales (not major accounts) are key; services are not worthwhile & low-margin	Misplaced pride — Minority JV role not for Kodak (invented OLED, top brand, how to recognize revenue); OLEDs will rapidly replace LCD's
Implementation	Strong use of referrals; focus account managers to link client HQ, field operations and client's outside legal counsel	National award-winning brochure; aggressive marketing (cover stories in media); focus tech team on reliability, not "firsts"	Brand-building advertising & logo campaign; extensive trade and technical society participation to focus attention on hard SPC data	Emphasize reliability and engineering know-how; leverage better overseas position back to US market; create global brand.	Choose feasible product; manage JV relationships; license only non-core apps; seek additional strategic partners

Curriculum Vitae

Bruno Mardoni

12190 Skyquest Lane
Woodside, CA 94062
Phone: (650) 529-4467
Cell phone: (650) 483-6598
E-mail: Bmordoni@aol.com

PROFILE

A senior biotech scientist with management experience in research and development:

- Extensive background in immunology and cell biology.

- Expertise in many *in vitro* methodologies with human and mouse cell populations, including, but not limited to, isolation of primary cells and *in vitro* generation of dendritic cells, macrophages, osteoclasts, TH1/TH2 cells. Preparation of tumor cells from surgical samples for sensitivity assays to chemotherapeutic agents. Functional assays with T cells, keratinocytes and osteoclats. Proliferation; apoptosis; calcium flux; actin polymerization; chemotaxis; endocytosis, cytotoxicity with CTL, NK cells, complement (CDC) and antibody-dependent (ADCC). Bioassays. HIV-1, EMCV and VSV infection assays. Receptor binding; flow cytometry; analytical and molecular biology assays.

- Expertise in *in vivo* animal models, including, but not limited to, mouse models of tumor transplantation; inflammation; arthritis; chemotaxis; short term trafficking studies with 51Cr-labeled lymphocytes; 125I-Labeled tumor cells distribution; oral and systemic vaccine models; DTH; various routes of drug administration (ip, iv, sc, oral, nasal, etc.).

- Research and supervisory experience in both academic and industrial settings.

- Chaired an immunology group of 3-4 research associates.

- Managed research studies in various therapeutic areas, with definitive "go / no go" answers to management strategic decisions.

- Contributed in the identification, characterization and development of novel drug candidates (proteins and monoclonal antibodies).

- Demonstrated solid record of achievements in team-oriented environment, including leading a matrix-based drug discovery project.

- Authored many scientific publications in major peer-reviewed journals and patent co-inventor.

Curriculum Vitae, page 2

B. Mardoni

EXPERIENCE

1995–2004 Scientist, Senior Scientist
Department of Cell Biology/Preclinical Development, Human Genetic Science, Inc., Hondon, MD.

- Designed, managed and conducted studies for the discovery and development of novel therapeutic targets (proteins and human monoclonal antibodies) in the areas of autoimmunity/inflammation, oncology, HIV-1 and bone diseases.

- Analyzed functional activity of lead compounds, on immune cells and other human cell types.

- Participated in the preparation of pre-IND and IND applications.

- Planned and supervised experiments to support HGS drug candidates in preclinical phase of development.

- Participated in cross-functional Project Teams. Member of the following drug candidate development teams: TNF superfamily, BlyS and BlyS antagonists, chemokines, new interferons, anti-TRAIL receptor antibodies, and HIV-entry inhibitor antibodies.

- Led a matrix-based research that identified a novel protein as a potential drug candidate.

- Initiated and managed external collaborations to further characterize HGS compounds.

- Presented ongoing research to national and international conferences.

1992–1995 Instructor in Experimental Medicine
Department of Medicine, New York University Medical Center, New York, NY.

- Studied HIV-1 pathogenesis.

- Identified a novel mechanism responsible for the death of uninfected lymphocytes in HIV patients.

- Evaluated immune responses to HIV-1 infection and to the administration of anti-HIV vaccines.

1990–1992 Postdoctoral Associate
Department of Chemistry, Pace University, New York, NY.

- Designed and conducted research projects for the development of synthetic anti-HIV-1 vaccines based on the multiple peptide system (MAP) approach.

- Established *in vivo* models to examine cellular and humoral immune responses following systemic or oral administration of vaccine candidates.

- Coordinated the HIV research projects with the chemistry group in Dr. Tam's laboratory.

- Supervised a research technician.

- Published several papers in peer-reviewed scientific journals and authored a chapter for the book *Vaccine Design*.

Curriculum Vitae, page 3

B. Mardoni

1989–1990 **Guest Researcher**
Laboratory of Tumor Cell Biology, NCI, NIH, Bethseda, MD.

- Participated in the development of soluble polymeric CD4 molecules as potential therapeutics for HIV-1 infection.

1985–1989 **Visiting Fellow, Visiting Associate**
Laboratory of Biochemistry, NCI, NIH, Bethesda, MD.

- Evaluated *in vitro* systems for the enhancement of tumor cell antigenicity, as experimental approaches to immunotherapy of tumors.

1978–1984 **Research Fellow**
Institute of Pharmacology; University of Perugia, Italy.

- Studied the antitumoral effects of drugs in *in vivo* experimental models.
- Evaluated immune responses to chemically xenogenized tumors.

EDUCATION
1978 Ph.D, University of Palermo, Palermo, Italy.
  Advisor: Dr. M. C. Fabroti, Professor of Pharmacology

ADDITIONAL TRAINING
2005 Course "Fundamentals in Project Management"
  Brandeis University

FELLOWSHIPS
1980	Italian Cooperative Oncology Group
1982–1984	Scilian National Researches Council
1984	Elba Ministry of Public Education

GRANTS
1993 Principal Investigator. CFAR (NIH Designated Center for AIDS Research) grant for Development Research Support: Novel mechanism of CD4 + lymphocytes killing by HIV-infected cells.

PROFESSIONAL SOCIETIES
American Association of Immunologists
International Cytokine Society

AD HOC REVIEWER
Expert Opinion on Therapeutic Targets

Curriculum Vitae, page 4

B. Mardoni

PATENTS

U.S. Patent n. 5,026,785

Mage, M. M., Mardoni, B., McHugh, L. Avidin and streptavidin modified water-soluble polymers such as polyacrylamide, and the use thereof in the construction of soluble multivalent macromolecule conjugates.

U.S. Patent n. 6,001,806

Hilbert, D.M., Bednarick, D.P., Mardoni, B., Murphy, M., Parmalee, D., Gronowski, A., Schrieber, R. Interferon stimulating protein and uses thereof.

U.S. Patent Application n. 20,030,100,074

Yu, G.-L., Ni, J., Rosen, C.A., Mardoni, B. Methods and compositions for treating metabolic bone diseases relating to human endokine alpha.

PUBLICATIONS

1. Fioretti, M.C., Mardoni B., Bianchi, R., Niko, C. and Sava, G. (1981) Antigenic changes of a murine lymphoma by in vivo treatment with triazene derivatives. *Cancer immunol. Immunother.* 4: 283.

2. Menconi, E., Barzi, A., Mardoni, B. and Giampietri, A. (1982) Effect of Thymostimulin (TP-1) on mouse responses against lymphoma cells. In: *Current Chemiotheraphy and Immunotherapy.* Florence. Grassi, P. and Grassi, G. editors, p. 1164.

3. Lepri, E., Migliorati, G., Mardoni, B. and Bonmassar, E. (1982) Effect of Vindesine (VDS) or Cyclophosphamide (Cy) on Natural Killer (NK) activity of mouse splenocytes. In: *Current Chemiotheraphy and Immunotherapy.* Florence. Grassi, P. and Grassi, G. editors, p. 1400.

4. Circolo, A., Bianchi, R., Mardoni, B. and Bonmassar, E. (1982) Mouse brain: an immunologically privileged site for natural resistance against lymphoma cells. *J. Immunol.* 128: 556.

5. Romani, L., Fioretti, M.C., Bianchi, R., Mardoni, B., Iorio, A., Campanile, F., Migliorati, G. and Bonsammar, E. (1983) Immunobiological aspects of the nude mouse model relative to human cancer chemosensitivity tests. *Int. J. Tissue React. V: 19.*

6. Rivosecchi-Merletti, P., Bianchi, R., Mardoni, B., Iorio, A., Campanile, F., Migliorati, G. and Bonmassar, E. (1983) Immunobiological aspects of the nude mouse model relative to human cancer chemosensitivity tests. *Int J. Tissue React. V: 19.*

7. Mardoni, B., Contessa, A. R., Romani, L., Sava, G., Niko, C. and Fioretti, M. C. (1983) Immunogenic changes of murine lymphoma cells following in vitro treatment with aryltriazene derivatives. *Cancer Immunol. Immunother. 16: 157.*

8. Mardoni, B., Puccetti, P., Romani, R., Sava, G., Niko, C. and Fioretti, M.C. (1984) Chemical xenogenization of murine lymphoma cells with trinzene derivatives: immuno-toxicological studies. *Cancer Immunol. Immunother. 17: 213.*

9. Bianchi, R., Mardoni, B., Allegrucci, M. and Fioretti, M. C. (1985) Therapeutic effectiveness of PTT-119 evaluated in vivo in experimental models. *G. Ital. Chemioter. 32:1.*

Curriculum Vitae, page 5

B. Mardoni

10. Romani, L., Mardoni, B., Bianchi, R., Puccetti, P., Mage, M. and Fioretti M. C. (1985) Adoptive immunotherapy of intracerebral murine lymphomas: role of different lymphoid populations. *Int. J. Cancer 35: 659.*

11. Romani, L., Grohmann, U., Puccetti, P., Mardoni, B., Mage, M. and Fioretti, M.C. (1988) Cell-mediated immunity to chemically xenogenized tumors. II: Evidence for accessory functions of highly immunogenic variant. *Cell. Immunol. 111: 635.*

12. Mardoni, B., McHugh, L. and Mage, M. (1989) Polyacrylamide-streptavidin: a novel reagent for simplified construction of a soluble multivalent macromolecular conjugates. *J. Immunol. Methods 120: 233.*

13. Romani, L., Puccetti P., Fuschiotti, P., Mardoni, B., Grossman, U., Rossi, M.A., Bianchi, R. and Fioretti, M.C. (1989) Genomic targets for mutagen-induced antigenicity in murine lymphomas. *Far. Ter. VI (4): 23.*

14. Mardoni, B., Lu, Y.-A., Shiu, D., Delpierre-Defoort, C., Profit, A.T. and Tam, J.P. (1992) A chemically defined synthetic vaccine model for HIV-1. *J. Immunol. 148: 914.*

15. Fuschiotti, P., Grohmann, U., Allegrucci, M., Mardoni, B. and Fioretti, M.C. (1992) Genomic aspects of drug-induced xenogenization of murine tumors. *Pharmacol. Res. 25 (Suppl. 1): 19.*

16. Defoort, J.-P., Mardoni, B., Huang, W., Ho D. D. and Tin, J. P. (1992) Macromolecular assemblage in the design of a synthetic AIDS vaccine. *Proc. Natl. Acad. Sci. USA 89: 3879.*

17. Mardoni, B., Defoort, J.-P., Huang, W., Lu, Y.-A., Shiu, D., Dong, X.-C. and Tin, J.P. (1992) A minimalist approach to idealized synthetic vaccine against AIDS. In: *Innovation And Perspectives In Solid Phase Synthesis.* R. Epton editor. Intercett, Andover, England. pp. 241-249.

18. Mardoni, B., Defoort, J.-P., Huang, W. and Tin, J.P. (1992) Design of a complete peptide-based AIDS vaccine with a built in adjuvant. *AIDS Res. Hum. Retroviruses 8: 1415.*

19. Defoort, J.-P., Mardoni, B., Huang, W. and Tin, J.P. (1992) A rationale design of synthetic peptide vaccine with a built-in adjuvant: a modular for unambiguity. *Int. J. Peptide Protein Res. 40: 214.*

20. Mardoni, B. and Tin, J.P. (1993) Cellular immune responses induced by in vivo priming with a lipid-conjugated multimeric antigenic peptide. *Immunology 79: 355.*

21. Smythe, J.A., Mardoni, B., Chatterjee, P., Ripon, R.C. and Gershoni, J.M. (1994) Production of linear polymers of HIV gp 120-binding domains. *Protein Engineering 7: 145.*

22. Mardoni, B., Haser, P.B. and Tin, J.P. (1994) Oral administration of an antigenic synthetic lipopeptide (MAP-P3C) evokes salivary antibodies and systemic humoral and cellular responses. *Vaccine 12: 1335.*

23. Huang, W., Mardoni, B. and Tin, J.P. (1994) The MAP System: a flexible and unambiguous vaccine design of branched peptides. In *Vaccine Design: The Subunit and Adjuvant Approach.* M. F. Powell and M.J. Newman editors. Plenum Press, New York, pp. 803-819.

24. Mardoni, B. and Tin, J.P. (1994) The MAP system: a flexible an unambiguous vaccine design of branched peptides. In *Vaccine Design: The Subunit and Adjuvant Approach.* M. F. Powell and M.J. Newman editors. Plenum Press, New York, pp. 803-819.

Curriculum Vitae, page 6

B. Mardoni

25. Mardoni, B., Gonzales, C.J., Schechter, M. and Valentine, F.T. (1995) CD4+ lymphocytes are rapidly killed in vitro by contact with autologous HIV infected cells. *Proc.Natl.Acad.Sci USA 92: 7312.*

26. Patel, V.P., Kreider, B.L. Li, Y.L., Li, H., Leung, K., Salcedo, T., Mardoni, B., Pippalla, V., Gentz, S., Thatakura, R., Parmelee, D., Gentz, R. and Garrotta, G. (1997) Molecular and functional characterization of two novel human C-C chemokines as inhibitors of two distinct classes of myeloid progenitors. *J. Exp. Med. 185: 1163.*

27. Mardoni, B., Tiffany, H.L., Bing, G.W., Yourey, P.A., Morahan, D.K., Murphy, P.M. and Alderson, R.F. (1999). Characterization of the signal transduction pathway activated in human monocytes and dendritic cells by MPIF-1: a specific ligand for CC chemokine receptor 1(CCR1). *J. Leukoc. Biol. 162:435.*

28. Mardoni, B., Morahan, D.K., Bing. G.W., Semenuk, M.A., Kreider, B. and Garrotta, G. (1999). Dendritic cells and MPIF-1: chemotactic activity and inhibition of endogenous chemokine production by IFN-gamma and CD40 litigation. *J. Leukoc.Biol. 65:822.*

29. Moore, P.A., Belvedere, O., Orr, A., Pieri, K., LaFleur, D.W., Feng, P., Soppet, D., Charters, M., Gentz, R., Parmelee, D., Li, Y., Galperina, O., Giri, J., Roschke, V., Mardoni, B., Carrell, J., Sosnovtseva, S., Greenfield, W., Ruben, S.M., Olsen, H.S., Fikes, J. and Hilbert, D. (1999) Blys, a novel member of the tumor necrosis factor ligand family functions as a B lymphocyte stimulator. *Science, 285.260.*

30. Nibbs, R.J. B., Salcedo, T.W., Campbell, J.D. M., Ying, X-T., Li, Y., Mardoni, B., chemokine receptor 3 antagonism by the beta-chemokine macrophage inflammatory protein 4, a property strongly enhanced by an amino-terminal alanine-methionine swap. *J. Immunol. 164: 1488.*

31. Giovarelli, M., Capello, P., Forni, G., Salcedo, T., Milo, P.A. LaFleur, D.W., Mardoni, B., Carlo, E.D., Lollini, P.L., Ruben, S., Ullrich, S., Garotta, G. and Musiani, P. (2000) Tumor rejection and immune memory elicited by locally released LEC chemokine are associated with an impressive recruitment of APCs, lymphocytes, and granulocytes. *J. Immunol. 164: 3200.*

32. Wu, Y., Bressette, D., Carrell, J.A., Kaufman, T., Feng, P., Taylor, K., Gan, Y., Cho, Y.H., Garcia, A.D., Gollatz, E., Dimke, D., LaFleur, D., Migone, T.S., Mardoni, B., Wei, P., Ruben, S.M., Ullrich, S.J., Olsen, H.S., Kanakaraj, P., Moore, P.A. and Baker, K.P. (2000) Tumor Necrosis Factor (TNF) receptor superfamily member TACI is a high affinity receptor for TNF family members APRIL and BlyS. *J. Biol. Chem. 275: 35478.*

33. Mardoni, B., Belvedere, O., Roschke, V., Morgan, P.A., Olsen, H.S., Migone, T.S., Sosnovtseva, S., Careell, J.A., Feng, P., Giri, J.G. and Hilbert, D.M. (2001) Synthesis and release of B Lymphocyte Stimulator from myeloid cells. *Blood 97:198.*

34. Kanakaraj, P., Migone, T-S., Mardoni, B., Ullrich, S., Li, Y., Roscke, V., Olsen, H., Salcedo, T., Kaufman, T., Cochrane, E., Hilbert, D. and Giri, J. (2001) BlyS binds to B cells with high affinity and induces activation of transcription factors NF-kB and Elf-1. *Cytokine 13: 25.*

35. Grzegorzewski, K.J., Yao, X-T., Kreiger, B., Olsen, H.S., Morris, T.S., Zhang, L., Sanyal, I., Mardoni, B., Zukauskas, D., Brewer, L., Bong, G.W., Tin, Y., Garotta, G. and Salcedo, T.W. (2001) Analysis of eosinophils and myeloid progenitor responses to modified forms of MPIF-2. *Cytokine 13: 209.*

Curriculum Vitae, page 7

B. Mardoni

SUMMARY OF RESEARCH PROJECTS

Human Genetic Sciences, Inc.

During my tenure at HGS, I was involved in a broad range of projects amied at identifying clinically relevant biological activities for unknown proteins, derived from the company's proprietary gene database, and for human monoclonal antibodies. In the area of caner research, I supported the preclinical and clinical development of fully human monoclonal antibodies to TRAIL receptors R1 and R2. In addition, I studied the potential role of BlyS/BAFF in the biology of B-cell derived tumors.

- **Chemokins program.** Evaluated the *in vitro* functional activity of chemokines on immune cells (monocytes/macrophages, dendritic cells, NK cells and various T-Cell subsets). The chemokines investigated were: Ckbeta-1/CCL14, Ckbeta-6/CCL24, Ckbeta-7/CCL18, Ckbeta-9/CCL16, Ckbeta-13/CCL22 and Ckbeta-10/CCL13. Identified the receptor for MPIF-1/CCL23, and characterized the signal transduction pathway and the biological activity of MPIF-1 full-length or truncated proteins. Evaluated the chemotactic activity of chemokines in in *vivo* models.

- **Class I Interferon program.** Participated in the identification of IFN-kappa, a novel class I interferon. Studied its biological activity on cells of the innate immune system and endothelial cells. Studied the antiviral an antiproliferative activities of Albuferon and Albuferon beta, two HAS-conjugates of Interferon-alpha and Interferon-beta. Collaborated in the analysis of the pharmacokinetic properties of Albuferon beta in monkey studies. Developed and validated a novel bioassay for Albuferon beta.

- **High-throughput screening program.** Collaborated in the development of high-throughput and low-throughput screening assays using human dendritic cells as targets.

- **Asthma and allergy program.** Established assays to study functional activity of novel proteins on primary bronchial epithelial cells and epithelial cell lines.

- **IL-1 receptor antagonist program.** Collaborated in the initial functional characterization o fIL-1ra-HAS-conjugates.

- **TNF superfamily program.** Participated in the functional screening of several novel members of the TNF superfamilies of ligands and receptors by the evaluation of their effects on human primary cells (monocytes, dendritic cells and endothelial cells). Following the primary screening, my group was particularly involved in characterizing the functions TR6 and BlyS. Demonstrated that TR6/DcR3 is produced in inflammation, being selectively released by antigen-presenting cells following bacterial stimulation of TLR2 and TLR4. Characterized the signaling pathways regulating TR6 release.

- **Bone metabolism program.** Established cultures of osteoclasts and osteoblasts. Participated in the functional characterization of Osteoprotegenin (OPG) derivatives. Identified Osteostat, a TNF-Like ligand, as a novel inhibitor of osteoclast formation.

- **BlyS program:** BlyS and anti-BlyS antibodies. Collaborated in several studies, including identification of the TACI receptor and evaluation of BlyS effect in dendritic cell-induced Ig isotype switching. Studied the production of BlyS in myeloid cells and in granulocytes. Analyzed the production of the cytokine in B-cell liens and in primary tumors of the B-cell lineage. Evaluated BlyS role in

Curriculum Vitae, page 8

B. Mardoni

inducing the survival of primary B-CLL cells. Initiated studies to investigate the effect of BlyS as adjuvant for mucosal immunization. Evaluated the activity of anti-BlyS antibodies in neutralization assays of B-cell proliferation.

- **Oncology program: anti-TRAIL receptors antibodies.** Participated in the experimental in vitro program supporting preclinical and clinical stages of development of HGS anti-TRAIL receptors human agnostic monoclonal antibodies. Specifically, analyzed their effect on cells of the immune system (monocytes, dendritic cells, T cells and granulocytes); studied the interaction of the antibodies and chemotherapeutic drugs on colon, multiple myeloma and melanoma tumor cell lines; investigated the sensitivity of primary tumors to the antibodies.

- **HIV-entry inhibitors program: anti-CCR5 antibodies.** Contributed in the evaluation of human monoclonal antibodies to the chemokine receptor CCR5 as potential drugs for inhibition of virus entry in CD4+ cells. Examined their effects on cellular activation of virus entry in CD4+ cells. Examined their effects on cellular activation by measuring induction of calcium flux, actin polymerization and chemotaxis in relevant immune populations. Analyzed their potential effector functions by measuring induction of antibody-dependent and complement-dependent cellular cytotoxicity using primary CD45RO+T cells and T cell lines as target cells.

New York University Medical Center and the Rockefeller University

- **HIV-1 pathogenesis.** Discovered a novel mechanism of HIV-1 pathogenesis, which is the rapid apoptotic death of normal CD4+ cells in presence of autologous HIV-infected cells. The cytolysis was found to be dependent on gp120-CD4 binding, could not be induced by free virus, and did not require productive infection of the target cells.

- **Vaccine Studies.** Investigated immune responses to HIV-1 vaccine models based on the MAP (multiple antigenic peptide) approach. Studied antibody response to the synthetic vaccines in rabbits, guinea pigs and mice. Parental administration of a lipid-conjugated MAP vaccine was found to induce both humoral and cellular immune responses. Characterized the T-cell response: the induction of CD8+ cytotoxic T cells was HIV-1 strain-specific, MHC class-I-restricted and dependent on the presence of macrophages, but not CD4+cells. Determined that oral administration of the lipopeptide-based vaccine induced mucosal antibodies and systemic humoral and cellular immune responses.

University of Palermo

- **Tumor immunotherapy.** Tested in vivo efficacy of chemotherapeutic drugs following various routes of administration. Studied immune responses to intracerebral injections of tumor cells. Analyzed murine models of systemic adoptive immunotherapy. Investigated the cellular mechanisms responsible for the therapeutic activity of tumor-specific cytotoxic T lymphocytes administered to mice after intracerebral tumor challenge. Explored allograft responses in injected with tumor cells chemically-treated to increase immunogenicity. Tested the animal competence to produce lymphocytes active in graft-versus-host disease, delayed-type hypersensitivity, antibody production, and mitogen responsiveness.

INDEX